The Sustainable Development Goals and Human Rights

The Sustainable Development Goals (SDGs) were adopted in 2015. The SDGs make the central promise to Leave No One Behind and include a dedicated goal to reduce inequalities. Human rights advocates have put great hopes in the SDGs as an instrument for transformative change. But do they bring about the much-needed paradigm shift? Or were the extensive consultations and negotiations much ado about nothing?

Sustainable Development Goals and Human Rights: A Critical Early Review follows two central lines of inquiry. Firstly, the chapters examine the extent to which the SDGs live up to the promise to reduce inequalities and promote policies that address the needs of marginalized populations. Secondly, they suggest transparent and binding accountability processes and mechanisms to ensure that the SDGs are more than lofty goals and bring power to their promise.

The book begins with three chapters that focus on different aspects of SDG 10 and the commitment to reduce inequalities. From this cross-cutting SDG, the following three chapters look at the translation of equality and accountability into specific sectors: health (SDG 3) and labour (SDG 8).

The chapters in this book were originally published in a special issue of *The International Journal of Human Rights*.

Inga T. Winkler is a lecturer in the Institute for the Study of Human Rights at Columbia University, USA. She leads the programming on economic, social and cultural rights. Prior to joining Columbia, Winkler was the Legal Adviser to the UN Special Rapporteur on the Human Rights to Water and Sanitation.

Carmel Williams, PhD, is a senior research officer in the Human Rights, Big Data and Technology project at the Human Rights Centre, University of Essex, UK. She is also the Executive Editor of the *Health and Human Rights* journal, published at the FXB Center, Harvard T.H. Chan School of Public Health, Boston, USA.

The Sustainable Development Goals and Human Rights

A Critical Early Review

Edited by
Inga T. Winkler and Carmel Williams

Routledge
Taylor & Francis Group

LONDON AND NEW YORK

First published 2018 by Routledge

2 Park Square, Milton Park, Abingdon, Oxfordshire OX14 4RN
52 Vanderbilt Avenue, New York, NY 10017

Routledge is an imprint of the Taylor & Francis Group, an informa business

First issued in paperback 2020

British Library Cataloguing in Publication Data
A catalogue record for this book is available from the British Library

ISBN13: 978-1-138-49529-6 (hbk)
ISBN13: 978-0-367-51979-7 (pbk)

Typeset in MinionPro
by diacriTech, Chennai

Publisher's Note
The publisher accepts responsibility for any inconsistencies that may have arisen during the conversion of this book from journal articles to book chapters, namely the possible inclusion of journal terminology.

Disclaimer
Every effort has been made to contact copyright holders for their permission to reprint material in this book. The publishers would be grateful to hear from any copyright holder who is not here acknowledged and will undertake to rectify any errors or omissions in future editions of this book.

Contents

Citation Information

The chapters in this book were originally published in *The International Journal of Human Rights*, volume 21, issue 8 (October 2017). When citing this material, please use the original page numbering for each article, as follows:

Chapter 1
The Sustainable Development Goals and human rights: a critical early review
Inga T. Winkler and Carmel Williams
The International Journal of Human Rights, volume 21, issue 8 (October 2017)
pp. 1023–1028

Chapter 2
Tackling inequality through the Sustainable Development Goals: human rights in practice
Ignacio Saiz and Kate Donald
The International Journal of Human Rights, volume 21, issue 8 (October 2017)
pp. 1029–1049

Chapter 3
Vertical inequalities: are the SDGs and human rights up to the challenges?
Gillian MacNaughton
The International Journal of Human Rights, volume 21, issue 8 (October 2017)
pp. 1050–1072

Chapter 4
Leaving no one behind? Persistent inequalities in the SDGs
Inga T. Winkler and Margaret L. Satterthwaite
The International Journal of Human Rights, volume 21, issue 8 (October 2017)
pp. 1073–1097

Chapter 5
Evaluating the health-related targets in the Sustainable Development Goals from a human rights perspective
Audrey R. Chapman
The International Journal of Human Rights, volume 21, issue 8 (October 2017)
pp. 1098–1113

Chapter 6

Neglecting human rights: accountability, data and Sustainable Development Goal 3
Carmel Williams and Paul Hunt
The International Journal of Human Rights, volume 21, issue 8 (October 2017)
pp. 1114–1143

Chapter 7

Economic growth, full employment and decent work: the means and ends in SDG 8
Diane F. Frey
The International Journal of Human Rights, volume 21, issue 8 (October 2017)
pp. 1164–1184

For any permission-related enquiries please visit:
http://www.tandfonline.com/page/help/permissions

Notes on Contributors

Audrey R. Chapman is Professor of Community Medicine and Healthcare and holds the Healey Memorial Chair in Medical Ethics and Humanities at the UConn School of Medicine, USA. She also has an adjunct appointment at the UConn School of Law and is an affiliate of the UConn Human Rights Institute, USA.

Kate Donald is the Director of the Human Rights in Development Program at the Center for Economic and Social Rights. Donald holds a Masters in Human Rights from the London School of Economics, UK.

Diane F. Frey is a lecturer in labour and employment studies at San Francisco State University, USA, and teaches negotiations at Harvard Extension and Summer Schools. She is an affiliate of the Economic and Social Rights Group of the Human Rights Institute at the University of Connecticut, USA.

Paul Hunt is Professor of Law, Human Rights Centre, University of Essex, USA.

Gillian MacNaughton is an assistant professor at the School for Global Inclusion and Social Development and a Senior Fellow in the Center for Peace, Democracy and Development, both at the University of Massachusetts, Boston, USA.

Ignacio Saiz is the Executive Director of the Center for Economic and Social Rights. Saiz holds an LLM in international human rights law with distinction from the University of Essex, UK.

Margaret L. Satterthwaite is a Professor of Clinical Law at NYU Law School, the Director of the Global Justice Clinic, the Faculty Director and Co-Chair of the Center for Human Rights and Global Justice, and the Faculty Director of the Robert L. Bernstein Institute for Human Rights, USA.

Carmel Williams, PhD, is a senior research officer in the Human Rights, Big Data and Technology Project at the Human Rights Centre, University of Essex, UK. She is also the Executive Editor of the *Health and Human Rights* journal, published at the FXB Center, Harvard T.H. Chan School of Public Health, Boston, USA.

Inga T. Winkler is a lecturer in the Institute for the Study of Human Rights at Columbia University, USA. She leads the programming on economic, social and cultural rights. Prior to joining Columbia, Winkler was the Legal Adviser to the UN Special Rapporteur on the Human Rights to Water and Sanitation.

Notes on Contributors

The Sustainable Development Goals and human rights: a critical early review

This special issue on the Sustainable Development Goals and human rights developed from a workshop of the Economic and Social Rights Group at the Human Rights Institute at the University of Connecticut in early 2016. This was shortly after the United Nations General Assembly had adopted 'Transforming Our World: The 2030 Agenda for Sustainable Development'[1] and its Sustainable Development Goals (SDGs). This now seems a somewhat distant, optimistic, and different political environment.

This is not to say human rights advocates were generally and universally satisfied with the 2030 Agenda, its goals, targets and monitoring mechanisms. Indeed, there was considerable disappointment that the SDGs had not reflected the advice provided by global leaders and grassroots activists to keep human rights central to the new development era.[2] Irrespective, there was a sense that the SDGs were a unifying agenda, applicable to all countries, despite criticisms of being too vague and too numerous.[3] There was hope that, with careful choice of indicators and appropriate measures of accountability, which were still unsettled at the time of adoption and remain so today, the Goals might bring real change, and actually reduce the rampantly increasing inequalities between and within most countries.

In the lead-up to the SDGs, the human rights community, along with civil society more generally, had engaged in the negotiations for the new development agenda at an unprecedented level, especially when compared to the Millennium Development Goals (MDGs). The MDGs were developed at a technocratic level extracted from previous commitments,[4] and the human rights community was a late-comer to the discussion. By the time human rights advocates engaged, they were left with the role of largely criticizing the MDGs for prioritising progress at an aggregate level without targeting the most marginalised populations and without addressing inequalities.[5]

For the SDGs, human rights NGOs and researchers, and other stakeholders sought to engage meaningfully throughout the process of developing, discussing and deliberating on the goals for a new more rights-based development era. There was plenty of opportunity for such engagement during a broad and long process including early thematic and country consultations,[6] the Rio+20 negotiations,[7] and the Open Working Group on the SDGs.[8] Many NGOs were deeply engaged in the process, National Human Rights Institutions outlined what their position and role might be,[9] and UN treaty bodies[10] and Special Rapporteurs sought to influence the process to keep human rights at the centre.[11]

Not even two years post adoption, the fanfare and optimism at the 2030 Agenda launching has waned. While ministers from nearly every state, both high- and low-income, embraced the SDGs enthusiastically at the UN Summit in 2015, the SDGs do not appear to be maintaining national interest in many of the better resourced countries since. For example, they were not election issues in the US and were referred to fleetingly and only by the Labour Party in the British election.[12] The Goals, which after all, focus on sustainability, and acknowledge the risk posed to all and especially the poorest people by climate change (SDG 13), have not just been ignored by the US, but the science behind them denied. Similarly, the SDGs addressing gender equality (SDG

5) and sexual and reproduction health and rights (SDG 3.1, 3.7) have been dealt serious blows, with US funding cuts both domestically and internationally for sexual health services hurting the poorest women the most. This matters not only for the US but globally, because without support from high income countries the goal of leaving no one behind cannot be achieved.

While the world in September 2015 celebrated the commitment to sustainable development for all, the very notion of survival, let alone sustainability, is under threat as reflected by the Doomsday Clock published by the Bulletin of Atomic Scientists, which has edged even closer to midnight.[13] At two and a half minutes to midnight – the closest it has been since 1953 – it reflects that 'the international community failed to come effectively to grips with humanity's existential threats, nuclear weapons, and climate change'.[14]

Contemporary human rights crises, including climate change and refugee crises, demand vigilance and response, and could be seen to be of more immediate concern than the development goals of the *2030 Agenda*. On the other hand, and without denying the immediacy of these concerns, sustainable development provides the framework for addressing all these challenges in an interconnected and comprehensive manner. It goes beyond piecemeal measures that only address the symptoms. Sustainable development as defined by the Brundlandt Commission 30 years ago is 'development which meets the needs of current generations without compromising the ability of future generations to meet their own needs'.[15] The *2030 Agenda* is built on the dimensions of people, planet, prosperity, peace and partnerships. Making the connections and finding comprehensive solutions is complex – but that is the strength of having the *2030 Agenda* grounded in human rights. International human rights law provides a scaffolding, and accountability mechanisms, that allow a systems-based and consistent response to sustainable development that can bring about transformative, structural change to reduce inequalities and challenge power imbalances. Because the world adopted the SDGs, they offer one of our best, contemporary global opportunities to oppose social injustices that human rights advocates can use as a tool.

Therefore, it is crucial that despite the urgent demands on the time, energy and resources of human rights NGOs, advocates and researchers, attention is not diverted away from the promises of the SDGs, and importantly, from the processes necessary to ensure that 'no one is left behind'.

This special issue provides early critical reflections on the SDGs.[16] Characteristic of the SDG deliberations were broad-based collaborations between grassroots activists, NGOs, think-tanks, academics and UN mechanisms, combining research, advocacy and policy-influencing. This special issue reflects these diverse voices.

It is too early to evaluate whether the SDGs live up to their potential and promise. Indicators and monitoring processes are still being developed, leaving a fair degree of confusion not just about the disaggregates required within specific indicators, but also about the indicators themselves. The first States have undergone voluntary review, and national strategies are still being drawn up, and very few countries have determined how and what indicators they will report on. It is an opportune time to reflect on these developments at a time where indicators, national strategies and review processes can still be influenced.

We identify two important themes arising from the papers in this issue: the first addresses the challenges within and between the goals, targets and indicators, that leave many of the SDGs frustratingly short of their promise, in particular with regard to leaving no one behind. In response to the MDGs' failure to prioritise the most disadvantaged populations, one of the key demands of the human rights community for the SDGs became, and remains, a commitment to ensuring equality. The human rights community and others called for a stand-alone goal on equality, as well as equality being integrated within the sectoral goals and targets. Importantly, they also called for indicators to be disaggregated so inequalities could be monitored to ensure that human rights entitlements are progressively realised, and inequalities ultimately eliminated.[17] The language of the SDGs makes this commitment to equality central. One of the key lines of inquiry addressed in the special issue is the critical interrogation of the extent to which the SDGs are likely to live up that promise.[18]

The second central premise of the articles in this special issue is that a focus on human rights can open spaces to keep the SDGs on task, and on the global agenda – bringing power to their promise. Accountability is a central theme in human rights analysis of development and social justice issues. If the SDGs are to be more than lofty global goals, it is necessary to have transparent and binding accountability processes and mechanisms in place. How such processes can be improved is the second central theme addressed in a number of articles in this special issue.

The issue starts with three papers that focus on different aspects of SDG 10 and the commitment to reduce inequalities. From this cross cutting SDG, the following four papers look at the translation of equality and accountability into specific sectors: health (SDG 3) and labour (SDG 8).

In one of the three papers examining SDG 10 on equality, Saiz and Donald observe its lack of alignment with human rights and note 'imprecise language or distortions that could jeopardise implementation'. They suggest the Goal is 'vulnerable to strategic neglect or even backlash, given that of all the goals it will arguably require the most profound and lasting changes to the "business-as-usual" economic and development model'. The authors suggest that human rights standards and tools could guide two crucial policy areas to reduce inequality: social protection and taxation. Importantly, they conclude that 'human rights advocates do not have to sacrifice their priorities in order to engage with SDG implementation and monitoring; quite the contrary, the imperative is to inject precisely those priorities into these efforts.'

MacNaughton in her interrogation of SDG 10 looks particularly at vertical inequalities, those 'inequalities of wealth, income or social outcome, including inequalities in health, education, housing and political power'. She finds that despite the overwhelming evidence of the negative impact of extreme economic inequalities, the SDGs fail to address them adequately. She cites target 10.1 which addresses economic inequalities and poverty reduction. It focuses on the bottom 40% of the population but does not address the disparity between this bottom 40% and the top 10% or the top 1%. MacNaughton puts a challenge to the human rights community: she calls for further interpretation and development of human rights norms. She argues human rights fail to address vertical inequalities, and thus are not setting limits on the 'rising gaps between rich and poor'. The global adoption and endorsement of the SDGs provides the urgency and rationale to take up this challenge.

Winkler and Satterthwaite turn to the indicators in the SDG framework, arguing that these metrics pegged to targets are not just technical, but political, and hugely influential. Indicators determine what data will be gathered, what we will know about inequalities and ultimately 'what matters' in the implementation of the SDGs by concentrating effort and attention. The authors put a particular focus on race and ethnicity as inherently related to processes of power and marginalisation and find that the SDG indicator framework to date fails to address these two key dimensions of discrimination, and therefore cannot translate the commitment to 'leave no one behind' into reality. They acknowledge the limitations of existing data and concerns over the risks of such data collection, but conclude that with political will much greater collection and analysis of disaggregated data is feasible.

Chapman's article applies the test of human rights standards to SDG 3 targets, and finds them lacking. The article focuses on the health rights of children; sexual and reproductive health and rights; the underlying determinants of health; achieving universal health coverage; and access to affordable essential medicines. She finds SDG 3 has largely failed in integrating human rights into its targets. For example, rights-based approaches make individual autonomy and decision-making central to sexual and reproductive health, but, Chapman states, 'the reproductive health targets in the SDGs refrain from taking a rights-based approach, focus on a technical approach, and do not address underlying structural issues impeding women's right to equality and their ability to control their own lives'. Chapman laments the lack of rights-based approaches within the SDGs, and fears their absence will leave the most vulnerable and disadvantaged behind.

Williams and Hunt focus on a key challenge confronting global governance for health and SDG 3: accountability. They use a tripartite conceptualisation of accountability guided by the experience of the Commission on Information and Accountability for Women's and Children's Health (COIA) and then explore whether the agreed SDG 3 indicators promote the collection of data that could demonstrate health rights entitlements are being respected, protected and fulfilled. They identify gaps in the SDG indicators, especially around human rights principles of participation and quality of health care. Any monitoring of SDG progress demands data and the authors find data are frequently absent in countries and communities most 'left behind'. Furthermore, they challenge suggestions that Big Data could fill these statistical gaps, because such claims ignore the realities of poor information systems and the digital divide. Williams and Hunt emphasise the human rights obligations of international assistance and cooperation to build the capacity of national statistics offices to make accurate data available to track SDG progress, but note this is not by itself accountability.

Invisibility is explored by Davis in her paper on global health monitoring and the politics of data in the context of HIV and SDG target 3.3. Current data often leaves out key populations who are invisible due to stigma and criminalisation. Davis discusses the paradox of invisibility reinforcing invisibility. Political leaders in many countries deny the very existence of key populations such as men who have sex with men, while individuals and communities themselves prefer to stay invisible and uncounted in contexts where their behaviour is criminalised due to fears of persecution and violence. While these power dynamics are difficult to change, Davis demonstrates how advocates and community-based organisations are beginning to interrogate and challenge the politics of data. As part of measuring progress towards the ambitious SDG 3.3, key populations are demanding that studies be more inclusive, ethical, and attuned to their human rights.

Finally, Frey turns her attention to SDG 8 on Economic Growth and Decent Work – a combination she finds perplexing and fraught. In her paper, Frey critically examines the two conflicting visions of development: a market-centred business approach, informing the economic growth side of the goal, and the rights-based approach that focuses on decent work for all. Rather than resolving the conflict between these visions, the SDGs have merged them and make the realisation of SDG 8 dependent on economic growth. This, explains Frey, confuses ends and means. However, she acknowledges that the Goal still includes important levers for human rights advocates to demand accountability for realising decent work for all.

The collection of articles in the special issue alludes to the complexity and richness of the 17 Goals and 169 targets. While focusing on a few select Goals,[19] the articles point to underlying recurring themes, in particular around equality, participation, and accountability. These are human rights principles without which implementation of the SDGs will not achieve their goal to 'leave no one behind'.

The SDGs are the result of political negotiations and compromise.[20] On the downside, that means that they are far from perfect, ripe with inherent contradictions and gaps. On the upside, they have been negotiated and adopted by all UN member States representing a global commitment. As each of the articles identifies, the SDGs bring a global focus to inequalities – within and between countries, and across all sectors, and with an agenda that is universal in scope. In contrast to the MDGs, the SDGs apply to all UN member States, in the Global South and the Global North alike.[21] They require all countries to reduce inequalities, even where absolute deprivation is low and/or small pockets of people experience persistent marginalisation.

Human rights advocates achieved a lot in SDG negotiations: from the overall promise of 'leave no one behind', to references to human rights in the Declaration, to many of the targets which implicitly reflect human rights language. The challenge now is to keep the ongoing engagement of the human rights community to ensure that human rights guide the implementation of the SDGs so that their promise is translated into reality and governments are held accountable for their commitments, especially to the most discriminated against, marginalised, impoverished and vulnerable communities.

The articles identify leadership opportunities in human rights engagement in SDG processes. First, although the goals and targets are finalised, the indicators and monitoring frameworks are still being developed. Human rights principles can guide these decisions, so that 'invisible' populations are counted, and national statistics offices are supported to gather data that measure and reflect human values. Second, human rights can guide the implementation of the SDGs and inform policies. The slow uptake of SDG national plans and strategies is providing increased space and opportunity for human rights advocates to engage with the processes and influence national priorities. Finally, human rights instruments have an immense potential to strengthen accountability.[22] Human rights mechanisms could monitor SDG commitments, by combining both frameworks, and drawing on their mutual strengths.

At this moment in global politics, the SDGs provide a much needed space to address issues of human dignity and equality. These goals are not framed as being part of international human rights law, but they attempt to achieve a more equal, peaceful and sustainable world. Importantly, they apply to all countries, and while weak at this stage, there is some monitoring in place. The critical engagement of human rights can further inform SDG plans and programmes with the principles of equality, participation and accountability to help fulfil the promise of leaving no one behind.

Notes

1. UN General Assembly, *Transforming Our World: The 2030 Agenda for Sustainable Development* (New York: UN, 2015).
2. High-Level Panel of Eminent Persons on the Post-2015 Development Agenda, Report, *A New Global Partnership: Eradicate Poverty and Transform Economies through Sustainable Development* (New York: 2013); Post-2015 Human Rights Caucus, *Human Rights for All Post-2015: A Litmus Test* (New York: 2014).
3. See for example, William Easterly, 'The SDGs Should Stand for Senseless, Dreamy, Garbled', *Foreign Policy*, September 28, 2015, http://foreignpolicy.com/2015/09/28/the-sdgs-are-utopian-and-worthless-mdgs-development-rise-of-the-rest/ (accessed July 12, 2017).
4. Jan Vandemoortele, 'Making Sense of the MDGs', *Development* 51, no. 220–7 (2008): 221.
5. United Nations, *Claiming the Millennium Development Goals: A Human Rights Approach* (New York & Geneva: UN, 2008), 9.
6. United Nations Development Group, *The Global Conversation Begins, Emerging Views for a New Development Agenda* (New York: UNDG, 2013), http://www.undp.org/content/dam/undp/library/MDG/english/global-conversation-begins-web.pdf (accessed July 12, 2017).
7. United Nations, *The Future We Want*, A/Res/66/288, September 11, 2012.
8. Open Working Group on Sustainable Development Goals, https://sustainabledevelopment.un.org/post2015/owg (accessed July 12, 2017).
9. Steven Jensen, Allison Corkery and Kate Donald, *Realizing rights through the sustainable development goals: The role of national human rights institutions, Briefing paper about the Sustainable Development Goals and human rights – and the role of national human rights institutions* (Danish Institute for Human Rights, 2015).
10. Joint Statement of the Chairpersons of the United Nations Human Rights Treaty Bodies on the Post-2015 Development Agenda, January 18, 2015, http://www.ohchr.org/EN/NewsEvents/Pages/DisplayNews.aspx?NewsID=15505&#sthash.y5QacpyZ.dpuf (accessed July 12, 2017).

11. Special Procedures of the Human Rights Council, *If Rio+20 is to Deliver, Accountability Must Be at its Heart*, http://www.ohchr.org/Documents/HRBodies/SP/BNSustainableDevelopment.pdf (accessed July 12, 2017).
12. Labour Party Manifesto 2107, *For the Many, Not the Few* May 2017, p. 122.
13. Bulletin of the Atomic Scientists, May 2017, http://thebulletin.org/timeline (accessed July 12, 2017).
14. Ibid.
15. United Nations, *Report of the World Commission on Environment and Development: Our Common Future*, A/42/427, August 4, 1987.
16. *Gender & Development* has published a special issue on the SDGs in March 2016: http://www.genderanddevelopment.org/page/current-issue (accessed July 12, 2017). The *Health and Human Rights Journal* has published an extensive series of blog posts on the SDGs that provide interesting insights: https://www.hhrjournal.org/2015/09/sdg-series-what-might-the-sdgs-mean-for-health-and-human-rights-an-introduction-to-the-series/ (accessed July 12, 2017).
17. United Nations, *Statement by 17 Special Procedures Mandate-Holders of the Human Rights Council on the Post-2015 Development Agenda, Grounding Development Priorities in Human Rights: Incentives to Improve Equality, Social Security and Accountability*, http://www.ohchr.org/Documents/Issues/Food/Post2015JointSubmission.pdf (accessed July 12, 2017).
18. See also Katja Freistein and Bettina Mahlert, 'The Potential for Tackling Inequality in the Sustainable Development Goals', *Third World Quarterly* 37, no. 12 (2016): 2139–55; Edward Anderson, 'Equality as a Global Goal', *Ethics and International Affairs*, June 10, 2015.
19. For a more comprehensive exercise, offering a spotlight on each SDG, see Reflection Group on the 2030 Agenda for Sustainable Development, *Spotlight on Sustainable Development* (2016).
20. For a critique of the final draft of the goals and targets prior to adoption see Thomas Pogge and Mitu Sengupta, 'The Sustainable Development Goals (SDGs) as Drafted: Nice Idea, Poor Execution', *Washington International Law Journal* 24, no. 3 (2015): 571–87.
21. See further Malcolm Langford, 'Lost in Transformation? The Politics of the Sustainable Development Goals', *Ethics & International Affairs* 30, no. 2 (2016): 167–76; for a more in-depth discussion, Graham Long, 'The Idea of Universality in the Sustainable Development Goals', *Ethics & International Affairs* 29, no. 2 (2015): 203–22.
22. Kate Donald and Sally-Anne Way, 'Accountability for the Sustainable Development Goals: A Lost Opportunity?', *Ethics & International Affairs* 30, no. 2 (2016): 201–13, 207 et seq.; Nadja Filskov, *SDGs and Human Rights Monitoring, Guidance for National Implementation* (Danish Institute for Human Rights, 2015); see also Global Initiative for Economic, Social and Cultural Rights, *Snapshot: The SDGs at the Human Rights Council* (March 2017), http://globalinitiative-escr.org/snapshot-the-sdgs-at-the-human-rights-council-march-2017 (accessed July 12, 2017).

Inga T. Winkler

Carmel Williams

Tackling inequality through the Sustainable Development Goals: human rights in practice

Ignacio Saiz and Kate Donald

ABSTRACT

In recent years, economic inequality has soared to unprecedented levels, presenting new threats to the full spectrum of human rights. Against this backdrop, Agenda 2030 includes a Goal aiming to reduce inequalities of all kinds, within and between countries. One of the most transformational aspects of the new sustainable development agenda, SDG10 has the potential to deliver an urgently needed paradigm shift in how development efforts are pursued to realise human rights and reduce inequality. This article analyses the strengths and shortcomings of SDG10 from a human rights perspective, and explores the political vulnerability of the Goal and the prospects for its implementation. It then explains how human rights norms, standards and tools can help to inform and guide actions towards these commitments, including how human rights monitoring mechanisms can play a role in tracking progress and providing a space for accountability.

Introduction

For many of the human rights organisations (and their allies in the development sector) involved in the SDG negotiations, a central priority was the inclusion of an explicit focus in the new goals on tackling inequalities. This was in part a reaction to the MDGs, which were subject to much criticism from the human rights community for lionising aggregate progress while masking (or even encouraging neglect of) economic and social inequalities. While the international community and individual countries were able to declare success in meeting many of the MDGs, significant disparities remained between and within countries.[1] Meanwhile, income and wealth inequality grew in most regions during the MDG period, with global wealth inequality reaching levels unprecedented in recent history.[2]

Thanks to persistent advocacy and despite strong resistance from some Member States, the final SDGs adopted in September 2015 did include a stand-alone goal on reducing inequality, along with an overarching pledge to 'Leave No One Behind' in the implementation of the agenda.[3] In many ways, this represents a considerable success and opportunity for the human rights movement. Sustainable Development Goal 10 (SDG10) is one of the most striking and groundbreaking elements of the 2030 Agenda when compared to the

Millennium Development Goals. In Goal 10, states formally commit to tackling inequality *within* and *between* countries. This goal includes associated targets on income inequality, social and political empowerment, discrimination, fairer fiscal and wage policies, migration, financial regulation and more democratic governance of the global economy.

However, as inevitable in any intergovernmental political process, the focus and content of SDG10 was subject to several compromises. It is therefore not as aligned with human rights as it could be, and in several cases the targets and indicators contain imprecise language or distortions that could jeopardise implementation.[4] Moreover, Goal 10 is particularly politically vulnerable to strategic neglect or even backlash, given that of all the goals it will arguably require the most profound and lasting changes to the 'business-as-usual' economic and development model.[5] At the same time, SDG10 has no obvious thematic body or set of institutions at the national or international level whose mandate is to drive actions and funding to this goal, monitor its achievement and hold decision-makers to account for any lack of progress (unlike other sustainable development goals which have dedicated UN agencies, mechanisms or committees). While the World Bank has made Goal 1 and Goal 10 the focus of its work on the SDGs, its approach to Goal 10 is shaped by its institutional priority to promote 'shared prosperity' rather than embracing a more comprehensive need to tackle income and wealth inequality.[6] The lack of an institutional 'home' for Goal 10 is indicative of the higher risk of it remaining an 'orphan' goal – hostage to the ebbs and flows of competing international development priorities and diverging national interests.

Therefore, there are real risks that SDG10 will be neglected or implemented half-heartedly, ineffectively or in a manner that does not align with human rights priorities. Building on the Center for Economic and Social Rights' briefing *From Disparity to Dignity*,[7] this article will analyse the strengths and shortcomings of SDG10 from a human rights perspective, before going on to explore how human rights norms, standards and tools could inform and guide effective implementation and monitoring efforts. In our view, SDG10 does have the potential to improve human rights realisation, but a robust, far-reaching and sustainable implementation of Goal 10 will only be possible if guided by human rights law and standards and animated by political will on the part of states to be held answerable for their commitments. In this regard, human rights tools and mechanisms could play a strategic role in incentivising states to bolster and drive forward implementation efforts, as well as hold governments and other actors accountable for their actions or omissions under the rubric of the SDGs.

What are the strengths and shortcomings of SDG10 from a human rights perspective?

From a human rights perspective, the inclusion of inequality as a priority 'development' issue is very welcome and long overdue. Human rights advocates have long been drawing attention to the way in which many development interventions – driven by a narrow focus on aggregate economic growth – have exacerbated inequalities of all kinds.[8] The human rights framework makes clear that an approach to development that pays attention only to absolute poverty and basic needs is far from sufficient. Tackling inequalities (of opportunity *and* outcome) and the systemic discrimination (direct and indirect) that fuel these disparities is also crucial if sustainable development is to serve the full realisation of human rights for all, as Agenda 2030 explicitly sets out to do. There-fore, the mere inclusion of Goal 10 in the SDGs represents an important watershed moment, in shifting the international development paradigm in a more human rights-friendly direction.

This commitment to reduce inequalities has universal applicability. The SDGs are explicitly intended to apply to *all* countries, including high-income, 'developed' states. SDG10 is perhaps the goal that most embodies this new universality. All countries in the world have stark and persistent inequalities, which in many cases have grown in recent decades.[9] All countries face significant policy and political challenges in dealing with this problem. Meanwhile, reducing inequalities *between* countries will by definition require action and solutions at the global level, especially from the wealthy countries that have the greatest influence over the global economy and the way it is governed.

Leave no one behind

If Goal 10 represents the Agenda's 'stand-alone' focus on inequalities, 'Leave No One Behind' is the attempt to mainstream the concern with inequality. First proposed by the High-Level Panel on the Post-2015 Agenda in 2012,[10] the exhortation to 'Leave No One Behind' has become the overarching rallying cry of the 2030 Agenda.[11]

From a human rights perspective, it is in many ways heartening to see a pledge to avoid exclusion, marginalisation and neglect of the worst-off at the centre of the 2030 Agenda. However, the meaning of this new development trope remains imprecise and contested. Some actors seem to interpret it as encapsulating only the need to reach the poorest people (in terms of income) globally[12] – in essence recapitulating the MDGs' focus pri-marily on addressing extreme poverty. The discourse around 'Leave No One Behind' has remained strangely disconnected from the commitments under Goal 10, and even more from human rights.

However, if 'Leave No One Behind' is to be more than a rhetorical flourish camoufla-ging fundamentally exclusionary policies, governments will need to take proactive and timely steps towards achieving Goal 10 *and* address chronic and systemic human rights deprivations, in particular in addressing discrimination, social exclusion and economic inequality. Because the political and economic impacts of intense income and wealth con-centration at the top are extremely pernicious,[13] 'leaving no one behind' should entail pre-venting some from getting too far ahead at the expense of others. That is, it should be understood as a commitment to tackle inequality not just poverty, and therefore sustain-able development policies will need to grapple with the top end of the income and wealth spectrum.

Economic inequality

Inequalities of all types are a central concern of human rights. Traditionally, human rights advocates and standard-setting processes have focused mostly on horizontal inequalities – inequalities between groups with a shared identity, along such lines as gender, race, eth-nicity and age.[14] Until recently, vertical economic inequality (inequality in income and wealth between individuals and households) has been relatively neglected by human rights bodies. Increasingly, however, the human rights impacts of economic inequality are being explored, as a contributor to horizontal inequalities, social disparities and to other human rights deprivations.[15] Therefore, it is positive that SDG10 takes aim at economic inequality alongside other disparities.

Economic inequality produces many detrimental human rights effects,[16] perpetuating poverty and social exclusion and creating stark disparities in access to health, education, housing and other services essential to the enjoyment of economic and social rights. Economic inequality also hampers enjoyment of civil and political rights, for example distorting people's equal access to justice and the rule of law, whilst also driving insecurity and conflict.[17] Extreme inequality has been shown to undermine opportunities for political participation and accountability, often co-occurring with elite capture and unjust institutions that (re)create patterns of inequality.[18] In this way, extreme economic inequality is both a consequence and a cause of human rights deprivations. Certainly, as Alston writes, 'there are limits to the degree of inequality that can be reconciled with notions of equality, dignity and commitments to human rights for everyone'.[19] In addition, many of the key determinants of economic inequality the erosion of labour rights, the weakening of public services and the capture of democratic decision-making by elites can be framed as denials of internationally guaranteed human rights, including the right to decent work and to just and favourable conditions at work, the rights to health, education, water and sanitation, and the right to participation in public affairs.[20]

Addressing economic inequality through Goal 10 is therefore a central human rights concern. However, the Goal's approach is somewhat oblique. For example, rather than using more precise metrics (such as the Gini Coefficient or Palma Ratio)[21] to measure unequal economic outcomes, decision-makers chose the target (10.1) of boosting the income of the bottom 40% faster than the average,[22] echoing the World Bank's goal of shared prosperity.[23] Amongst other limitations, this target in no way measures income or wealth growth at the top, which is the leading determinant of domestic economic inequality.[24] This weakness in the target was compounded by a choice of indicator[25] (promoted by the World Bank)[26] which is not strictly speaking a measure of income inequality, with robust existing methods like the Gini coefficient or Palma ratio rejected.[27]

Indeed, all of the targets and indicators under Goal 10 that relate to economic inequality shy away from the crux of the issue. For example, target 10.4 is to 'Adopt policies, especially fiscal, wage and social protection policies, and progressively achieve greater equality'. The inclusion of this target and the naming of these policy areas was an important victory. Yet, the deliberate displacement of the word 'progressive' – previous drafts made clear that the fiscal, wage and social protection policies themselves should be 'progressive'– indicates the political sensitivity of this issue. As a result of the compromise language, the target gives little indication to states as to what kind of policies can be expected to 'progressively achieve greater equality'. One need only look to the effects of recent austerity measures in many countries to see that regressive social protection, fiscal and wage policies will only fuel inequality.[28]

Similar shortcomings are present in the targets to measure and incentivise policy efforts for SDG10. Despite consistent proposals that governments commit to measure their policy steps towards meeting the SDGs,[29] the targets under Goal 10 ultimately set out only a patchy policy action agenda for reducing economic inequality.[30]

Discrimination and unequal outcomes

Inequality goes hand-in-hand with discrimination, as inequalities in the enjoyment of rights are often the outcome of policies or practices which are discriminatory in their intention or effect. Goal 10 recognises and seeks to confront the problem of discrimination. Again, however, it does so somewhat obliquely. Target 10.2 promises to 'empower and promote the social, economic and political inclusion of all, irrespective of age, sex, disability, race ethnicity, origin, religion or economic or other status' (thereby listing many – but not all – of the respective grounds of discrimination found in international human rights law). This is followed by a target which commits to 'eliminating discriminatory laws, policies and practices and promoting appropriate legislation, policies and action in this regard', therefore recognising the need for positive as well as prohibitive measures (on the shortcomings of the associated indicator see Winkler and Satterthwaite in this volume).

Perhaps most notably, target 10.3 starts with the pledge to ensure equal opportunity *and reduce inequalities of outcome*. The recognition of the need to go beyond equal opportunity towards tackling disparities in outcome is a very important step, and very much in line with human rights approaches to inequality, in particular the concept of substantive equality which will be discussed further below. This aspect of Goal 10 has been overlooked by many but could be an important leverage point for human rights advocates.

Inequalities between countries

An equally crucial aspect of SDG10 is to reduce inequalities among or *between* countries. In a fundamentally interdependent global economy with gross financial and power imbalances between states, actions by individual countries – or decisions they make as stakeholders in international financial institutions (IFIs) – affect deprivation and inequality within other countries, and maintain global disparities between countries.[31] Currently many countries are constrained in their fiscal and policy space to tackle domestic inequalities.[32] International trade deals may affect policies on labour rights, climate change policies, financial regulation and public health protections, while a country's ability to tax multinational corporations operating on its territory may be affected by the availability of financial secrecy jurisdictions overseas, or unfair double taxation agreements.

Unlike the skewed accountability framework of the MDGs which placed the greatest burden on the poorest countries with the heaviest policy restrictions,[33] SDG10's insistence on challenging global inequality has the potential to compel countries to evaluate and address the degree to which their actions undermine sustainable development efforts in other countries. This is very welcome from a human rights perspective, taking into account the duty of international assistance and cooperation at the heart of international human rights law, and growing recognition and exploration of States' extra-territorial human rights obligations.[34] Specific SDG10 targets cover important areas relevant to tackling global inequality – such as improving the regulation of financial markets, enhancing the voice of developing countries in global financial institutions and encouraging official development assistance to those states that most need it.

However, overall these targets do not represent the needed step-change in international cooperation, such as shutting down tax havens, or better regulating transnational corporations. Moreover, they lack the proper indicators to measure and incentivise international action, despite the ready availability of more robust alternatives.[35] In particular, the indicators shy away from delineating the differentiated responsibilities of countries at different income levels, and instead focus on broadly defined outcomes – thereby failing to provide the policy direction so desperately needed. For example, the indicator for target 10.6 – 'proportion of members and voting rights of developing countries in international organisations' – fails to incentivise or pinpoint the action that specific actors need to take to reach it (such as concrete steps towards voting reform at the IFIs), and so all can easily absolve themselves of responsibility if progress is disappointing or non-existent. As a result, the policies and systems that drive inequalities between countries go largely unmeasured by the target and indicator framework, posing yet another hurdle to what are already serious political challenges to reducing inequalities.

How can human rights norms and standards bolster Goal 10 implementation?

In many cases, the deficiencies and weaknesses of the SDG10 targets could be redressed or ameliorated through careful use of human rights standards and tools in implementation and monitoring. In this section, we will analyse a number of strategies to achieve this and give various concrete examples of how specific human rights principles and standards could contribute to a more fulsome understanding and more effective implementation of Goal 10.

Human rights standards address inequality in ways that can provide important normative guidance to Goal 10 implementation programmes and other efforts under the SDGs to reduce inequality. First, an array of anti-discrimination treaties and declarations[36] set out a rights-based policy agenda to advance equality for women, persons with disabilities, migrants, indigenous peoples and those facing discrimination based on race, sexual orientation and other prohibited grounds. These aim at achieving substantive equality – including equality of outcomes, measured by levels of rights enjoyment, and not just equality of opportunity.[37] Second, these instruments are complemented by international standards regarding economic, social and cultural rights obliging states to devote the maximum of their available resources to achieving progressively the full realisation of these rights for all people (article 2 of the International Covenant on Economic, Social and Cultural Rights) – which includes real and potential resources that could be raised through tax or international cooperation (e.g. aid). In these efforts, states must prioritise the reduction of disparities and the universal attainment of basic thresholds which correspond to many of the SDG goals and targets – e.g. primary education completion for all.[38] Third, human rights norms also impose duties on states to cooperate internationally to ensure their policies and practices do not create human rights violations in other countries, including by fuelling deprivation and disparities.[39]

Interpreting 2030 Agenda commitments through the lens of substantive equality

A human rights-based understanding of equality goes beyond formal equality to emphasise equal enjoyment of human rights in practice. For example, laws and policies that *appear* to treat women and men equally are not enough to ensure that women are able to enjoy the same rights as men. Due to the legacy of historical inequalities, structural disadvantages, biological differences and biases in how laws and policies are implemented, this *formal equality* can never be sufficient.[40]

In response, the concept of *substantive equality* has been elaborated in key human rights treaties (most notably the Convention on the Elimination of Discrimination Against Women in articles 1 and 3, and in the CEDAW Committee's General Comment 25 on temporary special measures).[41] The concept of substantive equality takes into account a number of overlapping factors: discrimination is often indirect; inequality can be structural; both unequal outcomes and unequal opportunities must be scrutinised; and different treatment might be required to move towards equality in practice, including temporary special measures and affirmative action.[42]

Substantive equality is concerned with the results and outcomes of laws and policies; in the words of the UN Committee on Economic, Social and Cultural Rights, 'ensuring that they do not maintain, but rather alleviate, the inherent disadvantage that particular groups experience'.[43] As UN Women has stressed, to achieve substantive equality for women, therefore, requires both direct and indirect discrimination to be addressed. It also requires specific measures to be adopted that redress women's socioeconomic disadvantage and, in the longer term, the transformation of the institutions and structures that reinforce and reproduce unequal power relations between women and men.[44]

A human rights approach to inequality also emphasises the intersecting and mutually reinforcing nature of different forms of inequality. Because of the multiple dimensions of social identity – such as race, gender, class, age and ability – many people face discrimination on more than one ground. A focus on *intersecting inequalities* examines how different social disparities interact and how these shape or are reinforced by inequalities of income and wealth. As the UN Committee on Economic, Social and Cultural Rights has stated, while a person's economic status may in itself result in pervasive discrimination, 'cumulative discrimination has a unique and specific impact on individuals and merits particular consideration and remedying'.[45]

These mutually reinforcing human rights concepts can (and should) inform the way Goal 10 commitments are interpreted and implemented, in particular in guiding policy choices. For example, the process of designing policies to meet target 10.2 ('empower and promote the social, economic and political inclusion of all, irrespective of age, sex, disability, race, ethnicity, origin, religion or economic or other status') would be vastly enriched by the understanding that these grounds of discrimination often overlap and reinforce each other, and by designing impact assessments and interventions accordingly. An implementation of target 10.3 ('Ensure equal opportunity and reduce inequalities of outcome, including by eliminating discriminatory laws, policies and practices and promoting appropriate legislation, policies and action in this regard') which uses human rights to guide what legislation and policies are 'appropriate' and effective would include special measures and affirmative action to reach particular groups and would seek to avoid and tackle indirect discrimination, including through carefully disaggregated analysis of outcomes.

Human rights norms around equality and non-discrimination can also inform the interpretation and implementation of the overarching 2030 Agenda commitment to 'Leave No One Behind', which as noted above is currently subject to hazy and varying definitions.[46] Viewing 'Leave No One Behind' through the lens of human rights obligations should focus policy attention on the multiple and intersecting forms of discrimination which often affect the most marginalised and disadvantaged people, including those who are frequently neglected by government policy and traditional development interventions, and are often even invisible in official statistics – such as street children and sex workers. The human rights normative framework can help connect the concern for disparity to legal obligations on equality and non-discrimination and determine when disparities in development outcomes are unjust or inequitable, because they arise from human rights deprivations and discriminatory policy efforts.

Drawing on human rights norms and principles to guide implementation and policy

Here, we will address two policy areas, social protection and tax, to demonstrate how human rights standards can inform and guide SDG10 implementation efforts in specific policy areas which are critical in addressing the determinants of economic inequality. Elsewhere, we have also examined other policy areas such as financial regulation, care and family leave, labour rights, health and education.[47]

Social protection is included and emphasised in several of the SDG targets (e.g. targets 1.3, 3.8, 5.4 and 10.4). Target 10.4 commits States to moving progressively towards greater equality through social protection policies (as well as fiscal and labour policies). Social protection is a human right in itself (enshrined in the Universal Declaration of Human Rights [UDHR] and International Covenant on Economic, Social and Cultural Rights [ICESCR] article 9 as 'the right to social security'), and is crucial for the realisation of many other human rights. Social protection includes measures such as transfers and benefits, in cash or in kind, designed to reduce poverty, provide income security and protect against a range of risks, vulnerabilities and lifecycle contingencies including unemployment, old age, childhood, maternity or sickness. It is proven to promote social integration,[48] and to be a key policy in mitigating both economic and social inequalities.[49] For example, in OECD countries between 1985 and 2005, direct income taxes and social transfers (including programmes such as cash transfers, public works, unemployment benefits and pensions) reduced income inequality by about one third.[50]

From a human rights perspective, it is important to ensure that spending on social protection reaches the most disadvantaged and marginalised.[51] However, social protection spending in many Latin American countries, for example, tends to be skewed towards higher income groups.[52] Many policymakers respond by insisting on the need for 'targeting' social protection programmes at specific sections of the population, often those at certain levels of household income identified via means-testing. However, a human rights approach to social protection puts much more emphasis on the need for universal programmes, not least because they help to avoid stigmatisation and engender better social solidarity.[53] Moreover, the evidence shows that when compared to targeted schemes, universal and inclusive social protection programmes have higher quality implementation, with fewer people living in poverty being excluded and with much more effective impacts on poverty and inequality reduction.[54] For example, while Brazil's much-lauded targeted cash transfer scheme *Bolsa Familia* has undoubtedly played a role in tackling inequality, research has shown that it is actually the country's pension system (various schemes which together provide almost universal coverage of Brazil's older people) that has had the biggest impact on reducing income inequality.[55] The social protection programmes which truly 'leave no one behind' and uphold human rights are those that equalise upwards, through universal and non-contributory programmes.[56] Of course, in some cases universal programmes will be not be possible initially because of resource constraints (although eliminating means testing and targeting vastly reduces administrative costs); but the eventual goal should be universality, with very careful targeting in the meantime that avoids exclusion errors (a far more serious concern than over-inclusion), stigmatisation and indirect discrimination or perpetuation of inequalities.[57]

Human rights-informed social protection policies must also be carefully designed to be gender-sensitive, in particular to be responsive to women's unequal share of unpaid care work. The Committee on Economic, Social and Cultural Rights has stated that family and child benefits and paid maternity leave are essential planks of the right to social security.[58] However, many social protection programmes – even those that are supposedly designed to benefit women – do indirectly discriminate or exacerbate inequality.[59] Conditional cash transfer schemes, for example, are often paid to women on the basis of ensuring that their children participate in certain social services.[60] Despite good intentions, these conditions can add to the existing unpaid care work of women, especially those living at a distance from these services. This risks inadvertently increasing their time poverty and economic insecurity, as they could otherwise be undertaking paid work, education or self-care during this time. Frequently, the services that women are expected take their children to are geographically difficult to access, with long wait times and unaffordable out-of-pocket transit costs.[61] In this sense, social protection systems must be complemented by and integrated into quality public services that are physically and economically accessible even for the poorest people.

The second key policy area we will discuss here is tax. Tax policy is one of government's most powerful tools to reduce income and wealth inequalities,[62] both by redistributing market incomes as well as by producing public revenue for public services. Income inequality in advanced economies, for example, is on average one-sixth less than it would be in the absence of direct taxes.[63] However, the decline in marginal tax rates at the top end of the spectrum has been a key factor in the growth of inequality since the 1980s.[64]

Target 10.4 refers to the need to use fiscal policies to achieve greater equality, and tax is included as a crucial 'means of implementation' and source of financing in the targets and indicators for Goal 17. Increasing domestic resource mobilisation through taxation will be a crucial part of implementing the SDGs in all countries, given the significant boost in public revenues required.[65] Yet, blindly chasing revenue targets without consideration of the distributive consequences could result in perverse outcomes. Human rights tools, standards and mechanisms are increasingly being used to inform tax policy and to challenge unjust fiscal arrangements.[66] The human rights principles of equality and non-discrimination and the duty in the ICESCR to allocate the maximum of available resources to progressively realise economic, social and cultural rights give powerful ethical and legal force to demands for more equitable tax systems and provide a corrective to the myopic focus only on tax 'efficiency'.[67]

In order to tackle inequalities, taxation measures must be progressive in nature, ensuring the well-off contribute a larger proportion of their income than those with fewer resources. In contrast, increasing tax revenue through higher levels of often-regressive indirect taxes such as VAT – as 138 countries are reported to have done between 2010 and 2015 as part of fiscal austerity – is likely to be counterproductive as such taxes hit the incomes of the poor the hardest, and particularly affect poor women.[68] Indeed, a holistic income and gender equality lens on taxation measures is vitally important at a time when austerity measures are intensifying across the globe.

Another important step to equalising the effects of tax policy would be to substantially crack down on tax abuse and eliminate unjustifiable tax incentives that largely benefit wealthy individuals and large corporations.[69] Currently, low-income countries in particular lose billions of dollars in potential revenue through these channels, but even relatively wealthy countries could invest far more in tackling inequality and human rights deprivation were they to take concrete steps to crack-down on tax abuses. For example, in Spain austerity measures contributed to the gap between the rich and the poor growing 15% from 2007 to 2013, while the Spanish union of tax inspectors (GESTHA) estimated that the amount the government could have raised through tackling corporate tax evasion would have easily exceeded the total budget cuts in 2012.[70]

In efforts to reduce tax abuses, international cooperation will be necessary. Human rights norms can guide this cooperation, assign responsibility and strengthen accountability.[71] International law – anchored in the UN Charter and various international human rights treaties, declarations and jurisprudence – affirms that states have certain human rights duties that extend outside of their own territory. States have an unambiguous legal obligation to respect human rights internationally, meaning that they must not engage in policies or actions that serve to undermine human rights beyond their borders. States also have a duty to protect human rights against abuse by third parties they are in a position to control or regulate, be they multinational companies or private individuals. They are likewise obliged to proactively contribute to the fulfilment of economic, social and cultural rights beyond their borders, including through cooperation with other nations.[72] Though rarely invoked in SDG debates, these 'extraterritorial' human rights obligations can shed light on the common but differentiated responsibilities of states to reduce inequality and prevent deepening disparity.[73] Indeed, human rights duties related to international cooperation and actions that have ramifications beyond borders can help to pinpoint the distinct but concurrent responsibilities of different duty-bearers, including those rich countries most responsible for – but currently most resistant to – creating a fairer international tax system that can help to improve economic inequality within and between countries.[74]

Looking at these policy areas illustrates how using the lens and tools of human rights can enrich and inform the implementation of the SDGs, and illustrate the types of policies that will be necessary. This type of analysis and rationale (carefully assessing the likely and actual impacts of policies on inequalities and examining their root causes; shining a light on systemic obstacles at the national and international level; rooting out direct and indirect discrimination) can usefully be applied to policy-making across many areas crucial to the implementation of SDG 10.

How can human rights accountability tools and mechanisms help?

Aside from aiding in interpreting and implementing the goals, the human rights system can provide spaces and tools to pursue accountability for the 2030 Agenda. As discussed above, SDG10 is vulnerable to being swept under the rug of 'prioritisation' and institutional inertia. Consequently, SDG10 may face the same lack of accountability as many of the predecessor MDGs. While the MDGs undoubtedly affected development discourse, the crucial task of recognising responsibilities among the multitude of development actors actually affecting outcomes was never properly addressed.[75] At the core of the human rights framework is the availability of properly functioning accountability mechanisms, which can ensure responsibility, answerability and enforceability with regard to the commitments states have made.[76] Human rights mechanisms at the national (e.g. national human rights institutions [NHRIs]), regional (e.g. regional human rights courts and commissions) and international levels can contribute to accountability for the SDGs – especially the inequality dimensions – but here for reasons of space we will just explore briefly the national and international mechanisms.

Agenda 2030 encourages countries to develop SDG national action plans or strategies,[77] in which they will present how they intend to achieve the Goals. In principle, these provide an opportunity for civil society to be involved in formulating and interrogating these plans, and holding governments answerable for implementing them. The extent to which governments are doing this so far, of course varies greatly. Some countries (e.g. Germany, the Netherlands) have expressed their intentions to address SDG implementation both domestically, and overseas through both development cooperation and the impact of other policy areas abroad.[78] This could be a positive step in fostering more rigorous monitoring and accountability for the reduction of inequalities between countries.

The 2030 Agenda agreement also states that governments will conduct regular reviews of their progress on the SDGs.[79] While these national-level reviews could increase the responsiveness of SDG implementation, they are explicitly described as voluntary which may mean that in some countries they do not happen at all, or that certain sensitive or challenging issues like economic inequality get left aside. National review processes will rightly take different forms in every country, but some common elements should be present in all in order for them to be adequate and effective rather than tokenistic. The broad principles for follow-up and review set out in the 2030 Agenda are a reasonable starting point, but more should be done to increase coherence between development policy and human rights obligations, both in process and substance. On a practical level, regional and international human rights mechanisms collect and issue a wealth of information that would be relevant to these SDG reviews. So, at the most basic level, human rights reports collected for country reviews before the UN treaty bodies or the UPR – and the recommendations issued – could be fed into SDG reporting and review, and vice versa.[80] National reviews should consider the challenges identified and recommendations issued by human rights bodies, and how they impact on sustainable development and how they should inform and guide SDG planning and implementation. In addition, it will be important for these reviews to include analysis of the role of the private sector and in particular public-private-partnerships for sustainable development, and interrogate their effects on human rights. To this end, it may be useful to consider existing or proposed National Action Plans on Business and Human Rights in the context of SDG reviews.[81]

The SDGs are political commitments and not legally binding, but in some cases domestic legal accountability measures may be available where the goals and targets overlap with existing legal or constitutional provisions, or where these provisions are breached by SDG implementation efforts (for example if a constitutionally-protected right to housing is breached by informal settlement upgrading undertaken supposedly to comply with target 11.1). In such cases, therefore, it may be possible to make claims within national judicial mechanisms to hold governments accountable.[82] In addition, beyond formal national review processes, accountability initiatives led by communities, civil society and social movements will be crucial to ensure people's perspectives and demands are collected and heard. 'Social accountability' and citizen monitoring projects could be developed to generate pressure, demand answers or corrective action from authorities, and to empower national actors. For example, initiatives such as citizen oversight committees, community scorecards and community mapping are already used in many places to monitor quality of public services and their impact on human rights in the fields of health, education and water, and could be powerful to monitor SDG progress on the relevant goals. In addition, efforts such as participatory budgeting could be scaled up, to ensure that governments dedicate sufficient, equitable, and accountable financing to sustainable development.[83] There are already existing initiatives promoting citizen-led data collection and participatory monitoring for the SDGs.[84]

Many human rights-specific institutions and mechanisms also exist at the national level which could play a crucial role in improving and facilitating SDG accountability. For example, NHRIs, where they are adequately resourced and sufficiently independent,[85] can play a unique role in ensuring international commitments are upheld domestically. They should be supported to develop the tools and capacity necessary to monitor SDG implementation domestically, and to report on these findings to both national and international stakeholders.[86] Moreover, many NHRIs have a primary or explicit focus on inequalities, and many are increasingly engaging with questions of economic and social rights and economic policy, and therefore their contribution to accountability for Goal 10 could be particularly valuable. These mechanisms can help backstop monitoring, review and accountability for those SDGs which are particularly informed by standing human rights guarantees.[87] The German Institute for Human Rights, for example, is engaging in analysing and critiquing the government's strategy for implementing the SDGs from a rights-based approach, and urging the government to improve the participation of civil society.[88]

The national level should be the main focus of SDG accountability efforts. Still, given the inevitability that many governments will not put the resources and political will behind robust national-level accountability processes, and the fact that many of the structural underpinnings of inequality extend far beyond national borders, efforts to ensure accountability for meeting SDG10 cannot rely solely on national mechanisms. Institutional reforms will be needed at the regional as well as the global level.

In the 2030 Declaration, the High-Level Political Forum on Sustainable Development (HLPF) is identified as the global mechanism for follow-up and review of the 2030 Agenda.[89] Alongside regional and national follow-up and review systems, the HLPF is mandated to take stock of the progress made towards achieving the SDGs at the global level, provide guidance on implementation of the SDGs as well as promote policy coherence by sharing successes and challenges in SDG implementation.[90] The HLPF consists of both voluntary national reviews, where countries present their progress towards the 2030 Agenda, and thematic 'reviews' which at least at the 2016 HLPF were in fact merely discussion panels.

Despite broad agreement that one of the key reasons the Millennium Development Goals fell short in many areas was the lack of a robust global accountability mechanism, the HLPF is not the powerful accountability body civil society has been advocating for. The power of the HLPF to review and hold states accountable is weak and limited, especially given its reliance on voluntary self-reporting by states, and a total meeting time of only eight days per year, with only 1.5 days total for the national reviews in 2016. As the first HLPF since the adoption of the SDGs took place in July 2016 it became clear that the weak mandate and as yet unspecified structure of the HLPF risks undermining its effectiveness as the overarching forum for SDG accountability. The voluntary nature of the national review process, and the modest time allocated to it, placed a considerable constraint on its effectiveness in terms of accountability. The presentations by the 22 states that had volunteered to be reviewed seemed more focused on giving the most positive gloss than on sharing implementation challenges and strategies.[91]

Although the HLPF's potential role as a global oversight mechanism should not be entirely discounted, given its institutional weaknesses, other accountability mechanisms must also be engaged. In particular, the international human rights monitoring mechanisms must be encouraged and supported to play a key role. The Agenda 2030 Declaration confirms that the SDG commitments are rooted in human rights obligations, and the international human rights mechanisms already examine and report on countries' performance on many of the issues covered in the SDG agenda. Given the centrality of inequality and non-discrimination to all international human rights treaties and the bodies that monitor them, their role in bolstering accountability for Goal 10 could be particularly valuable.[92] Several UN treaty bodies have made strong recommendations or statements on policy areas that are crucial determinants of economic and social inequality: for example, fiscal policy,[93] social protection,[94] labour and wage policies,[95] and of course, the elimination of discriminatory laws, policies and practices and the promotion of measures to counter gender, racial and other forms of discrimination.[96] All of these are strongly related to targets included in Goal 10.

The Human Rights Council's Universal Periodic Review (UPR) could also play a useful role as a complementary mechanism for reviewing States' progress on the SDGs where they overlap with and are underpinned by existing human rights obligations. For instance, the UPR might examine whether domestic SDG implementation is taking place in line with human rights obligations. It can also serve as an (albeit imperfect) model for improving the procedures for national voluntary reviews under the HLPF,[97] for instance in the space and legitimacy accorded to civil society participation and shadow reporting. While susceptible to the political dynamics that arise in any inter-governmental forum, the certain modalities and characteristics of the UPR could nevertheless be an important reference point for future HLPF reviews.

Utilising existing international human rights mechanisms as a vehicle for SDG10 accountability would not just bring an extra procedural layer of accountability; it would also provide a different *type* of accountability and provide an alternative to relying on 'official' SDG indicators. Especially given the more robust and meaningful space given to civil society in human rights monitoring bodies as compared to the HLPF, engaging with human rights mechanisms could provide an alternative space for questioning some of the SDG data, methods, assumptions and narratives; focusing on individuals and communities rather than aggregate national progress; and drawing on civil society perspectives and expertise rather than relying solely on official statistics or 'big data'. Moreover, human rights standards can provide alternative benchmarks against which to judge progress. In many cases they are more ambitious and more rigorous than the SDGs, they are legally binding, and they are backed up by a wealth of jurisprudence and interpretation (for example in General Comments) which provide specific recommendations and policy guidance. In this sense they can be a qualitative complement to the quantitative SDG indicators. They are also arguably more focused on the structural issues and some of the causes of inequality which are mostly missing from the SDGs. Indeed, given the focus and content of human rights standards and the expertise of human rights bodies, using human rights processes will be particularly important in ensuring SDG implementation does adequately address inequalities and in interrogating who is being left behind.

In order to become a valuable complement to national follow-up efforts, international human rights mechanisms engaging with the SDGs should seek to examine the transnational dimensions of SDG implementation – for example, the impact that countries' policies are having beyond their borders. The framework of extraterritorial obligations is a useful tool in this sense, to analyse the human rights and sustainable development impact of countries' policies and actions abroad and draw clearer lines of responsibility. Although there was considerable political resistance among some industrialised countries to the principle of 'Common But Differentiated Responsibilities' (CBDR) being applicable to Agenda 2030,[98] there is little doubt that the SDG-era 'global partnership for development' (SDG17) needs to be more equitable and accountable than the commitments under MDG8, which were largely limited to the level of rhetoric. Applying the normative framework of extra-territorial obligations in the area of economic, social and cultural rights as a reference point for determining CBDR would be a positive step in fostering more rigorous monitoring and accountability for the reduction of inequalities between countries, as well as the commitments under Goal 17, for example on policy coherence.

Conclusion

Some see the SDGs as just the latest distracting 'fad' in international development, with little chance of really shifting the real centres of power or the prevailing development policy shibboleths.[99] Some fear that they will undercut existing human rights obligations, and moreover divert attention and resources from human rights institutions and programmes. These anxieties and critiques certainly have some basis, and there is no question that the 2030 Agenda is deeply flawed in several respects.[100] We for example remain concerned that for all the talk of 'transformation', the vision of development underpinning the SDGs remains premised on old (and unsustainable) models of export-oriented economic growth and industrial consumption and production. Meanwhile, given the blithely oversimplified view expressed in the agenda of the private sector as a solely positive force, and failure to include anything approaching oversight or accountability for negative corporate impacts on rights and development, there is a real risk of corporate capture which must be vigorously resisted.

However, it is our view that human rights advocates have much more to gain than to lose by engaging with the SDGs, including and in particular Goal 10. The goals and targets will drive development priorities and funding in countries across the globe over the next 15 years. These international commitments will therefore have an influence over economic and social policy that international standards on economic and social rights have rarely, if ever, had. They include several elements which could be very valuable openings for advocates looking to inject more human rights sensitivity and alignment into development efforts. This is particularly the case when it comes to the Agenda's inclusion of targets on inequality.

We have analysed several of the opportunities in this respect in this article. However, it is clear that proactive engagement and lobbying will be necessary to keep the Goal 10 commitments on the political agenda. Moreover, careful vigilance will be required to ensure that their implementation is shaped by and reinforces human rights obligations. Therefore, human rights advocates do not have to sacrifice their priorities in order to engage with SDG implementation and monitoring; quite the contrary, the imperative is to inject precisely those priorities into these efforts. Indeed civil society groups around the world are already seizing the opportunity to track progress on the SDGs through a critical human rights lens, pointing to the structural obstacles that risk getting left behind in SDG implementation. The Spotlight Report on Sustainable Development, for example, is a civil-society-coordinated global monitoring initiative that casts a human rights lens on the implementation of the SDGs, including SDG10.[101] At a time when civil society space faces increasing restrictions in many countries, the SDG monitoring process offers a potential new avenue for holding governments accountable to the human rights obligations underpinning their development commitments. It also offers an opportunity for human rights organisations to work with different kinds of partners and networks that are not necessarily engaged in human rights processes, and therefore to forge new and broader alliances.

Human rights frameworks, standards and tools have a lot to offer to ensure the interpretation and implementation of SDG10 does confront inequalities of all sorts in a more holistic and sustainable way. It is crucial now that human rights advocates and institutions, particularly at the national level, seize the opportunity to influence the implementation of the agenda, and to stake a claim for accountability through the human rights system.

Notes

1. United Nations, *The Millennium Development Goals Report 2015* (New York: United Nations, 2015).
2. Oxfam, *An Economy for the 99%* (Oxford: Oxfam, 2017).
3. United Nations (UN), *Transforming Our World: The 2030 Agenda for Sustainable Development* (New York: UN, 2015).
4. Kate Donald, 'SDG Targets Risk Missing the Mark on Inequality', Center for Economic and Social Rights (CESR) blog, 2016, http://www.cesr.org/sdg-targets-risk-missing-mark-inequality (accessed July 21, 2017).
5. Goal 10 is graded as an 'F', meaning that 'reversal will be needed – complete rethinks in approach, new commitments, and likely public pressure': Susan Nicolai et al., *Projecting Progress: Reaching the SDGs by 2030* (London: Overseas Development Institute, 2015).
6. Although the 2016 issue of the World Bank's new 'Poverty and Shared Prosperity' annual report does include analysis of inequality: see World Bank, *Poverty and Shared Prosperity 2016: Taking on Inequality* (Washington DC: World Bank, 2016). For a critique of the report, see Peter Bakvis, 'The World Bank's Inequality Omissions,' Inequality.org, posted October 3, 2016, https://inequality.org/research/world-bank-inequality-report-whats-missing/ (accessed July 21, 2017).

7. Center for Economic and Social Rights (CESR), *From Disparity to Dignity: tackling economic inequality through the Sustainable Development Goals* (New York: CESR, 2016).
8. Iain Levine, 'Building a Better World by "Righting" Development', Human Rights Watch blog, September 12, 2015, https://www.hrw.org/blog-feed/righting-development (accessed July 21, 2017).
9. Era Dabla-Norris et al., 'Causes and Consequences of Income Inequality: A Global Perspective', IMF Staff Discussion Note (Washington DC: International Monetary Fund, 2015).
10. High-Level Panel of Eminent Persons on the Post-2015 Development Agenda, *A New Global Partnership: Eradicate Poverty and Transform Economies Through Sustainable Development* (New York: United Nations, 2013).
11. UN, *Transforming Our World: The 2030 Agenda for Sustainable Development* (New York: UN, 2015): 1–3, 7, 12.
12. For example, although their official position is more expansive, in practice the UK government has pushed a very narrow definition of 'Leave No One Behind', addressing poverty in the Global South. Certainly it has not acknowledged the relevance that the concept might have to the UK: see Paul Okumu, 'Why We Must Change Strategy on SDG Implementation,' Africa Platform blog, 3 August 2016, https://africaplatform.org/news/why-we-must-change-strategy-on-sdg-implementation/ (accessed February 27, 2017); UK Department for International Development, 'Leave No One Behind: Our Promise', https://www.gov.uk/government/publications/leaving-no-one-behind-our-promise/leaving-no-one-behind-our-promise (accessed July 21, 2017).
13. See e.g. J. G. Palma, 'Homogeneous Middles vs. Heterogeneous Tails, and the End of the "Inverted-U": It's All About the Share of the Rich', *Development and Change* 42, no. 1 (2011): 87–153.
14. See e.g. the Convention on the Elimination of Racial Discrimination or the Convention on the Elimination of All Forms of Discrimination Against Women. On horizontal inequalities, see Frances Stewart, 'Horizontal Inequalities', *World Science Report* (2016): 51–4, http://unesdoc.unesco.org/images/0024/002458/245825e.pdf.
15. See e.g. Economic Inequality and Human Rights debate on OpenGlobalRights, https://www.opendemocracy.net/openglobalrights/economic-inequality-and-human-rights; Office of the UN High Commissioner for Human Rights (OHCHR), 'Report of the Special Rapporteur on extreme poverty and human rights, Philip Alston,' A/HRC/29/31, 2015.
16. OHCHR, 'Report of the Special Rapporteur on extreme poverty and human rights, Philip Alston,' A/HRC/29/31, pp. 11–13, 2015.
17. Todd Landman and Marco Larizza, 'Inequality and Human Rights: Who controls what, when, and how', *International Studies Quarterly* 53, no. 3 (2009): 715–36; Oxfam International, 'Working for the Few: Political Capture and Economic Inequality', Oxfam briefing paper (Oxford: Oxfam International, 2014).
18. Oxfam International, 'Working for the Few'; Sakiko Fukuda-Parr, 'It's About Values: Human Rights Norms and Tolerance for Inequality', *Opendemocracy.net*, posted December 22, 2015, https://www.opendemocracy.net/openglobalrights/sakiko-fukuda-parr/it-s-about-values-human-rights-norms-and-tolerance-for-inequalit.
19. Philip Alston, 'Extreme Inequality as the Antithesis of Human Rights', *Opendemocracy.net*, posted October 27, 2015, https://www.opendemocracy.net/openglobalrights/philip-alston/extreme-inequality-as-antithesis-of-human-rights.
20. Ignacio Saiz and Gaby Oré Aguilar, 'Introducing the Debate on Economic Inequality: Can Human Rights Make A Difference?', *Opendemocracy.net*, posted October 27, 2015, https://www.opendemocracy.net/openglobalrights/ignacio-saiz-gaby-or-aguilar/introducing-debate-on-economic-inequality-can-human-ri.
21. The ratio of the income share of the top 10% to that of the bottom 40% see Alex Cobham and Andy Sumner, 'Is It All About the Tails? The Palma Measure of Income Inequality' (CGD Working Paper 343, Center for Global Development, Washington DC, 2013).
22. Alex Cobham, Lukas Schlogl and Andy Sumner, 'Top Incomes Drive Inequality: So Why Does The Inequality Target Ignore Them?' *The Guardian* Global Development blog,

September 21, 2015, https://www.theguardian.com/global-development/2015/sep/21/top-incomes-drive-income-inequality-global-target.

23. Nobuo Yoshida and Juan Feng, 'Reducing Inequality By Promoting Shared Prosperity', World Bank Data Blog, June 2016, http://blogs.worldbank.org/opendata/ic4d/sustainablecities/reducing-inequality-promoting-shared-prosperity.

24. Thomas Piketty et al., 'Optimal Taxation of Top Labor Incomes: A Tale of Three Elasticities' (NBER Working Paper 17616, NBER, Cambridge MA, 2011). http://www.nber.org/papers/w17616.pdf.

25. Inter-Agency and Expert Group on Sustainable Development Goal Indicators, 'Final List of Proposed Sustainable Development Goal Indicators', E/CN.3/2016/2/Rev.1.

26. See UN Statistical Division's compilation of metadata for target 10.1: https://unstats.un.org/sdgs/metadata/files/Metadata-10-01-01.pdf (accessed July 21, 2017).

27. Faiza Shaheen, 'Inequality Within and Among Countries', in *International Norms, Normative Change, and the UN Sustainable Development Goals*, ed. Noha Shawki (London: Lexington Books, 2016), 99–114.

28. Jonathan Ostry, Prakash Loungani and Davide Furceri, 'Neoliberalism: Oversold?', *Finance and Development* 53, no. 2 (2016): 38–41.

29. CESR, 'A Matter of Justice: Securing Human Rights in the Post-2015 Sustainable Development Agenda' (New York: CESR, 2014), http://cesr.org/sites/default/files/matter.of_.justice.pdf.

30. Cobham et al., 'Top Incomes Drive Inequality'; also, Nora Lustig has argued that the SDGs are missing a target to 'ensure that the tax system does not reduce the income of the poor': Nora Lustig, 'A Missing Target in the SDGs: Tax Systems Should Not Reduce The Incomes Of The Poor', International Growth Center blog, 2015, http://www.theigc.org/blog/a-missing-target-in-the-sdgs-tax-systems-should-not-reduce-the-income-of-the-poor/.

31. See for example, Amartya Sen, *The Idea of Justice* (Cambridge, MA: Harvard University Press, 2011), 409–10: 'The distribution of the benefits of global relations depends not only on domestic policies, but also on a variety of international social arrangements, including trade agreements, patent laws, global health initiatives, international educational provisions, facilities for technological dissemination, ecological and environmental restraint, treatment of accumulated debts (often incurred by irresponsible military rulers of the past), and the restraining of conflicts and local wars'.

32. See e.g. UNCTAD, *Trade and Development Report 2014* (Geneva: United Nations, 2014); UN DESA Committee on Development Policy, *Global Governance and Global Rules for Development in the Post-2015 Era* (New York: United Nations, 2014).

33. CESR, 'A Matter of Justice'.

34. E.g. Maastricht Principles on Extraterritorial Obligations of States in the Area of Economic, Social and Cultural Rights (Heidelberg: FIAN International, 2013).

35. See CESR, 'The Measure of Progress: How Human Rights Should Inform the Sustainable Development Goal Indicators', CESR Human Rights Policy Brief, October 2015, http://cesr.org/sites/default/files/downloads/cesr_measure_of_progress.pdf.

36. For instance, the Convention on the Elimination of All Forms of Discrimination Against Women, the Convention on the Rights of Persons with Disabilities, and the Declaration on the Rights of Indigenous Peoples.

37. See e.g. CESCR General Comment 16; CEDAW General Comment 25.

38. CESCR Article 13 2(a) and SDG target 4.1.

39. See CESR and Third World Network, 'Universal Rights, Differentiated Responsibilities: Safeguarding Human Rights Beyond Borders to Achieve the Sustainable Development Goals' (CESR and TWN Policy Brief, April 2015).

40. *UN Women, Transforming Economies, Realizing Rights: Progress of the World's Women Report 2015–16* (New York: UN Women, 2015).

41. CEDAW Committee, 'General recommendation No. 25, on article 4, paragraph 1, of the Convention on the Elimination of All Forms of Discrimination against Women, on temporary special measures' (2004).

42. UN Women, *Transforming Economies, Realizing Rights*.
43. UN Committee on Economic, Social and Cultural Rights (2005), General Comment No. 16, E/C.12/2005/4.
44. UN Women, *Transforming Economies, Realizing Rights*. See Chapter 1 of the report for a detailed description of substantive equality.
45. UN Committee on Economic, Social and Cultural Rights (2009), General Comment No. 20, Non-discrimination in economic, social and cultural rights, E/C.12/GC/20.
46. For interpretations, see IIED, 'Unpacking What We Mean By Leave No One Behind', IIED website, May 2016 https://www.iied.org/unpacking-what-we-mean-leave-no-one-behind (accessed July 21, 2017); ODI, 'Leaving No One Behind: A Critical Path for the First 1,000 Days of the Sustainable Development Goals' (ODI Research Report, July 2016). A good exploration of the concept from a human rights perspective is provided in United Nations Chief Executive Board for Coordination, 'Equality and non-discrimination at the heart of sustainable development: a Shared United Nations Framework for Action' (Report of the High-Level Committee on Programmes), UN Doc CEB/2016/6/Add.1.
47. See CESR, 'From Disparity to Dignity: Tackling Economic Inequality Through the Sustainable Development Goals' (CESR Human Rights Policy Brief, October 2016).
48. UNESCAP, 'Time for Equality: The Role of Social Protection in Reducing Inequalities in Asia and the Pacific' (Bangkok: United Nations, 2015) http://www.unescap.org/sites/default/files/SDD%20Time%20for%20Equality%20report_final.pdf.
49. UNRISD argue that broad-based and inclusive coverage can reduce inequalities across income, class, gender, ethnicity, gender and location: see UNRISD, *Combating Poverty and Inequality: Structural Change, Social Policy and Politics* (Geneva: UNRISD, 2010), 161, http://socialprotection-humanrights.org/wp-content/uploads/2015/12/PovRep-small.pdf.
50. Francesca Bastagli, David Coady and Sanjeev Gupta, 'Income Inequality and Fiscal Policy' (IMF Discussion Note, Washington DC, 2012), 11. See also Economic Commission for Latin America and the Caribbean (ECLAC), 'Time For Equality: Closing Gaps, Opening Trails' (33rd session summary, Santiago, 2010), 225.
51. For a human rights analysis of social protection, see CESCR General Comment 19; Magdalena Sepúlveda and Carly Nyst, 'A Human Rights Approach to Social Protection' (Ministry of Foreign Affairs of Finland, Erweko Oy, 2012); and the Social Protection and Human Rights Resource Platform http://socialprotection-humanrights.org/.
52. See UNRISD, *Combating Poverty*, 143–4.
53. Sepúlveda and Nyst, 'Human Rights Approach to Social Protection'.
54. Stephen Kidd, 'The Political Economy of "Targeting" of Social Security Schemes', Pathways' Perspectives on Social Policy in International Development 19 (*Development Pathways*, 2015), http://www.developmentpathways.co.uk/resources/wp-content/uploads/2015/10/Political-Economy-of-Targeting-PP19-4.pdf.
55. Stephen Kidd and Karishma Huda, 'Bolsa Unfamiliar', Pathways Perspectives on Social Policy in International Development 9 (*Development Pathways*, 2013). http://www.developmentpathways.co.uk/downloads/perspectives/Pathways-Perspectives-9-BOLSA-unFAMILIAr.pdf.
56. Sepúlveda and Nyst, 'Human Rights Approach to Social Protection'.
57. Sepúlveda and Nyst, 'Human Rights Approach to Social Protection'.
58. CESCR, General Comment 19, The Right to Social Security.
59. See UN Women, *Transforming Economies, Realizing Rights*, Chapter 3.
60. Observatorio de Igualdad de Género de América Latin y el Caribe, *Los Bonos en La Mira: Aporte y Carga Para Las Mujeres* (Santiago: CEPAL, 2012).
61. Observatorio de Igualdad de Género, *Los Bonos en La Mira*.
62. See e.g. Francesca Bastagli, David Coady and Sanjeev Gupta, 'Income Inequality and Fiscal Policy' (IMF Discussion Note, Washington DC, 2012), 11.
63. Maura Francese, 'Harnessing the Power of Fiscal Policy to Mitigate Inequality' (IMF September, 2015). http://www.imf.org/external/pubs/ft/survey/so/2015/pol092515a.htm.
64. Piketty et al., 'Optimal Taxation of Top Labor Incomes'.

65. CESR and Christian Aid, 'A Post-2015 Fiscal Revolution' (policy brief, CESR and Christian Aid, New York & London, 2014). http://www.cesr.org/sites/default/files/fiscal.revolution.pdf.

66. See CESR, 'Human Rights in Tax Policy', CESR website, http://cesr.org/human-rights-taxation (accessed July 21, 2017); OHCHR, 'Report of the UN Special Rapporteur on extreme poverty and human rights, Magdalena Sepúlveda Carmona,' A/HRC/26/28.

67. For more on the 'maximum available resources' standard, see Radhika Balakrishnan et al., *Maximum Available Resources and Human Rights: Analytical Report* (New Brunswick: Center for Women's Global Leadership, 2011).

68. Kate Donald and Rachel Moussié, 'Redistributing Unpaid Care Work: Why Tax Matters for Women's Rights' (Institute of Development Studies and CESR Policy Brief, January 2016), http://www.cesr.org/sites/default/files/UnpaidCare_IDS_CESR.pdf.

69. Oxfam International, 'An Economy for the 1%: How Privilege and Power in the Economy Drive Extreme Inequality and How This Can Be Stopped' (210 Oxfam briefing paper, Oxfam International, 18 January 2016), https://www.oxfam.org/sites/www.oxfam.org/files/file_attachments/bp210-economy-one-percent-tax-havens-180116-en_0.pdf.

70. CESR, 'Spain Factsheet', CESR Factsheet No. 12 http://www.cesr.org/sites/default/files/FACT_SHEET_SPAIN.pdf (accessed July 21, 2017).

71. CESR and Third World Network, 'Universal Rights'.

72. See Maastricht Principles on Extraterritorial Obligations of States in the Area of Economic, Social and Cultural Rights (Heidelberg: FIAN International, 2013).

73. CESR and Third World Network, 'Universal Rights'.

74. CESR and Third World Network, 'Universal Rights'.

75. Aldo Caliari and Mac Darrow, 'International Cooperation, MDG 8, and Human Rights', in *The Millennium Development Goals and Human Rights: Past, Present and Future*, ed. Malcolm Langford, Andy Sumner and Alicia Ely Yamin (New York: Cambridge University Press, 2013), 316–59.

76. CESR and OHCHR, 'Who Will Be Accountable? Human Rights and the Post-2015 Development Agenda' (New York: United Nations, 2013), http://www.cesr.org/sites/default/files/who_will_be_accountable.pdf.

77. UN, *Transforming Our World*.

78. Federal Government of Germany, 'Report of the German Federal Government to the High-Level Political Forum on Sustainable Development 2016', 12 July 2016, https://sustainabledevelopment.un.org/content/documents/10686HLPF-Bericht_final_EN.pdf (accessed July 21, 2017)

79. UN, *Transforming Our World*.

80. Kate Donald and Sally-Anne Way, 'Accountability for the Sustainable Development Goals: A Lost Opportunity?', *Ethics and International Affairs* 30 (2016): 2.

81. In June 2013 the UN Human Rights Council called on all states to develop National Action Plans on Business and Human Rights. Several countries have now done so, and the process is underway in many others.

82. Landmark cases in Latin America, India, and South Africa have had a direct effect on social and economic policies in recent years and similar strategic litigation could be possible in the SDG context: see CESR and OHCHR, *Who Will Be Accountable?*, 39–42.

83. Donald and Way, 'Accountability for the Sustainable Development Goals'.

84. See, for example, Civicus' DataShift project, as discussed by Jack Cornforth and Kate Higgins in 'How Can Civil Society Collaborate to Bolster SDG Monitoring?', Civicus website, August 13, 2015, civicus.org/thedatashift/how-can-civil-society-collaborate-to-bolster-sdg-monitoring/.

85. The 'Principles relating to the Status of National Human Rights Institutions' (the 'Paris Principles', adopted by the United Nations General Assembly, resolution 48/134 of 20 December 1993) set out the standards for NHRIs.

86. CESR and Danish Institute for Human Rights, 'Realizing Rights through the Sustainable Development Goals: The Role of National Human Rights Institutions' (New York and

Copenhagen: CESR and DIHR, 2015), http://www.cesr.org/sites/default/files/NHRI_realizing_rights_sdgs_0.pdf (accessed July 21, 2017).

87. Twelfth International Conference of the International Coordinating Committee of National Institutions for the Promotion and Protection of Human Rights, 'The Mérida Declaration: The Role of National Human Rights Institutions in implementing the 2030 Agenda for Sustainable Development' (October 2015), http://nhri.ohchr.org/EN/ICC/InternationalConference/12IC/Background%20Information/Merida%20Declaration%20FINAL.pdf (accessed July 21, 2017).

88. Julia Kercher and Claudia Mahler, 'Sustainable Development Goals: An Opportunity for the Realisation of Human Rights in and by Germany', German Institute for Human Rights, Aktuell, 2015 no. 3, http://www.institut-fuer-menschenrechte.de/fileadmin/user_upload/Publikationen/aktuell/aktuell_3_2015_Sustainable_Development_Goals.pdf; German Institute for Human Rights, 'Germany's 2016 Report to the High Level Political Forum on Sustainable Development Comments by the German Institute for Human Rights' (2016), https://sustainabledevelopment.un.org/index.php?page=view&type=111&nr=10810&menu=35 (accessed July 21, 2017).

89. UN, *Transforming Our World.*

90. UN, *Transforming Our World.*

91. CESR, 'Accountability Left Behind in SDG Follow-Up and Review', CESR blog, August 2016, http://www.cesr.org/accountability-left-behind-sdg-follow-and-review.

92. Human rights advocates have already engaged with regional and international human rights mechanisms to challenge issues related to Goal 10, including discriminatory fiscal measures: see CESR, 'Spain's austerity criticized again in UN rights review,' CESR Blog January 2015, http://www.cesr.org/spain%E2%80%99s-austerity-criticized-again-un-rights-review (accessed July 21, 2017) and CESR et al., 'Política Fiscal y Derechos Humanos en las Américas: Movilizar los recursos para garantizar los derechos,' Report to the Inter-American Commission on Human Rights, October 2015, http://www.cesr.org/sites/default/files/cidh_fiscalidad_ddhh_oct2015.pdf (accessed July 21, 2017).

93. Committee on Economic, Social and Cultural Rights, 'Letter by the Chairperson of the Committee on austerity measures', May 16, 2012, http://tbinternet.ohchr.org/_layouts/treatybodyexternal/Download.aspx?symbolno=INT%2fCESCR%2fSUS%2f6395&Lang=en (accessed July 21, 2017); Committee on the Rights of the Child, 'General Comment No. 19 on public budgeting for the realization of children's rights (art. 4)', CRC/C/GC/19 (2016).

94. Committee on Economic, Social and Cultural Rights, 'General Comment 19: The right to social security' http://tbinternet.ohchr.org/_layouts/treatybodyexternal/Download.aspx?symbolno=E%2fC.12%2fGC%2f19&Lang=en.

95. Committee on Economic, Social and Cultural Rights, 'General Comment 23 on the Right to Just and Favourable Conditions of Work' (article 7 of the International Covenant on Economic, Social and Cultural Rights)', http://tbinternet.ohchr.org/_layouts/treatybodyexternal/Download.aspx?symbolno=E%2fC.12%2fGC%2f23&Lang=en (accessed July 21, 2017).

96. See much of the work of the CEDAW Committee, including on substantive equality and temporary special measures; see also CESCR, 'General Comment 20: Non-discrimination in Economic, Social and Cultural Rights', http://tbinternet.ohchr.org/_layouts/treatybodyexternal/Download.aspx?symbolno=E%2fC.12%2fGC%2f20&Lang=en (accessed July 21, 2017).

97. Amnesty International, CESR, Center for Reproductive Rights and Human Rights Watch, 'Accountability For the Post-2015 Agenda: A Proposal for a Robust Global Review Mechanism' (Briefing note, 2015), http://cesr.org/accountability-post-2015-agenda-proposal-robust-global-review-mechanism (accessed July 21, 2017).

98. Alvin Leong, 'The Principle of Common But Differentiated Responsibilities and the SDGs', Deliver2030.org blog, May 27, 2014, http://deliver2030.org/?p=5279.

99. Jason Hickel, 'The Problem with Saving the World', *Jacobin*, August 8, 2015, https://www.jacobinmag.com/2015/08/global-poverty-climate-change-sdgs/.

100. For several pertinent assessments and critiques, see the special issue of *Gender and Development* 24, no. 1, March 2016; see also the assessment of the Post-2015 Human Rights Caucus:

http://cesr.org/sites/default/files/HR_Caucus_Reaction_Agenda2030.pdf (accessed July 21, 2017).

101. Reflection Group on the 2030 Agenda for Sustainable Development (2016), 'Spotlight on Sustainable Development', https://www.2030spotlight.org/en (accessed July 21, 2017).

Acknowledgements

This article draws from and builds on 'From Disparity to Dignity: Tackling Economic Inequality through the Sustainable Development Goals', published by the Center for Economic and Social Rights in 2016. Nicholas Lusiani (Director of Human Rights in Economic Policy at CESR) was one of the authors of that briefing.

Disclosure statement

No potential conflict of interest was reported by the authors.

Vertical inequalities: are the SDGs and human rights up to the challenges?

Gillian MacNaughton

ABSTRACT

Extreme inequalities in income, wealth and social outcomes are one of the greatest human rights challenges that we face today as they threaten individual and community health, national political and economic stability and global peace. This article considers the extent to which the Sustainable Development Goals (SDGs), adopted on September 25, 2016, and international human rights norms are adequate to address the challenges of these extreme inequalities. It focuses specifically on SDG 10, which aims to reduce inequalities within and among countries, and finds the targets inadequate to address many of the most pressing inequalities. It then examines international human rights law to discern whether human rights standards might inform the SDGs to alleviate some of the shortcomings of SDG 10. The article concludes that interpretations of international human rights to date also fall short in terms of addressing income, wealth and social inequalities. It therefore calls for research on the legal interpretation of the multiple equality provisions in the International Bill of Human Rights in a manner that would address the greatest human rights challenges of our time.

Introduction

Extreme inequalities in income, wealth and social outcomes are one of the greatest human rights challenges that we face today.[1] Social movements, such as Occupy and Our Revolution, political upsets, such as Brexit and Trump, and scholars, such as Picketty, Atkinson, Stiglitz and Wilkinson, all point to the crisis of economic and social inequality in the world.[2] It is, therefore, not surprising to find that inequality is also a central concern in the resolution *Transforming Our World: The 2030 Agenda for Sustainable Development* adopted by the United Nations General Assembly on September 25, 2015.[3] At the UN Summit launching the 2030 Agenda, Zeid Ra'ad Al Hussein, the UN High Commissioner for Human Rights declared, 'Inequalities and discrimination are the defining challenge of our time'.[4] Noting the 'intolerable fact' that the 85 richest people in the world own as much as the poorest 3.5 billion people together, Zeid maintained that addressing inequalities and discrimination, is both a practical necessity and a binding legal obligation under international human rights law. At its heart, Zeid asserted, the 2030 Agenda has the 'human rights promise of equality and nondiscrimination'.[5] This article examines these contentions that (1) the 2030 Agenda aims to reduce economic and social inequalities rather then simply reduce poverty, and (2) that reducing such inequalities is grounded in international human rights law.

In his September 25, 2015 statement, UN High Commissioner Zeid referred to three types of inequalities that the global community must address to achieve sustainable development. The first kind, 'horizontal inequalities', refers to inequalities between social, ethnic, linguistic or other population groups.[6] Balakrishnan and Heintz have described horizontal inequalities as those 'between culturally defined or socially constructed groups', such as those based on gender, race, caste, religion or sexuality.[7] These inequalities are often the result of discrimination and historical disadvantage. They are addressed, in part, by treaties, such as the Convention on the Elimination of Racial Discrimination (CERD) and the Convention of the Elimination of Discrimination against Women (CEDAW); non-discrimination provisions, such as those set forth in article 2 of both the International Covenant on Economic, Social and Cultural Rights (ICESCR) and the International Covenant on Civil and Political Rights (ICCPR); and non-discrimination provisions in domestic law.[8] The international laws prohibit discrimination that has the 'purpose or effect' of preventing the equal enjoyment of human rights by people on the basis of 'race, colour, sex, language, religion, political or other opinion, national or social origin, property, birth or other status'.[9]

The second kind, 'vertical inequalities', refers to inequalities of wealth, income or social outcome, including inequalities in health, education, housing and political power.[10] For example, vertical inequalities include disparities between top and bottom income quintiles in life expectancy or educational attainment. Vertical inequalities have yet to be adequately addressed in international human rights law, however, human rights scholars and practitioners have recently recognised the urgent need to do so.[11] As a result, a new research agenda on human rights and vertical inequalities has been launched.[12] Notably, there is potential for human rights scholars and practitioners, including the UN human rights mechanisms, to address vertical inequalities, for example, under the equality provisions in article 26 of the ICCPR as well as under substantive provisions guaranteeing specific economic and social rights.[13] Indeed, at this time when vertical inequalities have risen to crisis levels, there is a pressing need for the human rights community to take up this glaring gap in conceptualisation of the right to equality in international human rights law.

The third kind of inequalities Zeid identified is global inequalities between countries.[14] Global inequalities include those inequalities in income, wealth and power, such as the imbalance of power replicated through inter-governmental organisations, including the World Trade Organisation, the World Bank and the International Monetary Fund. Human rights do not explicitly address such inequalities between countries; rather, they are generally claims of individuals, families, communities, unions and peoples against the government of a country. While human rights generally address intra-state issues, inequalities between countries may have substantial impact on the realisation of human rights as well as the achievement of sustainable development. Therefore, these inequalities must also be considered 'human rights issues'.

The 2030 Agenda, Zeid, maintained, 'is a powerful framework' that addresses these three kinds of inequality. Using this typology of inequalities, this article considers whether the SDGs are adequate to address these three challenges of extreme inequalities. Central to this discussion is SDG 10 – reduce inequality within and among countries – as well as the 10 targets enumerated under this goal. While SDG 10 ostensibly addresses all three kinds of inequality discussed by Zeid, this article focuses most particularly on the inclusion of 'vertical inequalities' as this is a new aspect to the global agenda in both development and human rights. Both horizontal inequalities and inequalities between countries were previously addressed, at least in part, in the Millennium Development Goals (MDGs): MDG 3 – promote gender equality and empower women, and MDG 8 – develop a global partnership for development.[15] The article also considers international human rights norms on equality, as interpreted to date, to determine whether they provide support for reducing the three kinds of inequalities or whether further conceptual work might be necessary to encompass the current global concerns.

Following this introduction, the article begins with an overview of the extreme vertical inequalities within and between countries and then outlines the research on the impact of such inequalities on human rights and development. Next, the article turns to the SDGs and focuses specifically on SDG 10 – reduce inequalities within and among countries – and examines the targets in light of the existing inequalities described in the previous section. The article then considers the rights to equality and non-discrimination in international human rights law to discern whether human rights standards might inform SDG 10 and thereby alleviate some of the shortcomings of the targets. It finds that linking targets related to horizontal inequalities to human rights norms and mechanisms improves their conceptual clarity and monitoring of their implementation. On the other hand, the article finds that interpretations of international human rights law to date fall short in terms of addressing vertical inequalities. Accordingly, the article concludes with a call to scholars and UN human rights mechanisms for conceptual work on the multiple equality provisions in the International Bill of Human Rights to address the inequalities that are the greatest human rights challenges of our time.

Vertical inequalities in the world

Inequalities in income, wealth and social outcomes

Globally, income distribution is extremely unequal. In 2010, high-income countries – with 16% of the world's population – generated 55% of global income.[16] Low-income countries – with 72% of the world's population – generated just over 1% of the global income.[17] The World Bank reports that in 2014 the gross national income (GNI) per capita was US$1,571 in low-income countries, US$6,002 in lower-middle-income countries, US$14,225 in upper-middle-income countries and US$40,732 in high-income countries.[18] This data reveals that the 2014 GNI per capita of high-income countries was 26 times that of the low-income countries.[19] Notably, the global GNI per capita in 2014 was US$14,942,[20] which was higher than the average for upper-middle-income countries. In other words, if income were evenly distributed among the world's population, everyone would have an income above the average person's income in an upper-middle-income country. Evidently, there is adequate income in the world to ensure that no one lives in poverty. The problem is that the income is concentrated among the few at the expense of the many.

Within countries, inequality of income – comparing wages of workers with those of management – is also staggering. The Economic Policy Institute brief on wages in the US reported that in 2014 the average annual CEO compensation in the top 350 publicly owned firms was US$16,316,000, while the average worker in those firms earned US $53,200. That is a ratio of 303.4 to 1.[21] This was not always the case. In 1965, the ratio of CEO to average worker compensation was 20 to 1.[22] Since 1978, annual compensation for the average CEO has risen 997.2% while that of the average worker has risen 10.9%.[23] Similar income inequality was reported in the UK, where the 2012 average income of the top 0.1% of households was £919,882, while that of the poorest 10% was £4,467, a ratio of 206 to 1.[24]

Inequality in wealth is usually much greater than the inequality in income because it reflects an accumulation of high income over time. The Global Wealth Report 2016, issued by the Credit Suisse Research Institute, indicates that the top 1% of adults in the world own 50% of global assets, leaving the remaining 99% of adults with the other 50% of global assets.[25] The bottom half of the global population collectively owns less than 1% of total wealth.[26] The average wealth per adult in the world is US$52,800, however, the average wealth of those in the bottom 50% is US$159.[27] For the bottom 20%, the average wealth is *negative* US$1,079.[28] Negative wealth results from the debt carried by 44% of this lowest quintile.[29] Most adults in the bottom 50% of wealth are in India and Africa, while North America has the least adults in this group.[30] Strikingly, however, those adults with negative wealth are distributed equally across world regions. Thus, 'even in North America, there are many people in the global bottom quintile'.[31]

Those adults with US$71,600 in assets are in the top 10% of global wealth holders and those with US$744,400 are in the top 1%.[32] The Global Wealth Report estimates that 50,800 people in the world are worth at least US$100 million and 5,200 are worth over US$500 million.[33] There is also wide variation across regions and countries.[34] Switzerland has the highest average wealth per adult at US$562,000 and Australia has the next highest at US$376,000.[35] In comparison, most of the countries in central Africa and south Asia, including India, have an average wealth per adult of less than US$5,000.[36] As these figures from the Global Wealth Report show, global wealth inequality is extremely high, indeed much higher than income inequality.[37] A January 2017 Oxfam report estimates that the eight wealthiest men in the world own more than the poorest 50% of the global population combined; this new estimate indicates a substantial rise in wealth inequality since High Commissioner Zeid's statement on September 2015.[38]

Extreme inequalities in income and wealth are often reflected in extreme inequalities in social outcomes both between and within countries.[39] For example, the life expectancy at birth in OECD countries is 80.2 years, while in Sub-Saharan Africa it is only 58.5 years, a disparity of 21.7 years.[40] The difference is even greater between Japan, the country with the highest life expectancy (83.5 years) and the Central African Republic (50.7 years), a disparity of 32.8 years.[41] Other health indicators show similar inequalities both between and within countries. For example, the maternal mortality ratio for many countries in Europe is 4 per 100,000 live births, while in Sub-Saharan Africa the ratio is 506 per 100,000 live births.[42] At the extremes, the ratio in Israel is 2 per 100,000 live births while in Sierra Leone it is 1,100 per 100,000 live births.[43] Save the Children reports that in the 10 top ranked countries, 1 in 12,160 women die of a maternal cause compared to 1 in 30 women in the bottom 10 ranked countries.[44] Such disparities also exist within countries. For example, in India, the 2013 maternal mortality rate in the State of Kerala was 61 per 100,000 live births, while in the State of Assam is was five times higher at 300 per 100,000 live births.[45] Child mortality (under age five) rates are similarly unequal across regions, ranging from 7.6 per 1,000 live births in OECD countries to 91.2 in Sub-Saharan Africa and 64.9 in South Asia.[46] In the same way, within India, the child mortality rate is 12 in the State of Kerala in comparison to 69 in Madhya Pradesh.[47]

In education, youth receive on average 11.5 years of schooling in OECD countries compared to 6.2 years in Arab States and 5.2 years in Sub-Saharan Africa.[48] Germany reports an average of 13 years of school, while Nepal indicates an average of 3.3 and Burkina Faso only 1.4 years.[49] Large disparities in schooling also continue within countries. For example, in Nigeria, the country with the largest population in Sub-Saharan Africa, the primary school net attendance rate is over 80% in the southeast but less than 50% in the northeast.[50] Moreover, the primary school completion rate is 97% for the second to highest wealth quintile but only 35% for the lowest quintile.[51]

These extreme inequalities in income, wealth and social outcomes have been called alarming, intolerable and obscene.[52] And it does not appear that the situation is improving. Overall global inequality between individuals has declined over the past several decades, largely due to rapid economic growth in China and India.[53] However, the global decline in inequality has been matched by an increase in inequality within countries.[54] Within most countries – including India, China and the majority of developed countries – there has been an increase in inequality.[55] Thus, more than two-thirds of the world's population lives in countries where inequality has risen in the last three decades and is continuing to do so.[56] Moreover, those countries that have managed to reduce inequalities – in particular many countries in Latin America – remain among the most unequal in the world.[57] In short, both within and across countries over the past two decades, wealthy people have gained disproportionately from economic growth.[58]

The impact of vertical inequalities

Extreme inequalities in income, wealth and social outcomes have risen to the top of the international agenda for several reasons. First, it is clear that the goal in *Transforming Our World* of ending extreme poverty by 2030 cannot be reached at current levels of economic growth.[59] The World Bank estimates that at the rates of global growth predicted, it would take longer than the remaining 13 years to eliminate extreme poverty. Relying on growth alone, therefore, is not an adequate solution to address the key global development challenges identified in the 2030 Agenda.[60] A reduction in inequality is necessary to reach SDG 1 – End poverty in all its forms[61] – as well as many of the other SDGs by 2030. Additionally, the UN Department of Economic and Social Affairs reports, 'In fact, the higher the level of inequality, the more difficult it is to reduce poverty'.[62] SDG 10, calling for reducing inequality within and among countries, is, therefore, central to the 2030 Agenda and deeply connected to achieving most, if not all, of the other SDGs.

Second, there is mounting evidence of the negative impacts of income and wealth inequality on the health and wellbeing of individuals and societies. To begin with, there is a large body of research showing a clear relationship between higher income inequality and higher levels of violent crime.[63] In particular, homicide rates are higher in more unequal countries; generally, the more unequal the country, the higher the rate of homicide.[64] There is a similar trend across states in the United States; more unequal states tend to have more homicides.[65] Income inequality is also associated with many indicators of poor health, including lower life expectancy, higher rates of infant mortality, poorer self-reported health and greater depression.[66] These correlations are again evident across developed countries and across states in the United States.[67] Many people sense intuitively that societies with greater inequality would be more violent and have worse health outcomes.[68] Today, the evidence supports this intuition.

Moreover, income inequality also negatively impacts on a range of other social indicators. For example, across the fifty states in the United States, greater income inequality is strongly associated with higher levels of racism.[69] Discrimination against women is also worse in more unequal societies; for example, the greater the income inequality in a country, the greater the disparity between women's and men's pay.[70] Further, ethnic minorities, women, indigenous people and youth tend to have significantly lower levels of political participation in more unequal societies.[71] Wilkinson and Pickett also documented that more unequal societies also imprison a greater proportion of their population, have more teen pregnancies, and record lower literacy rates, more obesity and worse mental health.[72] In sum, in societies with greater inequality, there is a higher level of violence, more discrimination, poorer health and less political participation. These poor outcomes are not just for those at the bottom of the economic ladder. More unequal societies have worse outcomes for everyone – rich and poor alike.[73]

Third, economic inequality is often entwined with political inequality.[74] Indeed, the unequal distribution of wealth tends to cause the unequal distribution of political power.[75] The Word Bank explained that 'in a society with large inequalities of assets and incomes, the rich will tend to have more influence and an advantage in adopting and distorting institutions to their benefit'.[76] Consequently, public policy is distorted to favour these few, rather than ensuring public services for all. When the wealthy are in a position to ensure institutions and policies favour them, they become wealthier and more powerful, ensuring the replication and entrenchment of economic and political inequality. Greater economic inequality leads to social stratification and residential segregation, undermines trust and social cohesion, weakens the social compact between groups and results in poorer social outcomes for all.[77] The problem of wealth is that it goes hand in hand with privilege and divisions in society. Ultimately, economic inequality can cause political, social and economic instability, which may result in conflict and violence.[78]

In contrast, the World Bank reports:

> A society with greater equality of control over assets and incomes will tend to have a more equal distribution of political power. It will therefore tend to have institutions that generate equality of opportunity for the broad masses. This will tend to spread the rewards and incomes widely, thereby reinforcing the initial distribution of incomes.[79]

Reducing inequalities is conducive to social cohesion, and therefore, to social and political stability.[80] Political equality also results in better public policy and better public services.[81] In sum, the World Bank concluded that 'simple patterns in cross-country data show that more equalitarian distributions of political power and income are associated with sustained and enduring prosperity'.[82] And more cohesive societies are less vulnerable to threats that may arise from extremism, political unrest or weak institutions.[83] From a human rights perspective, vertical inequalities of income and wealth impact negatively on a wide range of economic, social, cultural, civil and political rights. In short, extreme vertical inequalities are detrimental to realising human rights.

Finally, in addition to the instrumental value of equality to ending poverty, improving the health and well-being of individuals and communities, fostering social cohesion and political stability, and realising human rights, equality has intrinsic value.[84] It is a matter of social justice. People want to live in societies that are fair, and most people feel that high economic inequality is not fair.[85] Indeed, experimental studies reveal that people have 'a deep-rooted concern for fairness in outcomes'.[86] For example, research on attitudes toward wealth inequality in both Latin America and the United States – indicates that most people in these highly unequal societies would prefer their societies to be more equal.[87] Indeed, in a survey in 18 Latin American countries, 89% of respondents thought the distribution in their country was either unfair or very unfair.[88]

In the United States, a study of a nationally representative sample of respondents found that 92% of Americans prefer the wealth distribution in Sweden (one of the most equal distributions among OECD countries) over that in the United States (one of the most unequal distributions among OECD countries) when presented with unlabelled distribution pie charts to choose from.[89] Indeed, 77% of respondents preferred a totally equal distribution to the grossly unequal distribution in the United States.[90] Importantly, this overwhelming preference for more equal societies was robust across gender, party affiliation and income level.[91] A similar experiment in Australia found that Australians' views on the ideal distribution did not differ much from those in the United States.[92] Thus, while there are many instrumental reasons for promoting greater equality across societies, '[r]educing inequality is first and foremost a question of fairness and social justice'.[93] The intrinsic value of equality to people is reflected in the Universal Declaration of Human Rights, which enshrines equality rights from beginning to end.[94]

In sum, extreme vertical inequalities – in income, wealth and social outcome – are of increasing global concern. The UN High Commissioner for Human Rights, The World Bank, UNESCO, UNDP and UN DESA, among other intergovernmental organisations, have issued reports in the last four years sounding the alarm, warning of the dangers of extreme inequalities. Yet, neither the 2030 Development Agenda nor international human rights law – as currently interpreted – adequately addresses these vertical inequalities.

Inequalities and the Sustainable Development Goals

The SDGs provide a global framework for economic, social and environmental policy and action for the next fifteen years. Most of the SDGs stem from the Millennium Development Goals (MDGs) and targets, which set the framework for development from 2001 to 2015.[95] For example, SDG 1, end poverty in all its forms everywhere, and SDG 2, end hunger, achieve food security and improved nutrition and promote sustainable agriculture, both build upon MDG 1, eradicate extreme poverty and hunger. Similarly, MDG targets related to education, health, housing, water, sanitation, gender equality and environmental sustainability are reflected in the SDGs.[96] One new focus in the SDGs, however, is the concern about inequality. SDG 10 states simply 'reduce inequalities within and among countries'.[97] Although the MDGs addressed gender inequality, they did not address horizontal inequalities beyond gender, nor did they address vertical inequalities of income, wealth or social outcome.

This shift in the SDGs to address 'vertical inequality', in addition to 'poverty' is significant. Addressing inequality requires substantially deeper structural changes to society than those required to address poverty. In this respect, it is a more radical agenda. As Freistein and Mahlert explain:

> Generally speaking, a focus on inequality is different from the development focus on poverty in that it is holistic, or structural. A concern with inequality is a 'concern with how society as a whole is structured, not just with the outcome for those that are worst off'.[98]

Freistein and Mahlert contend that the SDGs are remarkable as they encompass the most comprehensive framework to date for incorporating equality into the global development agenda.[99] Yet, upon examination of the targets for SDG 10, Faiza Shaheen concludes that 'this is a goal that is radical in namesake but placid in reality'.[100] Others agree.[101] A closer examination of the SDG 10 targets, listed in Table 1, reveals how they reach this conclusion.

The first four targets (1–4) ostensibly set benchmarks for reducing inequalities within countries, both vertical and horizontal inequalities. The next three (5–7) set benchmarks for reducing inequalities between countries. The final three targets (a, b and c), as is the case for other SDGs, are intended to address the *means* for achieving the goal and targets. In the case of SDG 10, however, many of the *targets* are actually *means* to reduce inequality or reduce poverty, rather than quantifiable measures with specific endpoints, which are necessary to evaluate whether or not a reduction in inequality has been achieved. Additionally, some targets do not actually specify 2030 or any other deadline to achieve them. A 2015 scientific evaluation of the SDG 10 targets concluded that they are inadequately developed, most are framed as activities instead of outcomes and most need to be revised to provide a measurable target.[102]

Table 1. SDG 10 – Reduce inequality within and among countries.[a]

Target 10.1	By 2030, progressively achieve and sustain income growth of the bottom 40 per cent of the population at a rate higher than the national average
Target 10.2	By 2030, empower and promote the social, economic and political inclusion of all, irrespective of age, sex, disability, race, ethnicity, origin, religion or economic or other status
Target 10.3	Ensure equal opportunity and reduce inequalities of outcome, including eliminating discriminatory laws, policies and practices and promoting appropriate legislation, policies and action in this regard
Target 10.4	Adopt policies, especially fiscal, wage and social protection policies, and progressively achieve greater equality
Target 10.5	Improve the regulation and monitoring of global financial markets and institutions and strengthen the implementation of such regulations
Target 10.6	Ensure enhanced representation and voice for developing countries in decision-making in global international economic and financial institutions in order to deliver more effective, credible, accountable and legitimate institutions
Target 10.7	Facilitate orderly, safe, regular and responsible migration and mobility of people, including through the implementation of planned and well-managed policies
Target 10.a	Implement the principle of special and differential treatment for developing countries, in particular least developed countries, in accordance with World Trade Organisation agreements
Target 10.b	Encourage official development assistance and financial flows, including foreign direct investment, to States where the need is greatest, in particular least developed countries, African countries, small island developing States and landlocked developing countries, in accordance with their national plans and programmes
Target 10.c	By 2030, reduce to less than 3 per cent the transaction costs of migrant remittances and eliminate remittance corridors with costs higher than 5 percent

[a]UNGA, *Transforming Our World*, 21.

Vertical inequalities

Target 10.1 is the key target in the SDGs to addresses vertical inequality within countries. It states, 'By 2030, progressively achieve and sustain income growth of the bottom 40 per cent of the population at a rate higher than the national average'.[103] For several reasons, this target fails to capture the problem of extreme income inequality. First, it addresses only the bottom 40% of the population and says nothing about the inequality between the bottom 40% as compared the top 10%, or indeed the top 1%. In fact, it does not address overall income inequality at all. To meet this target, the income of the bottom 40% might rise at a rate faster than the national average, while the inequality between the bottom 40% and the top 10%, and indeed the top 1%, continues to grow. Achieving target 10.1 would be completely consistent with growing income inequality. In this respect, the radical idea of including the SDG on reducing vertical inequality within countries was lost by the selection of an income target that actually ignores overall income inequality. The target is, in fact, concerned with poverty reduction, rather than reduction of vertical inequality.

Second, target 10.1 does not require any reduction in inequality unless there is income growth nationally. The bottom 40% merely receives a higher rate of income growth than the national average. If the national average does not grow, the bottom 40% would be entitled to nothing, and if the national average grows at an incredibly low rate, as is the case in many developed countries, the bottom 40% is entitled to little more than this low rate. Tying the reduction of inequalities to national income growth guarantees nothing to the bottom 40% in terms of reducing inequality. In this respect, the professed focus of SDG 10 on reducing inequalities is lost in target 10.1, which links any reduction in inequalities to economic growth. Pogge and Sengupta assert 'at the very least the demand should be that the income share of the poorest 40 percent will be substantially higher at the end of the period than at the beginning'.[104] They reflect that it is disheartening to see the important inequality goal 'defeated by the grotesque lack of ambition in its primary Target 10.1'.[105]

Third, target 10.1 is not a target at all. It is in fact a *means* for poverty reduction rather than a *benchmark* for a reduction in inequalities. As Drèze and Sen, explain, economic growth may enhance human development if the economic gains are used to address the needs of those worst off.[106] Nonetheless, it is important to be clear that economic growth is merely an instrumental *means* to achieve the *ends* of human development. A logical target for reducing income inequality, rather than that provided in Target 10.1, would be to progressively reduce the ratio of the income share received by the top 10% to the income share of the bottom 40% – the so-called Palma ratio – in all countries to less than 1 by 2030.[107] Numerous experts proposed a reduction of the Palma ratio as an SDG 10 target for reducing vertical inequalities, because unlike the Gini Index, which has been more commonly used by inter-governmental organisations to measure inequality over the past 100 years, the Palma ratio focuses effectively on extremes of inequality – a ratio of those at the top and the bottom.[108] The Gini, on the other hand, is more sensitive to changes in inequality in the middle of the income scale. As a result, there has been a movement to replace the Gini with the Palma ratio as it focuses on the inequalities that are most pressing today for policy to address.[109] A Palma ratio of 1 is 'an ideal reached only in a few countries', such as those in Scandinavia, which 'do not seem to suffer from the liabilities associated with extreme inequalities'.[110] As a result, the Palma ratio of less than 1 was often cited during the consultations on the SDGs as a target for SDG 10.

Variations of this target – reduce the Palma ratio to less than 1 – were recommended to the UN General Assembly's Open Working Group on Sustainable Development Goals by the Women's Major Group, the Worker and Trade Union's Major Group and the NGO Major Group,[111] as well as by the International Council for Science.[112] Indeed, during the consultations, NGOs, scholars and human rights practitioners consistently expressed concern that none of the targets under consideration specifically aimed at assessing economic inequality – the main point of SDG 10.[113] Human rights advocates called for a 'concrete target to reduce economic inequality by a said amount per year through enhanced use of progressive taxation, tracked in reference to one of the widely accepted metrics of income inequality'.[114] The International Council for Science reported:

> By addressing economic inequalities within countries, target 10.1 is essential to progress on other targets as well as for SDG 1. Because of its centrality, target 10.1 must be articulated as precisely as possible so it is clear, easily measured, and stands as an ambitious target facilitating progress across the entire sustainable development agenda.[115]

In the end, however, among the SDG targets '[t]here is nothing to require specifically that the level of income inequality in 2030 be lower than in 2015'.[116]

Horizontal inequalities

Targets 10.2 and 10.3 address horizontal inequalities. While the MDGs addressed gender inequality, they did not address the inequalities experienced by other status groups. Accordingly, targets 10.2 and 10.3 signify progress in this respect. Both targets, however, have significant shortcomings. Target 10.2 states, 'By 2030, empower and promote the social, economic and political inclusion of all, irrespective of age, sex, disability, race, ethnicity, origin, religion or economic or other status'.[117] Like target 10.1, this target has no measurable benchmark. Further, the use of the words 'empower and promote' in contrast to, for example, 'end', 'achieve' or 'enforce' that are used in other SDGs and targets, makes the target extremely vague. As a result, it is not clear how progress toward the target can be measured, nor how it can be determined when the target is met. If countries merely 'promote' but do not 'achieve' inclusion, is this sufficient to meet this target? The indicator for this target is 'Proportion of people living below 50 per cent of median income, by age, sex and persons with disabilities'.[118] Like target 10.1, the indicator focuses primarily on poverty rather than inequality.[119]

Target 10.3 states, 'Ensure equal opportunity and reduce inequalities of outcome, including eliminating discriminatory laws, policies and practices and promoting appropriate legislation, policies and action in this regard'. This target is also vague as it provides no measurable benchmark and no deadline to meet the list of undefined outcomes. On the positive side, the indicator for the target is 'Percentage of the population reporting having personally felt discriminated against or harassed within the last 12 months on the basis of a ground of discrimination prohibited under international human rights law'.[120] As the main target on non-discrimination, such linkages to international human rights laws could play an important role in defining measurement of progress toward the target. On the other hand, relying solely on personal opinion to determine whether horizontal inequalities have been reduced is rather limited.[121] The assessment under Target 10.3 could be improved, for example, by adding an indicator that explicitly requires an increase in national compliance with international human rights laws as measured by the international human rights treaty bodies.

Target 10.4 states, 'Adopt policies, especially fiscal, wage and social protection policies, and progressively achieve greater equality'. This target is perhaps the most vague of the four targets on reducing inequality within countries. There is no deadline to achieve this target and no measurable target to achieve. Indeed, it is a *means* to achieve equality, not an equality benchmark or *target*. Interestingly, target 10.4 requires adopting fiscal, wage and social protection policies but it does not set any parameters for such policies. And the policies are in addition to, rather than for the purpose of, progressively reducing inequality. Of course, many policies – such as austerity measures – could be adopted that do not reduce inequality.[122] On the positive side, target 10.4 is improved by the indicator selected: 'Labour share of GDP, comprising wages and social protection transfers', which measures one aspect of vertical inequality.[123]

Inequalities between countries

Targets 10.5, 10.6 and 10.7 are addressed at reducing inequalities between countries. While each of these targets focuses on an important area for action in reducing economic inequalities, none of the three provides a specific measurable target or a deadline to achieve it. They all appear to be *means* to reduce inequalities, rather than *benchmarks* for reduced inequalities. Even more importantly, it is not clear who is accountable for these international targets. While the 'within country' targets are the responsibility of national governments, the 'among countries' targets do not have an obvious actor responsible for achieving them.

Target 10.5 provides: 'Improve the regulation and monitoring of global financial markets and institutions and strengthen the implementation of such regulations'.[124] No indicator for this target has been selected to date. Wilkinson and Rogers recommended an indicator that would accurately measure tax avoidance and evasion,[125] which have enabled the wealthy to evade paying their fair share for government services and allowed the siphoning of billions of dollars of potential revenue from developing countries.[126] Such a measure would be a great step forward for the 2030 Agenda as it would begin to tackle the problem of wealth accumulation, rather than focusing solely on poverty, which will be key to reducing vertical inequalities.

Target 10.6 provides: 'Ensure enhanced representation and voice for developing countries in decision-making in global international economic and financial institutions in order to deliver more effective, credible, accountable and legitimate institutions'.[127] The indicator for this target is 'Proportion of members and voting rights of developing countries in international organizations'.[128] This is the same indicator used to measure progress toward Target 16.8, which states: 'Broaden and strengthen the participation of developing countries in the institutions of global governance'.[129] These two targets and the indicator begin to address the inequality of power in the global economic structure, and therefore, it is unfortunate that the targets provide no benchmarks or deadlines to achieve them.

Target 10.7 provides: 'Facilitate orderly, safe, regular and responsible migration and mobility of people, including through the implementation of planned and well-managed policies'.[130] Progress toward this target is measured by two indicators. The first is 'recruitment cost borne by employee as a percentage of yearly income'.[131] The second is 'number of countries that have implemented well-managed migration policies'.[132] While this target and its indicators focus on important human development and social justice issues, they do not directly aim at reducing inequality between countries. Rather, the focus appears to be reducing the risk of low-income workers from low-income countries, who seek employment abroad, ending up in debt bondage or other forms of modern slavery.[133] As a result, the target and indicators might be more suitable for monitoring progress toward SDG 8, promoting full employment and decent work. In any event, target 10.7 and its indicators do not challenge the structures that perpetuate extreme inequalities between countries.

Means to reduce inequality

All three targets on the *means* to reduce inequality – Targets 10.a, 10.b and 10.c – focus on addressing inequality between countries. Like Target 10.1, they focus on raising the bottom, which may or may not reduce inequality, depending on what happens at the top. In short, they are means to reduce poverty, rather than means to reduce inequality. Target 10.a states, 'Implement the principle of special and differential treatment for developing countries, in particular least developed countries, in accordance with World Trade Organization agreements'.[134] This target overlaps with the three trade targets in SDG 17 on a global partnership for sustainable development, which are more specific and therefore stronger than target 10.a.[135] For example, Target 17.11 provides: 'Significantly increase the exports of developing countries, in particular with a view to doubling the least developed countries' share of global exports by 2020'.[136]

Target 10.b states,

> Encourage official development assistance and financial flows, including foreign direct investment, to States where the need is greatest, in particular least developed countries, African countries, small island developing States and landlocked developing countries, in accordance with their national plans and programmes.[137]

This target overlaps with Target 17.2, which is again more specific and stronger. It states:

> Developed countries to implement fully their official development assistance commitments, including the commitment by many developed countries to achieve the target of 0.7 per cent of gross national income for development assistance (ODA/GNI) to developing countries and 0.12 to 0.20 per cent of ODA/GNI to least developed countries.[138]

Given that 'the action targets relating to international inequality in Goal 10 are weaker than their counterparts in Goal 17', Edward Anderson 'calls into question their value-added in the overall SDG framework'.[139] As he notes, the absence of quantified targets with deadlines also undermines the potential of these targets to incentivize actors or provide any basis to hold them accountable.[140]

In contrast, target 10.c provides a quantified benchmark to achieve by a clear deadline. It states: 'By 2030, reduce to less than 3 per cent the transaction costs of migrant remittances and eliminate remittance corridors with costs higher than 5 percent'.[141] Remittances provide an important source of income for many people in developing countries, and the commitment to reducing transaction costs means that more of that income – estimated at about US$20 billion per year – will go to migrant workers' families.[142] The target, however, is only tangentially related to reducing vertical inequality within and among countries. Like target 10.7, it is more properly an issue of worker rights that might be better suited as a target for SDG 8 on full employment and decent work.

Proposed targets to reduce inequalities

Importantly, none of the targets under SDG 10 sets a specific benchmark for the reduction of vertical inequality within or among countries, although the need to reduce vertical inequalities – in addition to horizontal and between country inequalities – was one of the main reasons that NGOs, human rights practitioners and academics advocated for SDG 10. Several more appropriate targets – quantitative, measurable and more closely aligned with the goal of reducing income, wealth and social inequalities – were recommended by a variety of experts. A few of these recommendations are listed in Table 2. They illustrate that far better targets for reducing vertical inequalities might have been selected for SDG 10.

Illustrative target 1 – By 2030, reduce the ratio of the income share received by the top 10% to the income share received by the bottom 40% to less than 1 – is the Palma ratio target discussed above.[143] The specific target of 1 was recommended in the 2015 report of the International Council for Science.[144] In 2013, ninety economists, academics and development experts recommended the target: By 2030, halve the national Palma ratio of 2010, and dramatically reduce the global Palma ratio of 32.[145] In 2014, Doyle and Stiglitz recommended a similar target, 'By 2030, reduce extreme inequalities in all countries such that the post-tax income of the top 10% is no more than the post-transfer income of the bottom 40%'.[146] In 2015, Pogge and Sengupta suggested the target: By 2030, each country reduce income inequality to the square root of its present Palma ratio. 'Thus, countries with current Palma ratios of 4, 2.25 and 1.69 would commit to reaching by 2030, Palma ratios of 2, 1.5 ad 1.3, respectively: 'Countries with current Palma ratios of 1 or below would merely need to remain within this range'.[147]

To address vertical inequalities, the focus on reducing income inequality alone is not enough however. Social inequalities related to these income inequalities must also be addressed. Targets to reduce such social inequalities could address the enormous education and health gaps documented above in section 2, either under SDG 10 or under

Table 2. Illustrative targets for reduction of vertical inequalities.

1	By 2030, reduce the ratio of the income share received by the top 10% to the income share received by the bottom 40% to less than 1.[a]
2	By 2030, eliminate differences in life expectancy between top and bottom quintiles of income.[b]
3	By 2030, eliminate differences in years of educational attainment between top and bottom quintiles of income.
4	By 2030 reduce inequalities between countries to less than 10:1 ratio between the richest 10% and the poorest 10% of countries in per capita income.[c]
5	By 2020, establish a public commission in every country that will assess and report on the extent and effects of national inequalities.[d]

[a]Wilkinson and Rogers, 'Goal 10 – Reduce Inequality', 52.
[b]See ibid. The authors call for a target on differences in life expectancy but do not propose a specific benchmark.
[c]Ibid.
[d]Doyle and Stiglitz, 'Eliminating Extreme Inequality', 10.

the specific sector (education or health) SDG. Table 2 illustrates two such targets. Illustrative target 2 – By 2030, eliminate differences in life expectancy between top and bottom quintiles of income – was also proposed in the 2015 report of the International Council for Science.[148] The report calls for a target on reducing differences in life expectancy across income quintiles but does not propose a specific benchmark. Given that this proposed target implicates the right to life, it would seem that any inequality in life expectancy between income quintiles would be unacceptable. Illustrative target 3 – By 2030, eliminate differences in years of educational attainment between top and bottom quintiles of income – has not previously been proposed but again aims to ensure that income status does not impact on the right to education.

Illustrative target 4 – By 2030 reduce inequalities between countries to less than 10:1 ratio between the richest 10% and the poorest 10% of countries in per capita income – is drawn from the 2015 report of the International Council for Science.[149] Unlike the SDG targets 10.5, 10.6 and 10.7, this proposed target explicitly aims to substantially reduce vertical inequality of incomes between countries. Together with illustrative target 1, these two targets aim to reduce extreme income inequality between households and individuals both within and between countries. To achieve such reductions in vertical inequalities would require massive restructuring of governance and policy at both the international and national levels. Thus, while these are the changes that human rights NGOs, worker organisations, women's groups and indigenous people called for, it is not surprising that such targets were not adopted by the UN General Assembly in 2015.

Finally – illustrative target 5 – By 2020, establish a public commission in every country that will assess and report on the extent and effects of national inequalities – was proposed by Doyle and Stiglitz in 2014.[150] If ending extreme poverty is the primary goal of the SDGs, and this cannot be done by economic growth alone – at least by 2030 – then reducing inequality will be necessary. While almost all countries measure levels of poverty over time, a commission in each country to monitor the reduction of national inequalities over time seems like an important part of the 2030 Agenda that is missing. Although SDG 16 calls for building effective, accountable and inclusive institutions at all levels, it calls for equality only with respect to access to justice for all. A dedicated institution to measure vertical and horizontal inequalities over time would be a 'deliberate, concrete and targeted' step toward reducing inequalities.[151]

In sum, SDG 10 is a great step forward from the MDGs as it recognises that extreme inequalities must be reduced to end poverty and achieve other human development goals. Nonetheless, the SDG 10 targets fail to capture key inequalities that threaten achievement of many, if not all, the other SDGs, namely inequalities of income, wealth and social outcomes. In other words, SDG 10 has introduced inequalities onto the development agenda but the targets do not successfully address vertical inequalities. SDG 10 is more successful in addressing horizontal inequalities, as the indicators are linked to international human rights laws, which provide definition for the otherwise vague targets. The links to international human rights law could be substantially stronger, however, by for example requiring reporting to the human rights mechanisms progress on implementing laws, policies and practices on non-discrimination. It remains to be seen to what extent international human rights law will inform the implementation of SDG 10 and help to hold governments accountable for achieving any reductions in vertical or horizontal inequalities.

Inequalities and human rights

The UN resolution *Transforming Our World*, declares that the 2030 Development Agenda is grounded in international human rights law.[152] At its launch, UN High Commissioner for Human Rights Zeid asserted that it is an 'Agenda for Equality', and that human rights align with all three types of inequalities addressed in the SDGs, vertical inequalities, horizontal inequalities and inequalities between countries.[153] International human rights law certainly enshrines many standards to address horizontal inequalities, including non-discrimination provisions in every treaty and specific treaties focused on the elimination of discrimination against women and people with disabilities, as well as on the basis of race. As a result, the SDG 10 targets on horizontal equalities, targets 10.2 and 10.3, may link to international human rights standards to clarify the expectations and international human rights mechanisms to reinforce monitoring and accountability.

International human rights law, however, has little to say about vertical inequalities of income, wealth and social outcomes – either between or within countries. Although equality in dignity and rights is a central principle in the human rights framework and reducing economic and social inequalities is vital to ending poverty and realising human rights, the international human rights community has focused almost exclusively on horizontal inequality – non-discrimination – and paid far too little attention to vertical inequalities in income, wealth and social outcomes.[154] As a result, there are no human rights standards on vertical inequalities to inform SDG 10. And significantly, the SDG 10 targets do not address vertical inequalities.

This serious omission in human rights (and the SDGs) has recently been recognised by human rights scholars and practitioners. Notably, in 2015 Philip Alston, UN Special Rapporteur on Extreme Poverty and Human Rights, issued his annual report to the Human Rights Council on the subject of extreme inequality. Alston highlighted the human rights community's neglect of vertical inequalities:

> The international human rights community has largely reciprocated the economists' neglect [of human rights] by ignoring the consequences of extreme inequality in the vast majority of its advocacy and analytical work. It does so at its peril, however, since a human rights framework that does not address extreme inequality as one of the drivers of extreme poverty and as one of the reasons why over one quarter of humanity cannot properly enjoy human rights is doomed to fail.[155]

While Alston argues that extreme inequalities in income and wealth are incompatible with human rights, he characterises these vertical inequalities as merely instrumentally related to human rights. As he states, 'It is clear that economic inequalities severely affect a range of civil, political, economic, social and cultural rights'.[156] However, Alston contends, 'At present, there is no explicitly stated right to equality, as such, under international human rights law'.[157] He thus maintains, 'Formal recognition of the fact that there are limits of some sort to the degrees of inequality that can be reconciled with notions of equality, dignity and commitments to human rights for everyone would be an important step forward'.[158] He therefore calls for moving beyond 'the work of the treaty bodies [which] seems unduly confined to a focus on specific violations of non-discrimination' toward 'revitalizing the equality norm' in international human rights law in an effort 'to develop notions of distributive equality'.[159]

A small number of human rights scholars and practitioners research on vertical inequalities and human rights.[160] This is important work as vertical inequalities have tremendous impacts on human rights, as noted in section 2 above. Nonetheless, almost all of this work focuses on the impact of vertical inequalities – and the instrumental value of reducing these inequalities – on the realisation of human rights and the elimination of poverty.[161] In the absence of a recognised right to equality, that is economic and social equality, human rights scholars and practitioners rely upon other international human rights standards that could indirectly reduce vertical inequalities. The Center for Economic and Social Rights, for example, uses international human rights standards for non-discrimination, maximum available resources and international cooperation, to address the inequalities under the SDG 10.[162] These round-about human rights approaches to reducing vertical inequalities are necessary today because human rights has yet to address them head on.

Certainly, equality is fundamental to international human rights. In the human rights framework, equality has instrumental value – inequalities adversely impact on the enjoyment of a full array of civil, political, social, economic and cultural rights. But equality also has intrinsic value – equality in dignity and rights. As Sakiko Fukuda-Parr recently stated, the human rights principles of 'equality and nondiscrimination anchor an alternative framework for analysis of inequality, one that is based on the intrinsic value of equality as a social norm, and one that explores unjust institutions as the source of inequality'.[163] For both intrinsic and instrumental reasons, human rights must address both horizontal and vertical inequalities. The right to equality with respect to vertical inequalities – the right to economic and social equality – has, however, yet to be conceptualised and unpacked.

Indeed, there has been no concerted effort to consider whether there might be a right to economic and social equality in international human rights law and what standards this right might impose. By recognising a right to equality, distinct from a right to non-discrimination, human rights bodies could establish explicit legal obligations for addressing extreme vertical inequalities, such as specific limits on economic and social inequalities. There are at least three distinct pathways in international human rights law to recognising vertical inequalities of income, wealth and social outcome as violations of human rights, rather than merely social conditions that impact on human rights. First, UDHR article 7 and ICCPR article 26 have multiple equality and non-discrimination provisions that have yet to be deciphered and conceptualised. For example, it seems likely that 'equal protection of the law' might apply to all human rights, not just civil and political rights.[164] Second, vertical equality should be an essential element of each economic and social right. The CESCR has not made vertical equality a central feature of it conceptual framework, preferring to focus on minimum essential levels of rights. However, vertical equality is a key component of many civil and political rights – like the right to vote – and should be an essential component of economic and social rights as well.[165] Finally, non-discrimination on the basis of economic status – or 'property' as it appears in the English version article 2 of the ICESCR – should be developed conceptually and implemented in practice.[166] Taking any of these paths, a right to economic and social equality, with explicit limits on vertical inequalities, would truly make a contribution to achieving the SDGs as well as realising human rights for all.

To date, international human rights law has focused on eliminating horizontal inequalities between groups. It has not been construed to address extreme inequalities in income, wealth and social outcomes. By pursuing the three paths outlined above, the human rights community may discover that international human rights law does indeed directly address the extreme vertical inequalities that are central concerns in the 2030 Development Agenda. And by doing so, human rights may give critical definition to the notion of 'reducing inequality within and among countries' enshrined in SDG 10.

Conclusion

The MDGs did not address vertical inequalities of income, wealth or social outcome. In this respect, the SDGs are a substantial improvement. First, the SDGs include several universal or zero-based targets, including ending hunger and ending extreme poverty, which ultimately require the elimination of inequalities in these social outcomes for everyone.[167] Second, the SDGs place greater emphasis upon disaggregation of data by income, gender, age, disability, ethnicity, rural/urban location and other relevant categories.[168] Third, in the resolution *Transforming Our World*, all UN members pledge to leave no one behind.[169] The resolution further states:

> Recognizing that the dignity of the human person is fundamental, we wish to see the Goals and targets met for all nations and people and for all segments of society. And we will endeavour to reach the furthest behind first.[170]

Finally, the SDGs include a stand-alone goal, SDG 10, on reducing inequalities within and among countries. This goal and its targets recognise that reducing both vertical and horizontal inequalities will be necessary to achieve the other SDGs.

Nonetheless, SDG 10 has many shortcomings. Most importantly, it does not include a target for the reduction of vertical inequalities, which was one of the main reasons for adopting SDG 10. Second, most of the SDG 10 targets are vague, not measurable and provide no deadline to achieve them. As a result, the promise of SDG 10 was greatly reduced by the selection of targets. The selection of indicators – still not completed – will therefore be extremely important to the implementation of SDG 10 as they may link to other more definitive concepts of equality. Certainly, target 10.3 is greatly improved by the indicator, which links the achievement of the target to 'discrimination prohibited under international law'.[171] Indeed, human rights has much to offer in clarifying the targets and indicators that address horizontal inequalities.

Unfortunately, although the 2030 Development Agenda is grounded in international human right law, human rights has little to offer with respect to benchmarks or indictors for reducing vertical inequalities. This is a glaring omission in international human rights law as interpreted to date that is made more obvious by the focus of scholars and activists in recent years on vertical inequalities. SDG 10 again flags this equality gap in the human rights framework. There are, however, multiple paths to addressing vertical inequalities in the International Bill of Human Rights, which holds a rich source of equality provisions that should be distinguished and conceptualised. Among these provisions, human rights must speak to vertical inequalities and set limits on the rising gaps between rich and poor.

Notes

1. Zeid Ra'ad Al Hussein, 'An Agenda for Equality', Statement of the United Nations High Commissioner for Human Rights at the Summit for Adoption of the Post-2015 Development

Agenda (UN Headquarters, New York, 25 September 2015); Ignacio Saiz and Gaby Oré Aguilar, 'Introducing the Debate on Economic Inequality: Can Human Rights Make a Difference?' *Open-Democracy*, October 27, 2015, https://www.opendemocracy.net/openglobalrights/ignacio-saiz-gaby-or-aguilar/introducing-debate-on-economic-inequality-can-human-ri; Philip Alston, 'Extreme Inequality as the Antithesis of Human Rights', October 27, 2016, https://opendemocracy.net/openglobalrights/philip-alston/extreme-inequality-as-antithesis-of-human-rights.

2. Anthony B. Atkinson, *Inequality, What Can Be Done?* (Cambridge MA: Harvard University Press, 2015); Thomas Picketty, *Capital in the Twenty-First Century* (Cambridge MA: Belknap Press, 2013); Joseph E. Stiglitz, *The Price of Inequality: How Today's Divided Society Endangers Our Future* (New York: W. W. Norton & Co., 2012); Richard Wilkinson and Kate Pickett, *The Spirit Level: Why More Equal Societies Almost Always Do Better* (London: Allen Lane, 2009).

3. UNGA, *Transforming Our World: The 2030 Agenda for Sustainable Development*, resolution adopted by the General Assembly on 25 September 2015, UN Doc. A/Res/70/1 (2015).

4. Zeid, 'An Agenda for Equality'.

5. Ibid.

6. Ibid.; see also Inga Winkler and Margaret Satterthwaite, 'Leaving No One Behind? Persistent Discrimination against Marginalised Groups and the Imperative to Monitor Inequalities', *International Journal of Human Rights*, this volume.

7. Radhika Balakrishnan and James Heintz, 'How Inequality Threatens All Rights', *Open-Democracy*, October 29, 2015, https://www.opendemocracy.net/openglobalrights/radhika-balakrishnan-james-heintz/how-inequality-threatens-all-human-rights.

8. International Convention on the Elimination of All Forms of Racial Discrimination, G.A. res. 2016 (XX), Annex, 20 UN GAOR Supp. (No. 14) at 47, UN Doc. A/6014 (1966), 660 U.N.T.S. 195, entered into force January 4, 1969; Convention on the Elimination of All Forms of Discrimination Against Women, GA. Res 34/180, 34 UN GAOR Supp. (No. 46) at 193, UN Doc. A/34/46, entered into force September 3, 1981; International Covenant on Economic, Social and Cultural Rights (ICESCR), G. A. res. 2200A (XXI), 21 UN GAOR Supp. (No. 16) at 49, UN Doc. A/6316 (1966), 933 U.N.T.S. 3, entered into force January 3, 1976; International Covenant on Civil and Political Rights (ICCPR), G.A. res 2200A (XXI), 21 UN GAOR Supp. (No. 16) at 52, UN Doc. A/6316 (1966), 999 U.N.T.S. 171, entered into force March 23, 1976.

9. ICCPR article 2; ICESCR article 2.

10. Zeid, 'An Agenda for Equality'; Philip Alston, Annual Report of the Special Rapporteur on Extreme Poverty and Human Rights, UN Doc. A/HRC/29/31, May 27, 2015, para. 6.

11. See Saiz and Oré Aguilar, 'Introducing the Debate'; Alston, 'Extreme Inequality'; Balakrishnan and Heintz, 'How Inequality Threatens All Rights'; Sakiko Fukuda-Parr, 'It's About Values: Human Rights Norms and Tolerance for Inequality', *OpenDemocracy*, December 22, 2015, https://www.opendemocracy.net/openglobalrights/sakiko-fukuda-parr/it-s-about-values-human-rights-norms-and-tolerance-for-inequalit.

12. See for example 'Inequality: A New Challenge for Human Rights', The Bernard and Audre Rapoport Center For Human Rights and Justice, University of Texas at Austin, https://law.utexas.edu/humanrights/project-type/inequality-project/ (accessed July 12, 2017).

13. Gillian MacNaughton, 'Untangling Equality and Nondiscrimination to Promote the Right to Health Care for All', *Health and Human Rights Journal* 11, no. 2 (2009): 47–63, 51.

14. Zeid, 'An Agenda for Equality'.

15. United Nations Department of Economic and Social Affairs (UN DESA), Statistics Division, Millennium Development Goals and Indicators, http://mdgs.un.org/unsd/mdg/Host.aspx?Content=Indicators/OfficialList.htm.

16. UN DESA, *Inequality Matters: Report of the World Social Situation 2013* (New York: United Nations, 2013), 25.

17. Ibid.

18. The World Bank, *World Development Indicators 2016*, 52, https://openknowledge. worldbank.org/bitstream/handle/10986/23969/9781464806834.pdf (in purchasing power parity).
19. Ibid.
20. Ibid.
21. Lawrence Mishel and Alyssa Davis, 'Top CEOs Make 300 Times More Than Typical Worker', *Issue Brief #399*, Economic Policy Institute, June 21, 2015, 3.
22. Ibid.
23. Ibid.
24. The Equality Trust, 'The Scale of Economic Inequality in the UK', https://www.equalitytrust. org.uk/scale-economic-inequality-uk (accessed November 26, 2016).
25. Credit Suisse Research Institute, *Global Wealth Report 2016*, 11, http://publications.credit-suisse.com/tasks/render/file/index.cfm?fileid=AD783798-ED07-E8C2-4405996B5B02A32E (accessed July 12, 2017).
26. Ibid.
27. Ibid., 30.
28. Ibid.
29. Ibid.
30. Ibid.
31. Ibid.
32. Ibid., 11.
33. Ibid., 27.
34. Ibid., 9.
35. Ibid.
36. Ibid., 10.
37. Ibid., 11.
38. Oxfam, *An Economy for the 99%* (Oxfam Briefing Paper, January 2017), https://www.oxfam. org/sites/www.oxfam.org/files/file_attachments/bp-economy-for-99-percent-160117-en.pdf; Zeid, 'An Agenda for Equality'.
39. UNDP, *Humanity Divided: Confronting Inequality in Developing Countries* (New York: United Nations, 2013), 9.
40. UNDP, *Human Development Report 2015: Work for Human Development* (New York: United Nations 2015), 211.
41. Ibid., 208, 211.
42. UNDP, *Human Development Report 2015*, 227.
43. Ibid., 224, 227.
44. Save the Children, State of the World's Mothers, https://www.savethechildren.net/state-worlds-mothers-infographics (accessed July 12, 2017).
45. Vidit Munshi, Gavin Yamey and Stéphane Verguet, 'Trends in State-Level Child Mortality, Maternal Mortality, and Fertility Rates in India', *Health Affairs*, 35, no. 10 (2016): 1759–63, 1761.
46. UNDP, *Human Development Report 2015* , 241.
47. Munshi, Yamey and Verguet, 'Trends in State-Level', 1760.
48. UNDP, *Human Development Report 2015* , 211.
49. Ibid., 208, 211.
50. Education Policy and Data Center, *Nigeria Core USAID Education Profile* (2012), 2, https://www.epdc.org/sites/default/files/documents/Nigeria_coreusaid.pdf (accessed July 12, 2017).
51. Ibid., 5.
52. Balakrishnan and Heintz, 'How Inequality Threatens All Rights'; Zeid, 'An Agenda for Equality'; Alston, 'Extreme Inequality'.
53. UNESCO and the Institute for Development Studies, *World Social Science Report 2016 – Challenging Inequalities: Pathways to a Just World* (Summary) (Paris: UNESCO Publishing 2016), 7.
54. Ibid.

55. UN DESA, *Inequality Matters*, 29.
56. Ibid.
57. Ibid.
58. Ibid., 63.
59. World Bank Group, *Poverty and Shared Prosperity 2016: Taking on Inequality* (Washington, DC: The World Bank 2016), 7; Thomas Pogge and Mitu Sengupta, 'The Sustainable Development Goals (SDGs) As Drafted: Nice Idea, Poor Execution', *Washington International Law Journal* 24, no. 3, 571–87, 582.
60. UN DESA, *Inequality Matters*, 67.
61. World Bank Group, *Poverty and Shared Prosperity 2016*, 69.
62. UNESCO, *World Social Science Report*, 9.
63. Wilkinson and Pickett, *The Spirit Level*, 135.
64. Ibid.
65. Ibid., 136.
66. Ibid., 81.
67. Ibid., 81–3.
68. Ibid., x.
69. Richard G. Wilkinson, *The Impact of Inequality: How to Make Sick Societies Better* (London: Routledge, 2005), 51.
70. Ibid., 221.
71. UN DESA, *Inequality Matters*, 72.
72. Wilkinson and Pickett, *The Spirit Level*, 174.
73. Ibid., 181.
74. Gillian MacNaughton, 'Beyond a Minimum Threshold: The Right to Social Equality', in *The State of Economic and Social Rights: A Global Overview*, ed. Lanse Minkler (New York: Cambridge University Press, 2013), 271–305, 289.
75. The World Bank, *World Development Report 2006: Equity and Development* (Washington DC: The World Bank and New York: Oxford University Press, 2005), 108.
76. Ibid.
77. UN DESA, *Inequality Matters*, 70–1.
78. Ibid., 70.
79. The World Bank, *World Development Report 2006*, 108.
80. World Bank Group, *Poverty and Shared Prosperity 2016*, 73.
81. The World Bank, *World Development Report 2006*, 108.
82. Ibid.
83. World Bank Group, *Poverty and Shared Prosperity 2016*, 3.
84. Ibid., 70.
85. Ibid.; UN DESA, *Inequality Matters*, 22.
86. World Bank Group, *Poverty and Shared Prosperity 2016*, 70.
87. The World Bank, *World Development Report 2006*, 82-83; Michael I. Norton and Dan Ariely, 'Building America – One Wealth Quintile at a Time', *Perspectives on Psychological Science* 6, no. 1 (2011): 9–12.
88. The World Bank, *World Development Report 2006*, 82–3.
89. Norton and Ariely, 'Building a Better America', 10; OECD, 'Income Inequality Remains High in the Face of Weak Recovery', *Income Inequality Update* (November 2016), http://www.oecd.org/social/OECD2016-Income-Inequality-Update.pdf. Among OECD countries, Mexico and Chile are more unequal than the United States. Sweden is listed among the more equal societies along with other northern European countries, the Czech Republic, The Slovak Republic and Austria. Ibid.
90. Norton and Ariely, 'Building a Better America', 10.
91. Ibid.
92. Dan Ariely, 'Americans Want to Live in a Much More Equal Country (They Just Don't Realize It)', *The Atlantic* (online August 2, 2012).
93. UNESCO, *World Social Science Report*, 1.

94. See for example Universal Declaration of Human Rights (UDHR), G.A. res. 217A (III), UN Doc. A/810 at 71 (1948), article 1 (equal in dignity and rights), article 7 (equal before the law), article 16 (equal rights as to marriage), article 21 (equal access to public service); article 23 (equal pay for equal work).
95. Compare UNGA, *Transforming Our World* with United Nations Department of Economic and Social Affairs, Statistics Division, Millennium Development Goals Indicators, http://mdgs.un.org/unsd/mdg/Host.aspx?Content=Indicators/OfficialList.htm (accessed July 12, 2017).
96. Ibid.
97. UNGA, *Transforming Our World*, 14.
98. Katja Freistein and Bettina Mahlert, 'The Potential for Tackling Inequality in the Sustainable Development Goals', *Third World Quarterly* 37, no. 12 (2016): 2139–55, 2140.
99. Ibid., 2144.
100. Faiza Shaheen, 'Inequality Within and Among Countries', in *International Norms, Normative Change, and The UN Sustainable Development Goals*, ed. Noha Shawki (Lanham MD: Lexington Books, 2016), 99–113, 100.
101. For example Pogge and Sengupta, 'The Sustainable Development Goals', 583.
102. Richard Wilkinson and Deborah Rogers, 'Goal 10 – Reduce Inequality Within and Among Countries', in *Review of Targets for the Sustainable Development Goals: The Science Perspective*, ed. Anne-Sophie Stevance (International Council for Science in partnership with the International Social Science Council, 2015), 51. These critiques are also valid for other SDGs and targets. See for example Diane Frey and Gillian MacNaughton, 'A Human Rights Lens on Full Employment and Decent Work in the 2030 Sustainable Development Agenda', *Journal of Workplace Rights* 6, no. 2 (2016), 1–13.
103. UNGA, *Transforming Our World*, 21.
104. Pogge and Sengupta, 'The Sustainable Development Goals', 583.
105. Ibid.
106. Jean Drèze and Amartya Sen, *India: Development and Participation* (Oxford: Oxford University Press, 2002), 36–7.
107. Wilkinson and Rogers, 'Goal 10 – Reduce Inequality', 52.
108. Michael W. Doyle and Joseph E. Stiglitz, 'Eliminating Extreme Inequality: A Sustainable Development Goal, 2015–2030', *Ethics and International Affairs* 28, no. 1 (Spring 2014), 10.
109. Alex Cobham and Andy Sumner, 'On Inequality, Let's Do the Palma (because the Gini is So Last Century)', Oxfam Blog 'From Poverty to Power', March 19, 2013, https://oxfamblogs.org/fp2p/on-inequality-lets-do-the-palma-because-the-gini-is-so-last-century/; Alex Cobham, Luke Schlogl and Andy Sumner, 'Inequality and the Tails: The Palma Proposition and the Ration Revisited' (UN Department of Economic and Social Affairs, Working Paper No. 143), http://www.un.org/esa/desa/papers/2015/wp143_2015.pdf.
110. Doyle and Stiglitz, 'Eliminating Extreme Inequality'.
111. Final Compilation of Amendments to Goals and Targets by Major Groups and Other Stakeholders including Citizen's Responses to My World Priorities: To Inform the Thirteenth and Last Session of the Open Working Group on Sustainable Development Goals, July 14–18, 2014, https://sustainabledevelopment.un.org/content/documents/4438mgscompilationowg13.pdf.
112. Wilkinson and Rogers, 'Goal 10 – Reduce Inequality', 52.
113. Pogge and Sengupta, 'The Sustainable Development Goals', 580–4; Alex Cobham, Lukas Schlogl and Andy Sumner, 'Top Incomes Drive Inequality – So Why Does the Inequality Target Ignore Them?', *The Guardian* (September 21, 2015), https://www.theguardian.com/global-development/2015/sep/21/top-incomes-drive-income-inequality-global-target.
114. Joint Statement by over 45 NGOs and Worker Organizations, OWG Inches Closer to Human Rights for All Post-2015, But Still a Long Road Ahead, April 30, 2014, https://sustainabledevelopment.un.org/content/documents/8706HRsForAll.OWG11WP.may4.pdf.
115. Wilkinson and Rogers, 'Goal 10 – Reduce Inequality', 51.

116. Edward Anderson, 'Equality as a Global Goal', *Ethics & International Affairs* 30, no. 2 (2016): 189–200, 194.
117. UNGA, *Transforming Our World*, 21.
118. Report of the Inter-Agency and Expert Group on Sustainable Development Goal Indicators, UN Doc. E/CN.3/2016/2/Rev.1, Annex IV (March 2016), 13.
119. See further Winkler and Satterthwaite, 'Leaving No One Behind?'.
120. Report of the Inter-Agency and Expert Group (March 2016). Notably, the same indicator is used to measure progress toward target 16.b 'Promote and enforce non-discriminatory laws and policies for sustainable development' (ibid., 22).
121. See further Winkler and Satterthwaite, 'Leaving No One Behind?'.
122. Kate Donald, 'Will Inequality Get Left Behind in the 2030 Agenda?', in *Spotlight on Sustainable Development, Report by the Reflection Group on the 203 Agenda for Sustainable Development*, ed. Barbara Aams, Roberto Bissio, Chee Yoke Ling, Karen Judd, Jens Martens and Wolfgang Obenland, https://www.2030spotlight.org/en/published.
123. Report of the Inter-Agency and Expert Group, 13.
124. UNGA, *Transforming Our World*, 21.
125. Wilkinson and Rogers, 'Goal 10 – Reduce Inequality', 52.
126. Donald, 'Will Inequality Get Left Behind', 84.
127. UNGA, *Transforming Our World*, 21.
128. Report of the Inter-Agency and Expert Group, 13.
129. Ibid., 21.
130. UNGA, *Transforming Our World*, 21.
131. Report of the Inter-Agency and Expert Group, 13.
132. Ibid., 13.
133. Inter-Agency Expert Group on SDG Indicators, *Compilation of Metadata for the Proposed Global Indicators for the Review of the 2030 Agenda for Sustainable Development*, Metadata for Goal 10 (updated March 3, 2016), 9, http://unstats.un.org/sdgs/files/metadata-compilation/Metadata-Goal-10.pdf.
134. UNGA, *Transforming Our World*, 21.
135. Anderson, 'Equality as a Global Goal', 198.
136. UNGA, *Transforming Our World*, 27. Target 17.12 states: 'Realize timely implementation of duty-free and quota-free market access on a lasting basis for all least developed countries, consistent with World Trade Organization decisions, including by ensuring that preferential rules of origin applicable to imports from least developed countries are transparent and simple, and contribute to facilitating market access'.
137. Ibid., 21.
138. Ibid., 26.
139. Anderson, 'Equality as a Global Goal', 198.
140. Ibid.
141. UNGA, *Transforming Our World*, 21.
142. Inter-Agency Expert Group on SDG Indicators, *Compilation of Metadata*, 14.
143. Wilkinson and Rogers, 'Goal 10 – Reduce Inequality', 52.
144. Ibid.
145. Letter to Dr Homi Kharas, executive secretary of the secretariat supporting the UN Secretary-General's High Level Panel of Eminent Persons on the Post-2015 Development Agenda, March 19, 2013, http://www.post2015hlp.org/wp-content/uploads/2013/03/Dr-Homi-Kharas.pdf.
146. Doyle and Stiglitz, 'Eliminating Extreme Inequality', 10.
147. Pogge and Sengupta, 'The Sustainable Development Goals', 585.
148. See Wilkinson and Rogers, 'Goal 10 – Reduce Inequality', 52.
149. Ibid.
150. Doyle and Stiglitz, 'Eliminating Extreme Inequality', 10.
151. Committee on Economic, Social and Cultural Rights, General Comment No. 3: The Nature of the State Parties Obligations, UN Doc. E/1991/23, annex III at 86 (1990), para 2.

152. UNGA, *Transforming Our World*, para. 10.
153. Zeid, 'An Agenda for Equality'.
154. Saiz and Oré Aguilar, 'Introducing the Debate'.
155. Alston, Annual Report 2015, para. 3.
156. Ibid., para. 26.
157. Ibid., para. 54.
158. Ibid., para. 48.
159. Ibid., para. 54–5.
160. See for example Saiz and Oré Aguilar, 'Introducing the Debate'; Alston, 'Extreme Inequality';
     Balakrishnan and Heintz, 'How Inequality Threatens All Rights'; Sakiko Fukuda-Parr, 'It's
     About Values'; Donald, 'Will Inequality Get Left Behind'; MacNaughton, 'Untangling Equal-
     ity and Nondiscrimination'; MacNaughton, 'Beyond a Minimum Threshold'; Radhika Balak-
     rishnan, James Heintz and Diane Elson, *Rethinking Economic Policy for Social Justice: The
     Radical Potential of Human Rights* (New York: Routledge, 2016); Centre for Economic
     and Social Rights (CESR), 'From Disparity to Dignity: Tackling Economic Inequality
     through the Sustainable Development Goals' (CESR human rights policy brief, 2016),
     http://www.cesr.org/sites/default/files/disparity_to_dignity_SDG10.pdf.
161. See for example Balakrishnan, Heintz and Elson, *Rethinking Economic Policy*, 30–8.
162. CESR, 'From Disparity to Dignity', 2.
163. Fukuda-Parr, 'It's About Values', 3.
164. MacNaughton, 'Untangling Equality and Nondiscrimination', 52.
165. Ibid., 56.
166. Alston, Annual Report 2015, para. 55.
167. Shaheen, 'Inequality Within and Among Countries', para. 6.42; Anderson, 'Equality as a
     Global Goal', 189.
168. Ibid.; See Report of the Inter-agency and Expert Group, 2. But see Winkler and Satterthwaite,
     'Leaving No One Behind?', maintaining that the indicators address only gender, age and dis-
     ability, leaving out ethnicity, race, language and religion.
169. UNGA, *Transforming Our World*, para. 4.
170. Ibid.
171. Report of the Inter-agency and Expert Group, 13.

Acknowledgements

I wish to thank two reviewers for their insightful comments, and Angela Duger for her research assistance for this article. I am also grateful to Shareen Hertel and Susan Randolph, Co-Directors of the Research Project on Economic and Social Rights at the University of Connecticut, for the opportunity to present an earlier draft of this article at their Spring 2016 Workshop, and to those in attendance who provided thoughtful comments on the draft.

Disclosure statement

No potential conflict of interest was reported by the author.

Leaving no one behind? Persistent inequalities in the SDGs

Inga T. Winkler and Margaret L. Satterthwaite

ABSTRACT

With a rallying cry of 'leave no one behind', the Sustainable Development Agenda has moved inequalities centre stage. A number of the Sustainable Development Goals (SDGs) include a cross-cutting focus on inequalities and the advancement of some communities that have historically experienced discrimination. However, the litmus test for whether the SDGs will truly 'leave no one behind' is not the inclusion of such (aspirational) language, but whether this language will translate into implementation. In that regard, monitoring through indicators will play an important role. As metrics pegged to specific targets, indicators have the power to concentrate effort and attention. Moving beyond aggregate outcomes will require that the data related to these indicators be sufficiently disaggregated to demonstrate the existence, magnitude and interplay of multiple forms of inequalities. However, despite a mandate to produce disaggregated data, there has been little attention to disaggregation based on some of the most important axes of discrimination – especially race or ethnicity. Human rights call for focusing on those who are often pushed to the margins of society – through political, social and economic processes as well as by data collection and analysis itself.

Introduction

The Sustainable Development Agenda has moved inequalities centre stage. Compared to the Millennium Development Goals (MDGs), the Sustainable Development Goals (SDGs) provide a boost for equality and promote development that 'leaves no one behind'.[1] Numerous goals and targets include a focus on inequalities and the advancement of communities that have historically experienced discrimination. Goal 10 focuses on reducing inequalities within and among countries. In addition, Goal 5 specifically addresses achieving gender equality and empowering women and girls.

Parallel to these cross-cutting goals, many of the sector-specific targets include a focus on reaching marginalised individuals and groups. For instance, Target 2.3 on small-scale food producers refers specifically to indigenous peoples and pastoralists, among others, and highlights the need for equal access to land. Target 4.5 seeks to ensure equal access to education, including for persons with disabilities and indigenous peoples. Target 16.b emphasises the need to promote and enforce non-discriminatory laws. Other targets throughout the SDGs complement these examples.

However, the litmus test for whether the SDGs will truly 'leave no one behind' is not whether the SDG goals and targets include such (aspirational) language, but whether this language will translate into implementation of the goals on the basis of equality and non-discrimination. In that regard, monitoring will play an important role. As metrics pegged to specific targets, indicators have the power to concentrate effort and attention.[2]

Moving beyond aggregate outcomes will require that the data related to these indicators be disaggregated along lines sufficient to meaningfully demonstrate the existence, magnitude and interplay of multiple forms of inequalities. In this regard, perhaps the most important rights-related target is 17.18, which makes the connection between human rights and disaggregation clear by calling for capacity building to enable countries to produce data 'disaggregated by income, gender, age, race, ethnicity, migratory status, disability and geographic location and other characteristics relevant in national contexts'. This target makes clear that data-gathering and analysis for *all* goals and targets, where disaggregable, should aim at highlighting inequalities. But to what extent do the existing indicators incorporate the call for disaggregation? And what are the real possibilities – and the perils – inherent in this call for disaggregation? This article sets out to explore these questions.

Focus of the article

This article examines disaggregation as a tool for monitoring inequalities based on a number of axes of identity protected by human rights law that we find are not receiving sufficient attention. Specifically, the article focuses on race and ethnicity, since racial and ethnic variables have been largely ignored in the first few years of SDG monitoring, despite the fact that racial and ethnic discrimination are among the most prevalent and persistent forms of discrimination. The article also refers to language, religion, indigenous status, caste and other stratifiers on the grounds of which particular groups are marginalised. We acknowledge that emphasising particular axes of discrimination may not do justice to an individual's intersectional identities. People do not just belong to an ethnic minority or to a particular caste or an indigenous people – they may belong to multiple ethnicities, or experience discrimination based on their ethnicity as well as their gender, place of living, age and other axes of discrimination. Thus, it may seem that disaggregating data using such categories would encourage simplistic analyses in which the categories used for comparison are fixed and homogenous. However, feminist scholars have suggested otherwise. McCall argues that disaggregation is one of the methods most suited to intersectional analysis, and that it is capable of taking into account the many-faceted nature of human identity.[3] She explains that empirical studies that deploy multiple comparisons of data sequentially disaggregated by various axes of discrimination can allow for a textured understanding of intersecting forms of discrimination. Whether this kind of synthesis is possible in the realm of the SDGs depends to a large extent on the availability of sufficiently granular data to conduct multiple intersecting disaggregations.

In the context of the SDGs, there is significant discursive and substantive focus on specific axes of discrimination, in particular gender inequalities. In this connection,

Goal 5 provides a clear mandate to focus on gender inequalities and the gender dimension is increasingly being addressed in relation to other goals as well.[4] While we by no means intend to dismiss the importance of such monitoring, we find that inequalities based on race, ethnicity and similar factors do not receive the same attention.

The distinctions that justify the focus of the article are inherently related to processes of marginalisation and power structures that continue to be in evidence in the SDG framework itself. A focus on groups marginalised by factors such as ethnicity, caste or indigenous status relates to dimensions that are perceived to be inescapably political – or 'sensitive', as often described euphemistically by those rejecting calls to focus on these stratifiers. Human rights advocates must reject calls to remain out of the political fray by focusing on those who are often pushed to the margins of society – through political, social, and economic processes as well as by data collection and analysis (or the lack thereof) itself.

Methodology

This article is based on an original analysis of the official SDG indicators and major household survey questionnaires relied upon for SDG monitoring data. We systematically assessed each of the 230 SDG indicators to determine whether the indicator explicitly calls for disaggregation and if so, on what bases. While we acknowledge that the official SDG indicators are only part of a much larger set of monitoring processes by UN member States and UN agencies that will often be sector-specific, the official indicator framework is what holds the monitoring framework together and what sets the tone for other processes. Further, the indicator framework has the potential to issue a concerted push for systematically improved data collection across all sectors and will therefore be in the focus of the article's attention.

To understand whether and how core data are gathered concerning ethnicity and race, we examined standardised household surveys (the Demographic and Health Survey [DHS] and the Multiple Indicator Cluster Survey [MICS]) used by approximately 100 countries in the Global South. We analysed the questionnaires used in all countries that conducted them during two different time periods.[5] The survey instruments used in countries during this time were examined to see whether they gathered data on ethnicity or race, as well as whether this data was based on self-identification or categorisation by the enumerator. While there are other data sources for this information (discussed below), these surveys represent key data sets for monitoring of development progress; their contents and omissions are therefore quite important.

Map of the article

Following this Introduction, Section 2 emphasises the importance of data collection and analysis as monitoring tools and the role of indicators in that context. Against the backdrop of a consensus on 'leaving no one behind', Section 3 proceeds to examine to what extent that commitment has been translated into the SDG indicators to date. Section 4 demonstrates that monitoring progress for marginalised groups is far from impossible. Examining different types of data used for monitoring – with a focus on household surveys – we find that existing data sources are amenable to much more equality analysis than performed to date. However, such data collection and analysis is not without challenges and risks. Section 5 explores the dark sides of monitoring the progress of marginalised communities and recommends human rights safeguards on data privacy and confidentiality, self-identification, avoiding stigmatisation and countering the risk of criminalisation and persecution. Participation of disadvantaged individuals and groups emerges as the central requirement. Section 6 explores this imperative, highlighting the importance of involving people from the very beginning of any data gathering and analysis process, including in the determination and prioritisation of marginalised groups for monitoring purposes as well as in data collection efforts. Section 7 presents the conclusion and outlook.

Monitoring progress for marginalised communities

From rhetoric to reality: the importance of data collection and analysis

No one will be 'left behind' only when policies, programmes and specific measures to eliminate discrimination and advance progress for marginalised groups are adopted. Data, indicators and disaggregation – as technical as they may seem – play an essential role in facilitating and enabling the adoption of such measures to ensure that inequalities are reduced. As CIVICUS recently explained:

> Every information system renders certain aspects of the world visible and lets others recede into the background. Datasets highlight some things and not others. They make the world comprehensible and navigable in their own way.[6]

The UN has described data as 'the lifeblood of decision-making and the raw material for accountability'.[7] Focusing monitoring efforts on marginalised groups helps break the vicious cycle of invisibility and neglect. All too often, marginalised communities are not part of monitoring efforts because they are excluded from data gathering and rendered invisible in the resulting analyses. By collecting data on, and analysing disparities and inequalities between groups, these dynamics start to shift, and policy-makers are pressured to redress the impacts of marginalisation and discrimination.

The rationale for and importance of monitoring inequalities is best understood in relation to the purpose and effects of global development goals. Fukuda-Parr distinguishes the *governance effects* and the *knowledge effects* of global goals. In terms of governance, the broad policy purpose of global goals is to put issues on the agenda, and to increase attention and support for areas that are important for development but have thus far been neglected.[8] Goals are intended to promote changes in policy and implementation at the national level by creating incentives.[9] In this regard, global monitoring has been used for performance evaluation, as an accountability framework and as a basis for advocacy.[10] In addition to the governance effects, the *knowledge effects* must be considered. Target-setting – and the indicators associated with targets – have the potential to influence how norms themselves are defined and understood and how the narrative around their implementation is shaped.[11] Merry has argued that 'indicators produce readily understandable and convenient forms of knowledge about the world that shape the way policy makers and the general public understand the world'.[12]

The framing of indicators and the disaggregation they call for are therefore not just technical details; they have significant influence on what data governments and development partners will gather over the next 15 years or more and 'what matters' in the implementation of the Sustainable Development Agenda.[13] The SDG indicators will help shape what governments, development partners and people – disadvantaged or powerful – will *know* about discrimination, exclusion and equality. Therefore, it will be essential to incorporate a focus on monitoring progress for marginalised communities and reducing inequalities in the SDG indicators to ensure that no one is left behind.

Non-discrimination and equality are perhaps the most essential norms in the human rights framework and underscore the need for monitoring inequalities. The prohibited grounds of discrimination provide guidance on stratifiers that should be monitored. Article 2(2) of the International Covenant on Economic, Social and Cultural Rights states:

> The States Parties to the present Covenant undertake to guarantee that the rights enunciated in the present Covenant will be exercised without discrimination of any kind as to race, colour, sex, language, religion, political or other opinion, national or social origin, property, birth or other status.

The category of 'other status' is understood to encompass a wide range of grounds upon which people may experience discrimination in different contexts and time periods.[14]

Human rights treaty bodies have recommended that States collect and report on the progress of protected groups using disaggregated statistics.[15] For example, the Committee on Economic, Social and Cultural Rights has stressed that States have an obligation to monitor the measures they take to effectively implement their obligations, assessing both the process and the outcomes using relevant indicators that should be 'disaggregated on the basis of prohibited grounds of discrimination'.[16] While some States do provide such data, progress on disaggregation has been relatively slow. For this reason (and because compared to treaty body monitoring, significantly greater resources will flow into the SDG processes), SDG monitoring efforts have a great potential to overcome these barriers in the coming decades. On the flip-side, however, if the SDGs do not provide the framework for monitoring inequalities experienced by marginalised groups, the knowledge effects of the indicators may yield a redefined, much narrower understanding of inequalities and discrimination than the expansive definition under human rights law.

Rationale for focusing on marginalised communities

The former UN Independent Expert on Minority Issues emphasises that ethnic, religious and linguistic minorities face systematic discrimination and marginalisation in countries across the world.[17] Statistics in countries that gather data disaggregated by relevant groups capture the effects of such discrimination. In the context of national Human Development Reports, for example, Nepal has disaggregated data on the basis of caste and ethnicity. Human Development Index values for castes and ethnic groups were calculated for representation in the political process, literacy rates, nutritional status and many other indicators.[18] The report shows that Tarai/Madhesi Dalits had the lowest level of human development among social groups within the country, irrespective of geographical location.[19]

Some global monitoring initiatives also examine these kinds of disparities. The World Inequality Database on Education reports on inequalities based on ethnicity and religion (in addition to gender, urban/rural residences, region, and wealth).[20] The UNICEF-WHO Joint Monitoring Programme for Water and Sanitation (JMP) has also started to report on inequalities linked to language, ethnicity and religion. These initiatives point to significant disparities in sanitation and water access among ethnic, religious and linguistic minorities in some countries. For example, in Laos, sanitation coverage among linguistic minorities (30% coverage for Chinese-Tibetan and Mon-Khmer) is less than half that of the majority of the population speaking Lao-Tai (74% coverage).[21]

Analysis of disaggregated data, coupled with assessment of national and local socio-political processes, can demonstrate that marginalisation cuts across different fields of social development. In a recent study, the Overseas Development Institute (ODI) has pointed out that in Nigeria, 'Fulani are eight times less likely than Yoruba to have access to sanitation, three times less likely to have had a substantial education and more than twice as likely to belong to the bottom wealth quintile'.[22] A recent cross-country analysis of DHS survey data on health and education outcomes in 16 countries by ODI found that depending on the country, ethnicity as a factor explains anywhere between 5 and 25% of inequality.[23]

Beyond economic inequalities

Marginalised communities are frequently among the poorest in society. There are significant correlations between social marginalisation and economic disparities. Economic inequality based on income or wealth has become a major point of convergence for discussions of inequalities, even from the perspective of human rights.[24] Addressing economic inequalities is central to Goal 10 (but see MacNaughton in this volume).

However, in order to both understand and eliminate economic inequalities, monitoring other forms of inequalities is essential. The world's poorest people are not randomly distributed across gender, ethnic, caste and other characteristics – who lives in poverty is often the result of multiple, intersecting forms of discrimination and exclusion. Human rights experts have long maintained that the impact of discrimination and marginalisation needs to be holistically integrated into development processes. For instance, the Independent Expert on minority issues has argued in the context of poverty reduction that a generalised approach that does not target minority groups 'can fail to address the particular structure and causes of poverty experienced by minority groups'.[25] More recently, other organisations have started to take up these arguments. ODI explained that people belonging to ethnic and other minorities are overrepresented among people living in extreme poverty and those not having adequate access to health and education.[26] The organisation observes that understanding discrimination is crucial, since '[o]ften we know how to reach the income-poor, but not the marginalized'.[27]

Focusing on economic disparities only cannot fully address the root causes of exclusion from social development, and material solutions cannot fully address discrimination.[28] Where discrimination is at play, being left behind does not happen arbitrarily. It is inherently political. Without acknowledging this, the necessary normative, attitudinal, political and social change will be impossible to achieve. For this reason, analysing disparities in outcomes along lines of race, ethnicity and other axes of discrimination can function as an indication that discriminatory processes may be at work and that urgent attention is needed.[29]

Without targeting the most marginalised people among people living in poverty with adequate measures, people will continue to be excluded even when efforts target those living in poverty. A pilot analysis by the JMP correlates data on wealth quintiles in Bosnia-Herzegovina with data on access to water and sanitation among the country's Roma population. It shows that 82% of the general population in the poorest wealth quintile have access to water and sanitation, whereas only 32% of the Roma population in the poorest wealth quintile have access.[30] Similar results for Roma populations were found in relation to education.[31] Another study in 33 (low and lower-middle income) countries found that 'education and health poverty' was concentrated among ethnic minorities. In more than two thirds of households characterised as experiencing education and health poverty, the 'head of household' was a member of an ethnic minority group.[32]

The failure to translate 'leave no one behind' into SDG indicators

From the promise to 'leave no one behind' to the many targets that focus on reaching specific marginalised groups to the across-the-board call for disaggregated data in Target 17.18, the building blocks are present in the SDGs to tackle discrimination and its impacts. However, when it comes to translating these targets into monitoring frameworks, indicators and disaggregation, much emphasis has been placed on the difficult reality that disaggregation can be overwhelming, costly and fraught with logistical and political challenges.

The list of prohibited grounds of discrimination in international human rights law is not only long, but it is also formulated in open-ended terms to make clear that it applies to evolving forms of discrimination. While a quest to be comprehensive is important, in practice, a balance must be struck between over-simplification and demanding disaggregation that overburdens statistical offices. However, the work done thus far to develop indicators for the SDGs comes nowhere near striking such a balance. The rhetoric of 'leave no one behind' does not translate into the indicators that would allow monitoring progress for marginalised groups, as the following analysis will demonstrate.

Analysis of the final list of proposed SDG indicators

Our analysis of the Final List of Proposed SDG Indicators yields the following: among the 230 indicators[33] used to measure progress towards the SDGs, 46 indicators call for disaggregation by sex or require sex-specific data, 35 for disaggregation by age or age-specific data, and 11 for disaggregation by disability status.

As far as disaggregation by race and ethnicity is concerned, the findings of this analysis are distressing and disillusioning. Target 10.2. on promoting social, economic and political inclusion and target 17.18 on data and monitoring indicate that such disaggregation should take place, but not a single indicator among the final list specifically requires disaggregation by ethnicity or race – not one. The closest the indicators get to capturing inequalities related to such marginalisation is a small number of indicators that relate to 'indigenous status' (indicators 2.3.2 and 4.5.1), 'key populations' in the context of HIV/AIDS (indicator 3.3.1), 'most disadvantaged population' (indicator 3.8.1), 'migrant status' (indicators 8.8.1 and 8.8.2), 'population groups' (indicators 16.7.1 and 16.7.2), 'marginalized communities' (indicator 13.b.1) and 'poor and vulnerable groups' (indicator 1.b.1). One ambitious indicator (4.5.1) calls for the use of 'parity indices (female/male, rural/urban, bottom/top quintile and others such as disability status, indigenous peoples and conflict-affected[…])', in the context of education, but qualifies this with 'as data become available'.

Perhaps most striking is the indicator associated with target 10.2. The target language is robust, reading: 'By 2030, empower and promote the social, economic and political inclusion of all, irrespective of age, sex, disability, race, ethnicity, origin, religion or economic or other status.' The associated indicator 10.2.1, however, calls for monitoring of the 'proportion of people living below 50 per cent of median income, by age, sex and persons with disabilities'. Disturbingly, in the step of translating the target into the indicator, the dimensions of 'race, ethnicity, origin, religion or … other status' were dropped entirely. Given the explicit target language, this cannot be considered an oversight. While 'technical' issues concerning missing data or the difficulty in obtaining comparable data may be relevant here, such problems can be overcome as the analysis below demonstrates. This omission is, in fact, a decision to treat these stratifiers differently by excluding these dimensions. The reasons for this exclusion are likely to lie in the power of data: measurement of racial and ethnic inequalities may call attention to historic and ongoing injustices that those in power would prefer not to see highlighted in embarrassing data at the international level.

This is not the only way in which target 10.2. is reduced, watered down and depoliticised. The target itself refers to promoting the 'social, economic and political inclusion of all', yet the only dimension measured in the indicator is that of income. There could hardly be a clearer case of reducing a multidimensional target concerned with marginalisation and exclusion through a limited indicator. And given that none of the other indicators in the total of 230 specifically refer to the categories of race and ethnicity, there are no other measurements that would remedy this glaring shortcoming.

As far as target 10.3 is concerned, it calls on States to '[e]nsure equal opportunity and reduce inequalities of outcome, including by eliminating discriminatory laws, policies and practices and promoting appropriate legislation, policies and action in this regard'. It presents a combination of an outcome target and structural target, which should be reflected in a combination of indicators capturing these elements. However, while the associated indicator 10.3.1 is inclusive in its phrasing ('on the basis of a ground of discrimination prohibited under international human rights law'), it seeks perception data alone ('proportion of the population reporting having personally felt discriminated against or harassed within the last 12 months'). While this is valuable in itself and recognises people as experts on their own experience, it does not adequately capture the reduction of inequalities in outcomes referred to in the target.[34]

As explained above, where complex global norms are simplified through single, far less complex indicators, there is a danger that the indicator alone – separate from the target – will be taken up in messaging as it presents a more compelling, more intuitively comprehensible case.[35] If the global monitoring of inequalities focuses largely on economic inequalities combined with a limited number of disaggregations that do not capture the outcomes of crucial processes of marginalisation such as racism and ethnic discrimination, these forms of discrimination are likely to be sidelined in advocacy and policy efforts.

Indeed, the indicator framework poses a real danger of diluting the complex goal of redu-cing inequalities across multiple dimensions as reflected in Goal 10 to a simple focus on reducing economic inequalities (see MacNaughton in this volume for further critique of this dimension). Rather than falling for this over-simplification, the call for disaggregation across multiple stratifiers in target 17.18 must be taken seriously so that inequalities are monitored and reflected in their complexity.

The current list of SDG indicators has been approved by the UN Statistical Commission as a 'practical starting point'.[36] The indicators might – and should – be further developed. The Inter-Agency and Expert Group on Sustainable Development Goal Indicators, which is tasked with developing the indicators, agreed on data disaggregation as an overarching principle:

> Sustainable Development Goal indicators should be disaggregated, where relevant, by income, sex, age, race, ethnicity, migratory status, disability and geographic location, or other characteristics, in accordance with the Fundamental Principles of Official Statistics.[37]

When approving the indicator framework, the UN Statistical Commission stressed that 'improving data disaggregation is fundamental for the full implementation of the indicator framework and to respect fully the principle of leaving no one behind', and that efforts should be made to strengthen national capacities in this area and to develop the necessary statistical standards and tools.[38]

One important opportunity to further develop the indicators is through the Metadata sheets. These sheets provide information on the rationale behind the indicators, the meth-odology, data sources and data availability. As of March 2017, there is no metadata sheet yet for Target 10.2.[39] However, one of the proposals (by the Office of the High Commis-sioner for Human Rights – OHCHR) suggests that the

> indicator should be disaggregated by ethnicity, sex, age, geographic location, disability, reli-gion, migratory or displacement status, civil status, and other statuses relevant at the national level, which may for example include minority or indigenous status, language spoken at home, etc.[40]

Such proposals highlight the role that UN agencies can play at the technical level, through tools such as metadata sheets, to push for further disaggregation. However, they also demonstrate that the question of disaggregation has been pushed out of the limelight of the political process and into a highly technical and agency-driven process.

As of now, the indicators fail to reflect the erstwhile commitment to 'leave no one behind'. They will fail to produce knowledge about which ethnic and racial population groups are left behind to start with, where progress is needed most, and whether measures taken to achieve the SDGs are successful in reducing existing inequalities. Without such knowledge, the needed governance effects will also be missing. The revision and expansion of indicators is therefore of utmost importance.

Analysis of the first Sustainable Development Goals Report (2016)

The first *Sustainable Development Goals* Report ('*SDGs* Report'), released in July 2016, demonstrates that the actual reporting is even worse than it appears from a conceptual review of the indicator framework. Of the 230 indicators, the 2016 *SDGs Report* reports on only 66 – 'those for which there are sufficient data available to provide an overview at the regional and global levels'.[41] Only 17 of the indicators used in the *SDGs Report* were disaggregated in any way in the main part of the report – and this is an over-count, since it includes group-specific data presented without comparisons. Sex-disaggregated or sex-specific data were presented for nine indicators; age-specific or age-disaggregated data were presented for five indicators; income or wealth-disaggregated data for three; and location-disaggregated data (e.g. urban/rural) for three. Not a single indicator was disaggregated by disability, race or ethnicity, religion, language, sexual orientation, gender identity or migration status.

The report includes a short section at the end entitled 'Leaving no one behind', which decries the lack of data that is disaggregable by relevant stratifiers and presents examples of indicators and their relevant disaggregations. This section is followed by a 'Note to Readers' that explains that 'accurate and timely information about certain aspects of people's lives are unknown, numerous groups and individuals remain "invisible", and many development challenges are still poorly understood'.[42] This holds true certainly for groups that are marginalised on grounds of race, ethnicity, caste or similar identities, who do not appear at all in the report.

Thus, while the revision of indicators is relatively straightforward from a conceptual perspective, and the addition of stratifiers by which data should be disaggregable would be a significant improvement, many assert that the greater challenge is collecting the necessary data on marginalised groups. As the Secretary-General explained in his June 2016 report on 'Progress towards the Sustainable Development Goals':

> The disaggregated information needed to address all vulnerable groups, as specified in the 2030 Agenda, remains scarce. For example, few of the current indicators can be disaggregated for migrants, refugees, persons with disabilities, minorities and indigenous people. A global effort to improve data availability for all population groups, including through improvements in the integration of data sources, has already begun. Further work is needed to enhance the coverage, quality and frequency of data to ensure that the most vulnerable and marginalized people are the first to be reached.[43]

The remainder of the article discusses and questions the degree to which data availability is indeed a major obstacle and how the collection of disaggregated data on marginalised groups can be improved. As will be demonstrated, the problems involve both a lack of data and a lack of political will to use available data in disaggregated analyses.

Household surveys and beyond: disaggregation and the missing millions

Work is still underway to determine the best sources of data for all of the SDG indicators.[44] While there is a need to expand well beyond the data sets used for MDG monitoring, core sources will remain important,[45] among them censuses and statistically representative household surveys.[46] The Sustainable Development Solutions Network (SDSN) estimates that 'surveys (household, consumption, agricultural, and labor force surveys) will be the key source of information for producing more than 26 percent of the SDG indicators'.[47]

However, as is plain from this SDSN assessment, additional data sources will be essential in monitoring the SDGs. This is partly due to the limitations of survey data, and partly due to the expansion of topics and the increased complexity of the SDGs as compared with the MDGs. The SDSN emphasises the need not only for survey data, but also for administrative data (for instance public records in the context of welfare, taxes, health and education), civil registration data, economic statistics such as labour force participation, and geospatial data, among other types of data.[48] In addition, Big Data has been suggested by many as a source with great potential, though it also carries significant risks.[49] Due to space constraints, this article will largely focus on household surveys to illustrate the potential for strengthened inequality-sensitive analyses, as there is the most experience with such data sets, and because they will retain a key role moving forward.

Data available – and not – through household surveys

The data sets resulting from major household surveys include a wide variety of variables related to ethnicity, race, religion and language that could be used more systematically, though real and perceived obstacles have stood in the way of such an effort.

Our analysis of the two major household surveys (the DHS and MICS) found that almost half of both pre- and post-2012 surveys examined included a question about race, ethnicity or colour. With respect to religion, almost two-thirds of the pre-2012 surveys examined asked about religion, while the proportion grew to just over two-thirds in the later period. This means that it is likely that in about half of the recent major household surveys conducted in the Global South, data are available that are disaggregable by these key grounds of discrimination. While it would be important to continue to expand the number of countries where data is disaggregable by race or ethnicity, this proportion of surveys is an excellent starting point for global SDG monitoring. The fact that about half of the surveys allow for disaggregation by race or ethnicity demonstrates its feasibility, in striking contrast to the broad-ranging claims about the lack of data available for disaggregation and the difficulty in collecting such data.

The DHS, MICS and similar surveys are not carried out in most countries of the Global North. Monitoring in these countries, however, is now increasingly relevant as the SDGs apply to all countries of the world. Monitoring inequalities is of particular significance in countries where only small specific groups continue to be left behind. In a number of developed countries, this data can be obtained through censuses and other national surveys. For instance, the US census collects data on race ('White, Black or African American, American Indian or Alaska Native, Asian, and Native Hawaiian and Other Pacific Islander') and Hispanic origin.[50] In Europe, the European Union Minorities and Discrimination Survey has collected data on several minority groups per country.[51] In brief, data sources exist in countries across the world that could be used much more widely.

Certainly, significant methodological issues present themselves in the drive to report at the global level on country data that contains enormous variation. For example, could findings concerning different ethnic groups in separate countries be compared or combined? Could a group defined by religion in one country be compared or combined with findings about an ethnic group of the same religion in another? While these are complex problems, they are the kinds of issues that social scientists deal with frequently, and there are ways to handle such challenges. For example, reporting could focus on 'disadvantaged' groups in each country, instead of specific population groups, with relevant 'disadvantaged' groups determined at the national level, which would allow for global comparisons.

Despite the differences, ethnic and racial inequalities are present in some form or another in virtually every country across the globe. While the specific forms may vary and the groups subject to discrimination define themselves differently across the world, the reality of marginalisation, exclusion and discrimination is global. Illustrating the effects of these intersecting forms of marginalisation and deprivation through the tools of global monitoring can convey a powerful message highlighting discrimination as a structural problem, helping ensure efforts are targeted to the benefit of the most marginalised groups and individuals.

Ongoing monitoring initiatives demonstrate that such comparisons are feasible. The World Inequality Database on Education mentioned above allows for comparisons across countries. When queried, the database displays the disparity between the most privileged group and the most deprived group in each country, presenting these groups on a continuum and displaying the group names as nationally defined. For example, in Nigeria (based on data from the DHS 2013) the primary education completion rate for the Kambari is 10% compared to 98% for the Igala, which places Nigeria as the country with the highest absolute disparity (out of the countries for which data is available).[52]

A contextualised analysis of the socioeconomic, legal and historical status of different groups and the data gathered is necessary if re-coding into 'advantaged' or 'privileged' and 'disadvantaged' or 'deprived' groups is to be undertaken. Such re-coding first requires determining which are the factors that determine a group's identity (whether it is language, caste, religion, race, ethnicity or several such factors), and second determining which groups are disadvantaged in each national context. In the context of health-related goals, researchers have developed a methodology for re-coding population groups into 'dominant', 'secondary dominant' and 'non-dominant' groups, thereby creating three categories.[53] Such re-coding could be done on a country-by-country basis to be context-specific and determine the relevant forms of marginalisation.

In Europe, the Fundamental Rights Agency has taken a similar approach in conducting the European Union Minorities and Discrimination Survey that was based on selecting two or three minority groups per country. Selection criteria for the groups included being a large group and being at risk of discrimination.[54] Using such methodologies creates categories that can be used for cross-country analysis and thus helps overcome the challenge of comparability.

While the existing data could be used much more widely, data on ethnicity and similar factors is currently not available for all countries. Still, this should not be seen as discouragement to pursue monitoring in this area, but rather as an incentive to develop it further. The data availability discussion needs to be unpacked and addressed as not only a technical problem, but a deeply political one. Where there is data, there is a way to analyse processes of marginalisation and discrimination. And where there is political will and proven methodologies, there is usually a way to gather such data.

Missing millions

But what about instances when there really is not any relevant data or established methodology for gathering it? A number of specific population groups are typically not captured through household surveys at all. A recent study by Carr-Hill estimates that as many as 300–350 million people might be missing from standard household surveys.[55] Related to the overall size of the world's population, this figure might not seem unacceptably high; however, people left out of surveys are likely to be among the most marginalised. A number of groups are often excluded from household surveys by their very design. These include homeless populations, populations in institutions such as prisons or refugee camps, and mobile, nomadic or pastoralist populations. In addition, difficult-to-reach populations will typically be underrepresented, including persons in fragile households, people living in informal settlements and people living in areas that are considered to pose a risk to security for enumerators.[56] Carr-Hill relates the figure of 300–350 million to the lowest wealth quintile, arguing that the undercount in this quintile is up to a quarter of these populations, making 'a mockery of monitoring development progress'.[57] We currently do not know what proportion of these missing millions are also members of groups marginalised by race, ethnicity or similar identities, but it is a fair bet that the proportion is significant in many countries.

There is another issue that poses particular problems for efforts to use disaggregation as a tool for equality analysis: sample size and statistical power. Because household surveys are based on nationally representative sampling, the resulting data sets tend to include relatively small numbers of respondents representing minority groups. This is not a problem for aggregate, national analyses. When data are disaggregated into multiple intersecting axes of discrimination – precisely the analysis that would be most meaningful from a human rights perspective – however, the numbers can become too small to yield adequate statistical power for meaningful analytical findings. There are numerous solutions to this kind of challenge, such as deliberate oversampling of minority groups, targeted surveys of such groups and recoding of multiple groups into aggregate stratifiers like advantaged/disadvantaged, discussed above, but these methods need to be actively used.[58]

Beyond household surveys

Many of the SDG indicators demand data that is not captured in standardised forms across the globe. As noted above, the 230 indicators draw on data to be captured via not only household surveys, but also perception and opinion polling, administrative data, qualitative scoring and methods designed to capture information about illicit activity. Some could be based on – or integrate – Big Data, crowdsourced data and data collected using participatory methods. Examining all of these potential sources is beyond the scope of this article, but it is worth noting some of the most important obstacles and perils involved in using these – as well as more traditional – sources and methods for disaggregated analysis of inequalities experienced by ethnic, racial and other marginalised communities. These are explored in the next section.

Human rights safeguards and the dark sides of data collection

Monitoring inequalities and progress for marginalised communities holds tremendous promise for ensuring that these communities are not left behind, and for tailoring programmes to fit their needs. At the same time, however, this monitoring and targeting also entails significant risks. Race, ethnicity and similar factors can be highly political, with power imbalances often following divisions along these lines.

A commonly voiced concern is that the very act of collecting and presenting data on race, ethnicity and similar factors can violate human rights by infringing on the right to privacy, or can reinforce group-related inequalities through stereotyping certain groups[59] and reifying otherwise fluid ethno-racial categories.[60] Due to the sensitive nature of the data on ethnicity and similar factors, human rights law stipulates particular requirements for data collection and disaggregation using such categories. These prerequisites serve as safeguards to mitigate risks posed by the dark sides of data collection.

This section points out some of the risks associated with data collection and analysis and includes a brief overview of some measures that can be used to mitigate the risks where possible. This article cannot possibly catalogue all the relevant risks; instead, it intends to raise awareness of some of the dangers inherent in the push to uncover and measure inequalities, and to point out some of the human rights principles relevant to addressing those perils.

Informed consent, data privacy, confidentiality and anonymity

Many scholars have addressed the potential tensions between the right to privacy and efforts to promote equality through the collection of disaggregated data.[61] Some countries, such as France, have long been opposed to collecting data on race and ethnicity.[62] These States have traditionally argued that collecting data on ethnicity and similar factors for inclusion in official statistics may threaten and expose the very communities and individuals who are ultimately meant to benefit from improved monitoring.[63]

However, collecting data on ethnicity and similar factors does not violate human rights *per se* as long as data are collected and protected in accord with human rights principles. Among the most important principles is that data must be gathered with the informed consent of the data subject.[64] This means that the persons from whom data are being gathered must be given sufficient, comprehensible information about the purpose, risks and benefits linked to the data-gathering process to allow them to freely and knowingly decide whether to participate or not.[65] Second, human rights require that safeguards be put in place for dealing with sensitive data and avoiding their misuse. Above all, data privacy and confidentiality must be ensured.[66] Simon argues:

> The very nature of statistical analysis, which involves making an 'impersonal use of personal data', suggests that it cannot harm individuals if procedures for ensuring anonymity of data are properly followed, and confidentiality is scrupulously respected throughout the process of collecting and producing data.[67]

Simon therefore concludes that the aims of guaranteeing data protection and collecting information on ethnic and other minority groups to benefit the realisation of their human rights can and must be reconciled.[68] However, anonymisation is a complex and often imperfect process, since many seemingly impersonal variables can be analysed together to re-identify data. For this reason, those engaging in data collection or analysis that uses categories that are subject to social or political risk must engage in a risk analysis concerning re-identification and ensure that they have a robust anonymisation protocol in place before data are collected and shared or published.[69]

Even then, it must be acknowledged that the collection of such data gives rise to a potential for abuse and misuse. Especially where individuals are (re-)identified, they can be subject to discrimination and persecution. A change of government, law or policy framework can turn a once innocuous data set into a potential weapon for racist or exclusionary policies.[70]

Categorisation and self-identification

Another concern relates to the categorisation of population groups. Demographic categories such as race, ethnicity and colour are not straightforward, as they are bound up in processes of power and identity. They are social constructs that are produced through a combination of objective and subjective, communal and individual, historical, legal, material and cultural factors.[71]

Human rights require that people have the opportunity to determine the identifiers they have applied to themselves as a matter of respect for their personal identity and autonomy.[72] This requires allowing respondents themselves to determine which categories they identify with in surveys and other data-gathering exercises.[73] Respondents must have the opportunity to provide a free response if they do not identify with one of the suggested categories, and must have the opportunity to choose multiple identities.[74] Beyond these immediate steps, human rights principles require that categories used in surveys are developed through participatory approaches that include the country's entire population.[75]

Our analysis of the pre-2013 DHS and MICS household surveys showed that while the majority of surveys examined asked respondents to identify themselves, some surveys did not follow the principle of self-identification, but rather asked the enumerator to observe the respondent's ethnicity.[76] In other instances, respondents were asked to choose *one* single group, which is problematic for people who consider themselves having a mixed ethnicity or origin.[77]

Taking a step back, the categorisation of groups and the process of determining nationally relevant groups themselves presents challenges. Which choices are presented in questionnaires for ethnicity, race, religion, language and other factors? How have these choices been determined? Do they adequately cover and represent the relevant groups in a given country?

The 'Principles and Recommendations for Population and Housing Censuses: The 2020 Round' call for the involvement of 'scientists and specialists in the field of ethnography, as well as organizations dealing with indigenous people' in the determination of relevant ethnic groups.[78] However, more important than experts, the relevant groups themselves should be involved in the identification of groups through a participatory process. In this regard, OHCHR stresses that '[d]ecisions concerning data collection on particularly vulnerable or marginalised groups, including, "legally" invisible groups for instance, should be made in close partnership or consultation with the group concerned to mitigate associated risks'.[79] In the context of household surveys, such participation is not ensured. Rather, questions and responses concerning ethnicity, race, religion, tribe, caste and language – like all variables that vary across contexts – are left to the discretion of the national agencies that implement the surveys.[80]

Avoiding stigmatisation

A further risk lies in the fact that the very act of requesting or holding data about individuals' identification as members of particular groups can be used or misused to stigmatise those groups. The OHCHR stresses that data collection must not 'create or reinforce existing discrimination, bias or stereotypes exercised against population groups'.[81]

In contexts of intense discrimination, marginalisation or criminalisation, even identification with a particular group can be perceived as stigmatising. This risk again highlights the importance of the participation of the groups to be monitored themselves in the process of defining the categories to be used in monitoring and, for instance, using terminology that individuals belonging to a particular group use to describe themselves instead of that used by outsiders.

Many of the challenges related to stigmatisation are concerned with the misuse of data from surveys. Data can be used selectively or certain findings can be misrepresented. A common example of such stereotyping is the misuse of crime statistics linked to the Roma population, who have been stereotyped as 'criminals' in some countries.[82] Similarly, data on the disadvantages that Roma populations face in relation to education, work or access to water and sanitation often underline the neglect they face as a population in government measures, but have also been misused to label and stigmatise Roma as 'dirty' and 'lazy'.

Once data are available, it is difficult to control who uses and potentially misuses them, what kind of correlations are drawn and how cause and effect might be misrepresented. At the very least, the potential for misuse highlights the need for responsible, unbiased presentation of data. It also shows the value – and indeed necessity – of linking outcome data with process data and structural data. For instance, the fact that Roma have limited access to water and sanitation in many countries can be presented much more powerfully as a result of government neglect when linked with evidence of structural discrimination in policies and other measures. This highlights the need to combine quantitative data with qualitative studies that can go deeper into understanding the causes of disparities.

Limits to data collection: criminalisation and risk of persecution

Data can be used to identify groups that experience discrimination to ensure that policies and measures reach the intended beneficiaries, but with targeted programming becoming possible, data can also be used for oppression and exclusion.[83] Individuals may realise or fear that stating their association with a marginalised and/or criminalised group puts them at risk of further discrimination or even persecution.[84] In many countries, enumerators are public officials,[85] which reinforces the (real or perceived) threat for many populations. How should monitoring efforts be crafted when it is important to track the progress of marginalised groups, but identification with these groups can itself place individuals and communities at risk?

Human rights law emphasises that individuals and groups have a right to be who they are without fear of persecution. LGBTQ people, for example, have the right to exist and to express their identities without fear of prosecution under sodomy or 'proselytisation' laws.[86] Similarly, HIV-positive individuals must be able to live full lives without facing forced disclosure, sterilisation, dismissal from the workplace or other persecution. And individuals whose activities are criminalised, such as sex workers or drug users in some contexts, have the right to be free from violence, discrimination and arbitrary detention. Countries that continue to subject LGBTQ people, HIV-positive individuals, sex workers or drug users to persecution on the basis of their identity are committing human rights violations, and this should be made plain in the course of SDG monitoring.

In such contexts of entrenched harm and persecution, marginalised groups may decide that they do not want the State or other powerful actors to categorise and monitor them at all. In such settings, alternatives such as community-based data collection and analysis[87] can be considered as a way of upholding the principles of self-identification, privacy and autonomy while also ensuring these groups are not persecuted. Such efforts would ensure that marginalised groups are not part of the 'missing millions' (see further Davis in this volume). Further, monitoring and advocacy efforts will be needed at the international level to pressure abusive governments to change discriminatory behaviour, law and policy.[88]

Exacerbated and unique risks posed by Big Data

Many of the challenges addressed above are exacerbated in the context of Big Data, where enormous datasets are created using consumer data, data 'exhaust', social media postings and data from service providers that contains information about individual habits, purchases, health status and social networks. These data sets are collected, analysed, bought and sold – often without the participation or even knowledge of the individuals who are the subject of the data. Big Data users such as merchants and service providers can often identify individual characteristics like sex, race, age, disability status and social class from these data, and when they cannot, they may infer these characteristics using predictive analytics.[89]

Big data has been hailed as a potentially rich source for monitoring in the SDGs context.[90] For example, 'strongly anonymized data' about mobile communications has been used in combination with public health information to produce highly detailed epidemiological models for malaria prevention and response.[91] Such techniques might be helpful in assessing and tracking health-related SDGs (but see further Williams and Hunt in this volume).

But should SDG monitoring include the use of such data sets if they include data that does not respect human rights principles? What about the data subject's consent, which is missing when data are used for purposes other than those for which it was originally gathered?[92] These are difficult questions, since Big Data would be analysed in the development monitoring context without any intent to re-identify individuals, rendering the potential harm imposed on any given individual through using such data largely theoretical or abstract. Can consent be inferred in some settings, like the use of social media or images gathered in public? And what is the likelihood that machine learning and data mining may produce erroneous imputations of race and ethnicity, leading to poor data not well suited for monitoring of development outcomes?[93] More importantly, do human rights principles require the rejection of any data that uses predictive analytics to impute racial and ethnic categories since such imputation violates the principle of self-identification?

A related concern when using Big Data is the creation of new types of invisible populations through the digital divide. Unconnected communities will be invisible in many Big Data sets. Data mining and predictive analysis presume that data sets are close to complete; these assumptions may be manifestly unjustified in settings where populations are offline.[94] These and other complex issues need to be engaged as Big Data sources are considered for SDG monitoring purposes.

Embedding participation at all levels as a way forward

From the analysis above, participation emerges as a central theme that needs to be embedded in any ongoing and future efforts for collecting, disaggregating, and analysing data on marginalised groups. Meaningful participation of those concerned is a key human rights principle that helps to reduce risks inherent in data collection and analysis. Embedding participation in data processes is crucial as SDG monitoring moves towards a 'pluralistic ecosystem of data'[95] that goes beyond one defined set of centrally defined indicators and captures a variety of overlapping and complementary processes at different levels. These different processes – some official and State- or UN-sponsored, others led by civil society or academia – hold the potential for broad participation. Without careful attention, however, they could reinforce existing processes of exclusion and marginalisation.

Determination and prioritisation of marginalised communities

Participation is essential from the very beginning, including in the determination of which groups to monitor. These fundamental decisions determine which groups might continue to be invisible and which groups will be elevated in the public eye. Participatory processes should ensure active, free and meaningful participation of all relevant population groups – especially those that are especially disadvantaged must have the opportunity to make their perspectives and opinions heard, including on whether they want to be subject to monitoring. National human rights institutions may have an important role in facilitating such processes, which should also involve civil society, community-based organisations and academia.

There is, of course, a danger that groups that experience discrimination will be overlooked or deliberately excluded in the process of identifying disadvantaged communities, even if the need for inclusiveness is stressed. These challenges are inherent in any effort to protect the rights of groups that experience discrimination. Depending on the circumstances, international pressure may help in protectively raising the profile of marginalised communities.

Human rights bodies provide important guidance for the process of identifying and engaging disadvantaged groups. Concerns raised in reports by the Special Rapporteur on minority issues, other relevant Special Procedures, Concluding Observations by various treaty bodies and recommendations adopted through the Universal Periodic Review process may include crucial recommendations about marginalised groups or information about specific country situations. The Universal Human Rights Index provides a tool to search for country-specific recommendations from various human rights bodies and allows for a search that focuses specifically on the rights of 'members of minorities' as well as 'indigenous peoples'.[96] Reporting by national human rights institutions, as well as domestic and international human rights groups can also be a valuable resource in this process.

Several countries have gained relevant experience in identifying marginalised groups for focused monitoring. Countries that have adopted a National Human Rights Action Plan (NHRAP) usually have undertaken a participatory process of identifying disadvantaged and marginalised groups in the country. For example, Australia held a large-scale community consultation in the elaboration of its Human Rights Framework that resulted in a Baseline Study, which was also informed by the UPR process. The NHRAP identifies priority areas and specific groups, including 'Aboriginal and Torres Strait Islander people' and 'people from culturally and linguistically diverse communities'.[97]

In the context of the SDGs, the Leave No One Behind Partnership coordinated by Project Everyone, Development Initiatives and CIVICUS facilitates national dialogues that are conducted in partnership with national civil society organisations with the aim of identifying the most marginalised groups in a given country.[98] It will be essential to ensure that these dialogues are linked to longer-term processes that involve all relevant actors involved in the implementation of the SDGs, including national governments.

In many instances, civil society organisations advocate for marginalised groups to be included in data-gathering processes such as censuses and in planning processes. For example, in Colombia, Brazil and other Latin American countries, civil society has advocated for the inclusion of 'Afro-descendants' as a category in survey instruments based on the participation of people of African descent in the design of censuses.[99] In the United States, civil rights advocates have been engaging on potential adjustments and improvements on data collection concerning race and ethnicity for the 2020 census, including a proposal to add a category for Middle Eastern/North African populations as well as a category on second generation immigrants.[100]

Participatory data collection

Another way in which marginalised communities are sometimes involved in monitoring efforts is through direct data collection. Slum/Shack Dwellers International has facilitated enumerations and mapping programmes in informal settlements across many countries, including Kenya.[101] Such enumerations support communities as they shape messages concerning their needs and priorities. Another example of a methodology for data collection that focuses on indigenous peoples (and is carried out in a participatory manner) is the 'Indigenous Navigator',[102] which has developed tools and frameworks for indigenous peoples to monitor the realisation of their own rights. The DataShift initiative by CIVICUS seeks to support civil society groups that engage in collecting and producing citizen-generated data with initial pilot locations in Kenya, Tanzania, Nepal and Argentina. What sets this initiative apart from others is the direct link to the SDGs. It seeks to inform data collection for the SDGs by feeding individual-generated data into policy processes at the global level.[103]

Community-driven data collection initiatives can be extremely empowering and powerful. Not only do they ensure that those being monitored are engaged in defining themselves, they can also raise awareness among the broader public and the government by documenting inequalities, neglect and exclusion from the perspective of those experiencing it. As such, they can be a compelling tool for accountability by holding State institutions responsible for meeting their obligations. However, States cannot abdicate responsibility for monitoring the progress of their whole populations by leaving such efforts to marginalised groups. Instead, these efforts should be complementary, and communities should be provided with resources and opportunities for capacity-building.

Conclusion and outlook

The SDGs represent a real break from the past by emphasising the need to reduce inequalities, but so far the difference is largely one of rhetoric and aspiration. The 'leave no one behind' mantra does not translate into indicators that capture progress for marginalised groups such as those defined by race and ethnicity. The indicators do not live up to the promise of the goals and targets. This is particularly disillusioning because the SDGs are the result of broad political and technical discussions. Despite extensive consultations on the need to monitor the reduction of inequalities in the lead-up to the SDGs, despite sector-specific processes that formulated proposals demonstrating the technical feasibility of monitoring progress for marginalised groups and even despite the call for specific disaggregations in the targets themselves, the SDGs risk – once again – ignoring, neglecting and excluding marginalised communities.

If the indicators are not significantly amended with disaggregations based on ethnicity, race, caste and similar factors added at least for key targets, we will not have the data needed in real time to close gaps in development outcomes. And if marginalised communities themselves are not included in ongoing monitoring and response, attempts to reduce inequalities will be stymied by lack of embedded knowledge and expertise, and could violate core human rights principles. This imperative is only more urgent in the context of rising nationalism, xenophobia and racism.

While there are technical challenges, monitoring the gaps in progress between dominant and marginalised groups is technically feasible. Groups are not always easily comparable, and specific precautions must be taken during data collection and disaggregation. We must acknowledge the dark sides of data collection. However, these are all issues that have solutions, and there simply can be no solution to inequalities until their contours are known.

The failure to produce such knowledge can only be ascribed to politics and power. The politics of data cannot be overestimated. Data are political because data are powerful. The hesitancy and even resistance to monitor progress specifically for groups based on ethnicity, race, religion and caste demonstrates precisely what a powerful instrument data can – or could – be. Once again, it has proven much easier to adopt aspirational language than to incorporate attention to inequalities and marginalisation where it matters most: in indicators, data sources and monitoring processes. This must be remedied, and our analysis shows that much greater collection and analysis of disaggregated data is feasible. It is not too late to amend the SDG indicators. Including additional disaggregations that are meaningful for dismantling inequality is an urgent step in moving the 'leave no one behind' mantra from rhetoric to reality.

Notes

1. United Nations General Assembly, *Transforming Our World: The 2030 Agenda for Sustainable Development*, A/RES/70/1 (21 October 2015), para. 4.
2. Kevin E. Davis, Benedict Kingsbury and Sally Merry, 'Indicators as a Technology of Global Governance', *Law and Society Review* 46, no. 1 (2012): 71–104.
3. Leslie McCall, 'The Complexity of Intersectionality', *Signs: Journal of Women and Culture in Society* 30, no. 3 (2005): 1771–800. See also Naila Kabeer, 'The Challenges of Intersecting Inequality', *Maitreyee* 24 (2012): 5–10; Amanda Lenhardt and Emma Samman, *In Quest of Inclusive Progress, Exploring Intersecting Inequalities in Human Development* (London: Overseas Development Institute, 2015), 18.
4. See e.g. Joni Seager, *Sex-disaggregated Indicators for Water Assessment Monitoring and Reporting. Technical Paper* (Paris: UNESCO, 2015), http://unesdoc.unesco.org/images/0023/002340/234082e.pdf. See also UN Statistics Division, 'Minimum Set of Gender Indicators', https://genderstats.un.org/#/home (accessed July 12, 2017); and Plan International, *Counting the Invisible: Using Data to Transform the Lives of Girls and Women by 2030* (Woking: Plan International, 2016).
5. For DHS: 1984–2011 and 2012–2015; for MICS: MICS 3, 2005–2011 and MICS 4, 2011–2013. Because there was greater variability among DHS questionnaires, a longer time period (including more countries) was chosen.
6. Jonathan Gray, Danny Lämmerhirt and Liliana Bounegru, "Changing What Counts: How Can Citizen-Generated and Civil Society Data Be Used as an Advocacy Tool to Change Official Data Collection?" (CIVICUS, 2016), http://civicus.org/thedatashift/wp-content/uploads/2016/03/changing-what-counts-2.pdf (accessed July 12, 2017).
7. Independent Expert Advisory Group (IAEG) on a Data Revolution, *A World That Counts: Mobilising the Data Revolution for Sustainable Development* (New York: United Nations, 2014), 2.
8. Sakiko Fukuda-Parr, 'Global Goals as a Policy Tool: Intended and Unintended Consequences', *Journal of Human Development and Capabilities* (2014): 118–31, 119.
9. Fukuda-Parr, 'Global Goals', 120.
10. Fukuda-Parr, 'Global Goals', 122–3.
11. Fukuda-Parr, 'Global Goals', 120.
12. Sally Engle Merry, 'Measuring the World: Indicators, Human Rights, and Global Governance', *Current Anthropology* 52 (2011): S92.
13. Center for Economic and Social Rights (CESR), 'From Disparity to Dignity: Tackling Economic Inequality through the Sustainable Development Goals' (CESR Human Rights Policy Brief, 2016), 33.
14. United Nations, Committee on Economic, Social, and Cultural Rights (UN CESCR), *General Comment No: 20, Non-discrimination in Economic, Social and Cultural Rights*, UN Doc. E/C.12/GC/20 (2009), para. 27 et seq.
15. See e.g. UN Human Rights Committee, *Guidelines for the Treaty-Specific Document to be Submitted by States Parties under Article 40 of the International Covenant on Civil and Political Rights*, UN Doc. CCPR/C/29/1 (2009), para. 25; UN Committee on Economic, Social and Cultural Rights, *Guidelines on Treaty-Specific Documents to be Submitted by States Parties under Articles 16 and 17 of the International Covenant on Economic, Social and Cultural Rights*, UN Doc. E/C.12/2008/2 (2008).
16. UN CESCR, *General Comment No. 20*, para. 41.
17. Gay McDougall, *The First United Nations Mandate on Minority Issues* (Leiden: Brill, 2016).
18. United Nations Development Programme (UNDP), *Nepal Human Development Report: State Transformation and Human Development* (2009), 153–76. Other national HDRs, including Brazil, India and Guatemala, have included similar types of disaggregation.
19. UNDP, *Nepal Human Development Report*, 155. For further examples of disaggregation according to minority status, in particular in relation to poverty see Gay McDougall, Report of the Independent Expert on Minority Issues, UN Doc. A/HRC/4/9 (2007), paras 25–37.

20. World Inequality Database on Education, http://www.education-inequalities.org/ (accessed July 12, 2017).
21. UNICEF Joint Monitoring Programme (JMP) for Water Supply and Sanitation, *Progress on Drinking Water and Sanitation: 2014 Update* (Geneva: World Health Organization/New York: United Nations Children's Fund 2014), 25.
22. Alainna Lynch and Tom Berliner, *Who is Being Left Behind in Sub-Saharan Africa? An Illustration in Benin and Nigeria* (London: Overseas Development Institute, 2016), 6.
23. Lenhardt and Samman, *In Quest of Inclusive Progress*, 18.
24. CESR, 'From Disparity to Dignity'.
25. McDougall, *The First United Nations Mandate on Minority Issues*, para. 83.
26. Tanvi Bhatkal, Emma Samman and Elizabeth Stuart, *Leave No One Behind: The Real Bottom Billion* (London: Overseas Development Institute, 2015), 1.
27. Elizabeth Stuart, 'How to Leave No One Behind: A Workable Plan for Ambitious Aims', posted February 3, 2016, https://www.odi.org/comment/10287-leave-no-one-behind-workable-plan-ambitious-aims (accessed January 31, 2017).
28. Lenhardt and Samman, *In Quest of Inclusive Progress*, 18.
29. This kind of analysis is not a replacement for, but a complement to the legal assessments required under human rights law. Such assessments demand contextual, qualitative, and legal information lacking in the development monitoring context.
30. JMP, *Progress on Drinking Water and Sanitation*, 26.
31. Bhatkal, Samman and Stuart, *Leave No One Behind*, 3.
32. Ibid.
33. While the framework includes a list of 241 indicators, there are only 230 unique indicators as some are used for multiple targets.
34. Danish Institute for Human Rights (DIHR), *Human Rights and Data: Tools and Resources for Sustainable Development* (2017): 16.
35. Fukuda-Parr, 'Global Goals', 120.
36. UN Statistical Commission, Report of the Inter-Agency and Expert Group on Sustainable Development Goal Indicators, UN Doc. E/CN.3/2016/2/Rev.1, Annex IV (2016).
37. Ibid., para. 26.
38. Ms Wasmália Bivar, Chair of the UN Statistical Commission, 'Remarks to the Economic and Social Council Coordination and Management Segment' (June 1, 2016).
39. Compilation of Metadata for the Proposed Global Indicators for the Review of the 2030 Agenda for Sustainable Development, Goal 10, p. 3, https://unstats.un.org/sdgs/files/metadata-compilation/Metadata-Goal-10.pdf (accessed July 12, 2017).
40. Ibid.
41. United Nations, *The Sustainable Development Goals Report 2016*, 50, http://unstats.un.org/sdgs/report/2016/.
42. Ibid.
43. United Nations Secretary-General, *Progress Toward the Sustainable Development Goals*, UN Doc. No. E/2016/75, 3 June 2016: para. 134.
44. See SDG Indicators Metadata Repository, http://unstats.un.org/sdgs/metadata/ (accessed July 12, 2017).
45. Sabina Alkire and Emma Samman, 'Mobilising the Household Data Required to Progress toward the SDGs' (OPHI Working Papers 72, University of Oxford, 2014).
46. See Alkire and Samman, *Mobilising the Household Data*.
47. Sustainable Development Solutions Network, *Data for Development: A Needs Assessment for SDG Monitoring and Statistical Capacity Development* (New York: Sustainable Development Solutions Network, 2015), 17.
48. Ibid., 12–13.
49. United Nations Statistical Commission, *Report of the Global Working Group on Big Data for Official Statistics*, UN Doc. E/CN.3/2015/4 (2015).
50. United States Census Bureau, American Fact Finder, http://factfinder.census.gov/faces/nav/jsf/pages/community_facts.xhtml (accessed July 12, 2017).

51. See European Union Agency for Fundamental Rights, EU-MIDIS: European Union Minorities and Discrimination Survey, http://fra.europa.eu/en/survey/2012/eu-midis-european-uni on-minorities-and-discrimination-survey; European Union Agency for Fundamental Rights, Roma Pilot Survey, http://fra.europa.eu/en/survey/2012/roma-pilot-survey (accessed 12 July, 2017).
52. See World Inequality Database on Education, http://www.education-inequalitie s.org/indicators/comp_prim_v2#?sort=disparity&dimension=ethnicity&group=all&age _group=comp_prim_v2&countries=all (accessed July 12, 2017).
53. Meg Wirth, Enrique Delamonica, Emma Sacks, Deborah Balk, Adam Storeygard and Alberto Minujin, 'Monitoring Health Equity in the MDGs: A Practical Guide' (CIESIN & UNICEF, January 2006), 21.
54. John Wrench, 'Data on Discrimination in EU Countries: Statistics, Research and the Drive for Comparability', *Ethnic and Racial Studies* 34, no. 10 (2011): 1715–730, 1723.
55. Roy Carr-Hill, 'Missing Millions and Measuring Development Progress', *World Development* 46 (2013): 37.
56. Carr-Hill, 'Missing Millions', 32.
57. Ibid., 37.
58. See Margaret Satterthwaite, 'JMP Working Group on Equity and Non-Discrimination Final Report (2012)', unpublished (on file with authors).
59. McDougall, *The First United Nations Mandate on Minority Issues*, para. 71.
60. Véronique de Rudder and François Vourc'h, 'Quelles statistiques pour quelle lutte contre les discriminations?', *Journal des Anthropologues* (2007): 110–11.
61. Julie Ringelheim, 'Ethnic Categories and European Human Rights Law', *Ethnic and Racial Studies* 34, no. 10 (2011): 1682.
62. See Wrench, 'Data on Discrimination', 1716.
63. Patrick Simon, '"Ethnic" Statistics and Data Protection in Council of Europe Countries: Study Report' (European Commission against Racism and Intolerance, Strasbourg, 2007), 7.
64. Romesh Silva and Jasmine Marwaha, 'Collecting Sensitive Human Rights Data in the Field: A Case Study from Amritsar, India' (Human Rights Data Analysis Group, 2013), https://hrdag. org/wp-content/uploads/2013/02/silva-marwaha-JSM-2011.pdf.
65. For an excellent example of informed consent in the context of risky data collection for human rights purposes, see Silva and Marwaha, 'Collecting Sensitive Human Rights Data'.
66. Office of the UN High Commissioner for Human Rights (OHCHR), *A Human Rights-based Approach to Data, Leaving No One Behind in the 2030 Development Agenda* (2016), 10, http://www.ohchr.org/Documents/Issues/HRIndicators/GuidanceNoteonApproachtoData. pdf.
67. Simon, '"Ethnic" Statistics', 12.
68. Ibid., 9.
69. Mark Elliot, Elaine Mackey, Kieron O'Hara and Caroline Tudor, 'The Anonymisation Decision-Making Framework' (2016), http://ukanon.net/wp-content/uploads/2015/05/The-Anonymisation-Decision-making-Framework.pdf.
70. See Zahra Rahman, 'Dangerous Data: The Role of Data Collection in Genocides', *The Engine Room*, November 21, 2016, https://www.theengineroom.org/dangerous-data-the-role-of-data-collection-in-genocides/.
71. Ringelheim, 'Ethnic Categories', 1685; Peter J. Aspinall, 'Answer Formats in British Census and Survey Ethnicity Questions: Does Open Response Better Capture "Superdiversity"?', *Sociology* 46 (2012): 354–64, 365.
72. OHCHR, *Human Rights-based Approach to Data*, 8; United Nations Committee on the Elimination of Racial Discrimination, *General Recommendation VIII concerning the interpretation and application of article 1, paragraphs 1 and 4 of the Convention* (1990); Simon, 'Ethnic' Statistics, 40.
73. OHCHR, *Human Rights-based Approach to Data*, 8.
74. Ibid.
75. Ibid.

76. Margaret Satterthwaite, 'Background Note on MDGs, Non-Discrimination and Indicators in Water and Sanitation' (JMP, 2012), 28, unpublished (on file with authors).
77. Satterthwaite, *Background Note*, 30.
78. United Nations Statistical Commission, 'Principles and Recommendations for Population and Housing Censuses: the 2020 Round. Revision 3 – Draft' (2015), 175, unstats.un.org/unsd/statcom/doc15/BG-Censuses.pdf.
79. OHCHR, *Human Rights-based Approach to Data*, 7.
80. See ICF International, 'Survey Organization Manual for Demograpic and Health Surveys' (2012), 5–9.
81. Ibid., 8.
82. Simon, '"Ethnic" Statistics', 14.
83. Ringelheim, 'Ethnic Categories', 1683.
84. Ibid., 1689.
85. Carr-Hill, 'Missing Millions', 31.
86. Same-sex sexual acts between consenting adults are criminalised in 74 countries across the world: see ILGA, 'Sexual Orientation Laws in the World: Criminalisation' (2016), http://ilga.org/downloads/04_ILGA_WorldMap_ENGLISH_Crime_May2016.pdf.
87. Good practice examples can be found in the HIV/AIDS field, where organisations serving key populations have conducted inclusive and participatory research into discriminatory barriers to service affecting sex workers, men who have sex with men, and drug users. See e.g. Bridging the Gaps, 'Operational Research with and for Key Populations', http://www.hivgaps.org/about/operational-research/.
88. Sara L. M. Davis, William C. Goedel and John Emerson, 'Punitive Laws, Key Population Size Estimates, and Global AIDS Response Progress Reports: An Ecological Study of 154 Countries', *Journal of the International AIDS Society* 20 (2017): 21386, http://www.jiasociety.org/index.php/jias/article/view/21386.
89. See e.g. Kate Crawford and Jason Schultz, 'Big Data and Due Process: Towards a Framework to Redress Predictive Privacy Harms', *Boston College Law Review* 55, no. 93 (2014); Michael Schrage, 'Big Data's Dangerous New Era of Discrimination', *Harvard Business Review* (January 29, 2014), https://hbr.org/2014/01/big-datas-dangerous-new-era-of-discrimination.
90. See United Nations Statistical Commission, 'Report of the Global Working Group on Big Data for Official Statistics', UN Doc. E/CN.3/2015/4 (2015).
91. Independent Expert Advisory Group on a Data Revolution, *A World That Counts*, 9.
92. OHCHR explains that human rights-based data principles require that 'Data collected to produce statistical information must be strictly confidential, used exclusively for statistical purposes and regulated by law': OHCHR, *Human Rights-based Approach to Data*, 10. This is often not the case with Big Data: see Jacob Mertcalf and Kate Crawford, 'Where are Human Subjects in Big Data Research? The Emerging Ethics Divide', *Big Data and Society*, January–June 2016, 1–14.
93. Crawford and Schultz, 'Big Data and Due Process'.
94. See Kate Crawford and Megan Finn, 'The Limits of Crisis Data: Analytical and Ethical Challenges of Using Social and Mobile Data to Understand Disasters', *Geojournal* 80 (2015): 491.
95. DIHR, *Human Rights and Data*, 31.
96. United Nations Human Rights Office of the High Commissioner, Universal Human Rights Index, http://uhri.ohchr.org/search/annotations (accessed July 12, 2017).
97. Commonwealth of Australia, 'Australia's National Human Rights Action Plan' (2012), 5, http://www.ohchr.org/Documents/Issues/NHRA/NHRPAustralia2012.pdf.
98. See Leave No One Behind Partnership website: http://action4sd.org/leavenoonebehind/.
99. Corinne Lennox and Carlos Minott, 'Inclusion of Afro-Descendants in Ethnic Data Collection: Towards Visibility', *International Journal on Minority and Group Rights* 18 (2011): 257–75, 262 et seq.
100. The Leadership Conference Education Fund, 'Race and Ethnicity in the 2020 Census: Improving Data to Capture a Multiethnic America' (2014), 15, http://civilrightsdocs.info/pdf/reports/Census-Report-2014-WEB.pdf.

101. See e.g. Irene Karanja, 'An Enumeration and Mapping of Informal Settlements in Kisumu, Kenya, Implemented by Their Inhabitants', *Environment and Urbanization* 22 (2010): 217–39.
102. Indigenous Navigator, http://www.indigenousnavigator.org/index.html#tools (accessed July 12, 2017).
103. Datashift, Building the Capacity and Confidence of Civil Society Organizations to Produce and Use Citizen-Generated Data, http://civicus.org/thedatashift. For further examples see DIHR, *Human Rights and Data*, 37.

Acknowledgements

Sections of the article are informed by the authors' work with the WHO/UNICEF Joint Monitoring Programme on Water Supply and Sanitation (JMP) on equality and non-discrimination, in particular through the 'Equity and Non-Discrimination Work Group', and they are thankful to the JMP team and all those who contributed to the discussions over the last years. Inga T. Winkler presented an earlier draft of the article at a Workshop of the Economic and Social Rights Group at the University of Connecticut and is grateful for the useful input received from participants. The authors would also like to thank the reviewers for the helpful comments as well as Ajani Husbands, Yolanda Borquaye and Pauline Brosch for the research assistance they provided.

Disclosure statement

No potential conflict of interest was reported by the authors.

Funding

Margaret Satterthwaite gratefully acknowledges the support of the Filomen D'Agostino Research Fund at NYU School of Law.

Evaluating the health-related targets in the Sustainable Development Goals from a human rights perspective

Audrey R. Chapman

ABSTRACT

This article evaluates the health targets identified in the Sustainable Development Goals (SDGs) adopted at a September 2015 UN summit from a human rights perspective. Although there is considerable overlap in the subject matter of these targets and human rights commitments, the SDG framers did not adopt a human rights approach to the realisation of the health-related targets. This article details human rights shortfalls and their implications for the implementation of the SDGs. Given the limitations of space, the article focuses on health targets of particular relevance to the right to health, specifically promoting the health rights of children; realising universal access to sexual and reproductive health services and reproductive rights; delivering the underlying determinants of health; achieving universal health coverage; and providing access to affordable essential medicines.

Introduction

The emphasis given to health goals in the Millennium Development Goals (MDGs) that informed global developments efforts between 2000 and 2015 has been reduced in the Sustainable Development Goals adopted at a September 2015 UN summit. Three of the eight MDG goals focused on health with a fourth including a health-related target. In contrast, the Sustainable Development Goals (SDGs) have 17 goals, only one of which deals with health. The single health goal, which is Goal 3, 'to ensure healthy lives and promote well-being for all at all ages'[1] is quite comprehensive both in its definition and its targets. It is operationalised through nine targets, three of which incorporate the three health goals in the MDGs but with more demanding objectives, and there are also four subsidiary targets. The targets identified for Goal 3 encompass a wide range of discrete and unrelated objectives, some of which have human rights parallels. As with the other 16 goals in the SDGs, none of the health targets is prioritised. Consequently, discrete targets like halving the number of global deaths and injuries from road traffic accidents (3.6) are on the same footing as far more significant and complex targets, as for example achieving universal health coverage with financial risk protection and access to quality essential health-care services (3.8).

This article assesses the health goals and targets in the Sustainable Development Goals from a human rights perspective. It does so for three reasons. First, the Declaration preceding the enumeration of the goals and targets purports that one of the goals of the SDGS is to be promoting human rights. According to the text of the Declaration:

> We envisage a world of universal respect for human rights and human dignity, the rule of law, justice, equality and non-discrimination; of respect for race, ethnicity and cultural diversity; and of equal opportunity permitting the full realization of human potential and contributing to shared prosperity.[2]

The Declaration resolves to do a number of things by 2030, among them to protect human rights and gender equality.[3] Second, the human rights community generated some of the most sustained criticism of the manner in which the Millennium Development Goals (MDGs), the predecessor set of international development goals applicable from 1990 to 2015, were designed, framed, and monitored. Their human rights critiques anticipated some of the key problems the MDGs were to encounter. Third, I believe that the adoption of a rights-based approach which focuses on the most vulnerable populations is key to achieving the objective to which the SDGs are ostensibly committed, to leave no one behind.

Importantly, despite the references to human rights in the Declaration suggesting the SDGs would seek to promote human rights, the SDGs do not adopt a human rights approach. None of the SDGs that are health-related, with one exception, target 5.6 to ensure universal access to sexual and reproductive health and reproductive rights, is framed in rights language. Moreover, target 5.6 does so in the context of referencing the commitments agreed to in the Programme of Action of the International Conference on Population and Development and the Beijing Platform for Action and not as the affirmation of a right. None of the SDGS are framed as a human rights entitlement guaranteeing that all people having a right to the services and benefits with governments accountable for its availability and for equal access.

Consistent with a human rights framing, the paper focuses on targets and issues which have particular relevance for vulnerable populations. It assesses the SDG health targets related to promoting the life and health of children, reducing maternal mortality and ensuring universal reproductive health services, achieving universal health coverage, and providing access to affordable essential medicines and vaccines.

Overview of the health goal and targets in the SDGs

The nine health targets and four subsidiary health targets in Goal 3 are listed in Table 1.

Some of these health targets have human rights parallels, but unlike their human rights counterparts the SDGs do not confer entitlements or require that the population be consulted as countries set policies and priorities to advance to the goals. Table 2 identifies the goals with human rights parallels recognised in international human rights instruments.

There are also health-related targets in several of the other goals, most importantly the target to ensure universal access to sexual and reproductive health and reproductive rights (5.6) and the various targets corresponding with what the UN Committee on

Table 1. Targets for Goal 3.

Major Health Targets
3.1: By 2030, reduce the global maternal mortality ratio to less than 70 per 1000,000 live births.
3.2: By 2030, end preventable deaths of newborns and children under five years of age, with all countries aiming to reduce neonatal mortality to at least as low as 12 per 1,000 live births and under-five mortality to at least as low as 25 per 1,000 live births.
3.3: By 2030, end the epidemics of AIDS, tuberculosis, malaria and neglected tropical diseases and combat hepatitis, water-borne diseases and other communicable diseases.
3.4: By 2030, reduce by one-third premature mortality from non-communicable diseases through prevention and treatment and promote mental health and well-being.
3.5: Strengthen the prevention and treatment of substance abuse, including narcotic drug abuse and harmful use of alcohol.
3.6: By 2020, half the number of global deaths and injuries from road traffic accidents.
3.7: By 2030, ensure universal access to sexual and reproductive health-care services, including for family planning, information and education, and the integration of reproductive health into national strategies and programmes.
3.8: Achieve universal health coverage, including financial risk protection, access to quality essential health-care services and access to safe, effective, quality and affordable essential medicines and vaccines for all.
3.9: By 2030, substantially reduce the number of deaths and illnesses from hazardous chemicals and air, water and soil pollution and contamination.
Subsidiary Targets
3.a: Strengthen the implementation of the World Health Organisation Framework Convention on Tobacco Control in all countries, as appropriate.
3.b: Support the research and development of vaccines and medicines for the communicable and non-communicable diseases that primarily affect developing countries, provide access to affordable essential medicines and vaccines, in accordance with the Doha Declaration on the TRIPS Agreement and Public Health, which affirms the right of developing countries to use the full provisions in the Agreement on Trade-Related Aspects of Intellectual Property Rights regarding the flexibilities to protect public health, and, in particular provide access to medicines for all.
3.c Substantially increase health financing and the recruitment, development, training and retention of the health workforce in developing countries, especially in least developed countries and small island developing states.
3.d: Strengthen the capacity of all countries, in particular developing countries, for early warning, risk reduction and management of national and global health risks.

Economic, Social and Cultural Rights termed the underlying determinants of health in its general comment interpreting the right to health.[4] These include providing access to safe and affordable drinking water for all (6.1), reducing poverty (SDG 1), ending hunger and ensuring access to safe, nutritious and sufficient food (2.1), and ensuring access for all to adequate, safe and affordable housing (11.1). While all of these can potentially contribute to the realisation of improved health, their placement in other goals makes it unlikely that policymaking on these targets will take their health impacts into account.

Table 2. SDG health targets with human rights parallels.

SDG Health Target	Human Rights with Similar Content
3.1 reduce maternal mortality	Right to life (ICCPR article 6)
3.2 reduce child mortality	Reduction infant mortality (ICESCR, article 12 (2) a)
	Right to life (ICCPR article 6)
	Child's inherent right to life (CRC article 6)
	Diminish infant & child mortality (CRC article 2.a)
3.3 end epidemic AIDS	prevention & treatment epidemic & endemic diseases, assure medical service (ICESCR, article 12 (2) b, c &d)
3.4 reduce mortality non-communicable diseases	Improvement environmental hygiene; prevention & treatment epidemic & endemic diseases, assure medical service (ICESCR, article 12 (2) b, c &d)
3.7 universal access reproductive services	Right of women to health services, including family planning (CEDAW 12 (1))
3.8 universal health coverage	Right to health (ICESCR article 12 (2)) d)

Notes: ICESCR – International Covenant on Economic, Social and Cultural Rights;
ICCPR – International Covenant on Civil and Political Rights; CRC – Convention on the Rights of the Child.

Promoting the life and health of newborns and children

In most countries in the world children, particularly the girl child, are one of the most, if not the most, vulnerable groups. The Convention on the Rights of the Child recognises the right of the child to the enjoyment of the highest attainable standard of health and to facilities for the treatment of illness and rehabilitation of health.[5] The general comment on children's health of the Committee on the Rights of the Child reflects the perspective that all children should have opportunities to survive, grow and develop in an environment conducive to physical, emotional and social wellbeing. It interprets children's right to health as an inclusive right, extending not only to timely and appropriate prevention and access to curative, rehabilitative and palliative care services, but also to a right for children to grow and develop to their full potential and to live in conditions that enable them to attain the highest standard of health through the implementation of programmes that address the underlying determinants of health.[6] UNICEF had proposed that a first priority for the SDGs should be reaching the poorest and most disadvantaged children and paying special attention to removing barriers that currently prevent girls from accessing basic services. It also called for targeted investments on disadvantaged children.[7] But the SDGs do not do so.

While the SDGS have a variety of goals and targets relevant to children's well-being the single target for children in Goal 3 focuses exclusively on lowering child mortality. SDG target 3.2 requires countries by 2030 to end preventable deaths of newborns and children under five years of age, with all countries aiming to reduce neonatal mortality to at least as low as 12 per 1,000 live births and under-five mortality to at least as low as 25 per 1,000 live births.

While substantial progress with lowering child mortality was made during the duration of the MDGs, in 2015 the global under-five mortality rate stood at 43 deaths per 1,000 live births, mostly from preventable causes. The decline in neonatal mortality has been slower than the child mortality reduction. It was 19 deaths per 1,000 live births in 2015. Neonatal deaths can often be avoided with simple, cost-effective, and high-impact interventions for mothers and newborns,[8] but there is no sign that the countries in Africa and South Asia with high neonatal mortality rates will adopt these interventions in the near future.

Aware that children growing up in the poorest 20% of households are twice as likely as those in the richest 20% to die before reaching their fifth birthday and nearly twice as likely to suffer from stunting, UNICEF had advocated for the use of disaggregated data for monitoring. It proposed that data be disaggregated on the basis of all grounds of discrimination prohibited by international human rights law and called for the active and meaningful participation of civil society in order to achieve transparent monitoring and accountability.[9] However, the two indicators selected for target 3.2 as of November 2016 – the under-five mortality rate and the neonatal mortality rate – do not incorporate any disaggregation.[10] Moreover, aside from a possible assessment of coverage of child health services (as yet not identified), none of the other indicators selected for health targets require disaggregation by age in order to permit assessments of children's health status.

Reducing maternal mortality and providing universal sexual and reproductive health care

Sexual and reproductive rights are central to women's right to health and their well-being. While reproductive health is an important component of health for both women and men, it is more critical for women. A major burden of disease in females is related to their reproductive function.[11] Article 12 of the Convention on the Elimination of All Forms of Discrimination Against Women (CEDAW) enumerates the obligation of state parties to take all appropriate measures to eliminate discrimination against women in the field of health care so as to ensure their access to health care services including those related to family planning and those connected with pregnancy, confinement and the post-natal period.[12] These requirements are elaborated in the UN Committee on the Elimination of All Forms of Discrimination Against Women's General Recommendation 24 on Women and Health.[13] The Committee on Economic, Social and Cultural Rights also recently adopted a general comment that proceeds from the recognition that the right to sexual and reproductive health is an integral part of the right to health enshrined in article 12 of the International Covenant on Economic, Social and Cultural Rights and other international human rights instruments.[14]

Rights-based approaches consider individual autonomy and decision-making as being central to sexual and reproductive health. For example, the general comment of the Committee on Economic, Social and Cultural Rights seeks to strengthen women's freedom to make free and responsible decisions and choices, free of violence, coercion and discrimination, regarding matters concerning their body and sexual and reproductive health.[15] It also broadens the obligations of state parties to provide access to and the availability of a wide range of services relevant to sexual and reproductive health including the need for safe abortion care and the elimination of restrictive abortion laws.[16]

There are two health targets in Goal 3 relevant to sexual and reproductive health. Target 3.1 calls for the reduction of the global maternal mortality ratio to less than 70 per 100,000 live births by 2030, but an improvement in the global maternal mortality ratio could take place with many countries still suffering from high maternal mortality ratios. The initiative to end preventable maternal mortality also specifies that no country should have a maternal mortality ratio greater than 140 per 100,000. Meeting this goal would require some countries achieving at least a two-thirds reduction in their maternal mortality ratio between 2010 and 2030.[17] The second of the relevant targets, target 3.7, seeks to ensure universal access to sexual and reproductive health-care services, including for family planning, information and education and the integration of reproductive health into national strategies and programmes. This target parallels human rights obligations. Targets 3.1 and 3.7 continue the focus of MDG 5 with more ambitious targets. Additionally, SDG Goal 5, to achieve gender equality and empower all women and girls, has a target (5.6) to ensure universal access to sexual and reproductive health and reproductive rights, as agreed in the Programme of Action of the International Conference on Population and Development and the Beijing Platform for Action.

MDG 5 was one of the MDGs with the greatest shortfalls.[18] While the global maternal mortality ratio declined by 44%, this was well short of the targeted 75% fall called for in MDG 5A. It is estimated that there were 303,000 maternal deaths in 2015, most of them preventable.[19] This makes maternal mortality the second leading cause of death after HIV among women ages 15 to 49. In the African Region maternal mortality is particularly high, 540 per 100,000 live births, which combined with the high levels of fertility in the region translates into a lifetime risk of dying from maternal causes of 1 in 37.[20] Not only are there scandalous inequalities between countries – from a maternal mortality rate of one per 100,000 in Finland to 1,360 per 100,000 in Sierra Leone – but there are huge national inequalities as well both between the wealthiest and poorest regions and individuals.[21] Reflecting differences in the availability of high quality health services, the lifetime risk of dying from pregnancy and childbirth related complications, including unsafe abortions, is 80 times higher in low-income than in high-income countries. These data underscore that the failure to deal with preventable causes of maternal mortality constitutes a human rights violation of the right to life as well as a violation of the right to health.

The target of achieving universal access to reproductive health also seems unrealistic. Contraceptive prevalence with a modern method rose from 48 to 58% among married or in-union women between 1990 and 2015, resulting in a slight decline in unintended pregnancies.[22] However, a few regions where contraceptive use was particularly low in 1990 had even lower rates of use in 2015. Sub-Saharan Africa with a 28% use rate was notably low. Moreover, these figures likely underestimate the unmet need. Women who are sexually active but not married or in a stable union were not included in these data,[23] but a human rights approach does not permit discrimination in access to sexual and reproductive health-care services and information based on marital status and type of relationship.

The international women's movement perceived the MDGs to be a betrayal of the commitments that emerged from the 1994 Cairo International Conference on Population and Development and the 1995 Beijing World Conference on Women that recognised the promotion of women's health required the restructuring of social relations, along with changed laws and policies, and not just technical fixes.[24] MDG 5 was much criticised as 'a parable of politics, betrayals, regroupings, and most fundamentally, the perpetual challenges to meaningfully empowering women through development initiatives'.[25] In a 2014 article, Alicia Ely Yamin and Vanessa Boulanger document how the narrow focus of the MDG goal on maternal health care and on maternal mortality rather than women's rights or women's right to health and the targets and indicators adopted were converted into national planning tools and priorities for international aid, and in the process sidelined broader dimensions of gender equality and women's sexual, reproductive and health rights.[26] And like MDG 5, the reproductive health targets in the SDGs refrain from taking a rights-based approach, focus on a technical approach, and do not address underlying structural issues impeding women's right to equality and their ability to control their own lives.

What is promising though is that SDG goal 5, to achieve gender equality and empower all women and girls, is much stronger and more inclusive than its counterpart, MDG 3. SDG Goal 5 includes targets to end all forms of discrimination against women and girls; to eliminate all forms of violence against all women and girls in the public and private spheres; to eliminate harmful practices such as child, early and forced marriage and female genital mutilation; to undertake reforms to give women equal rights to economic resources; to ensure women's full and effective participation and equal opportunities for leadership at all levels of decision-making in political, economic and public life; and to adopt and strengthen sound policies and enforceable legislation for the promotion of gender equality and the empowerment of all women and girls, and there are a wide range of proposed indicators to measure progress. If even some of these objectives are met, it would strengthen women's status in society and their likelihood of achieving control of their sexual and reproductive health.

In terms of measurement, target 3.1 has just two indicators: the maternal mortality ratio and the proportion of births attended by skilled health personnel. Target 3.7 is to be measured by the proportion of women of reproductive age who have their need for family planning satisfied with modern methods and the adolescent birth rate (aged 10–14; aged 15–19) per 1,000 women in that age group. Goal 5.6 has two indicators to assess its fulfilment: (1) proportion of women aged 15–49 years who make their own informed decisions regarding sexual relations, contraceptive use and reproductive health care (which has yet to have an assigned methodology to calculate) and (2) number of countries with laws and regulations that guarantee women aged 15 to 49 years access to sexual and reproductive health care, information and education. However, both of these are tier III indicators which means there is no established methodology and standards or methodology to use for measurement or standards are being developed.[27]

Universal health coverage[28]

Target 3.8 directs countries to 'achieve universal health coverage, including financial risk protection, access to quality essential health-care services and access to safe, effective, quality and affordable essential medicines and vaccines for all'.[29] There has been a growing interest in recent years to the goal of achieving universal health coverage (UHC) so it is not surprising that UHC was selected as a target for Goal 3. Although universal coverage is only one of nine substantive targets and four additional targets labelled as means of implementation that are related to Goal 3, it is considered to be the target that underpins and is key to the achievement of all the others.[30] UHC also receives special attention in the Declaration for Transforming Our World endorsed by heads of government that precedes the identification of the SDGs: UHC is linked with the central commitment in the SDGs to leave no one behind: 'To promote physical and mental health and well-being, and to extend life expectancy for all, we must achieve universal health coverage and access to quality health care. No one must be left behind.'[31]

Of the various targets related to Goal 3, the universal health coverage target arguably reflects the right to health the most closely. UHC has been termed 'a practical expression of the right to health'.[32] It is explicitly enumerated as a core obligation related to children's right to health,[33] and the commitment to universality in access to key health services is implicit in other international and regional human rights instruments. Significant progress toward UHC, consistent with the requirements of the right to health, could have the potential of enabling the approximately one billion people currently estimated to not have access to the health services they need the opportunity to obtain them and to do so affordably.

However, paths to UHC and the way the goal is conceptualised are not necessarily consistent with international human rights principles, and target 3.8 falls short of human rights requirements in key ways. While the four components of target 3.8 overlap with dimensions of the right to health, as interpreted in UN Committee on Economic, Social and Cultural Rights' General Comment 14,[34] there are important human rights omissions as well. The most important of these is the failure to confer priority to providing access to health services to poor and disadvantaged communities in the process of expanding health coverage and in determining which health services to provide. Human rights are predicated on giving priority to the poor and disadvantaged. Simply expanding health coverage, especially if it continues to exclude poor and vulnerable communities, is not sufficient from a human rights perspective.

Financial risk protection, a second component of target 3.8, also overlaps with right to health requirements. According to General Comment 14, economic accessibility, conceptualised as health facilities, goods and services being affordable for all whether privately or publicly provided, including for socially disadvantaged groups, is an essential element of the right to health.[35] The text of the general comment further notes that equity considerations demand that poorer households should not be disproportionately burdened with health expenses as compared to more affluent households.[36] This implies either that health services, at least basic health services, will be provided free of cost or that poor and disadvantaged groups will be heavily subsidised. The SDGs do not have a similar requirement.

Importantly, the way in which financial risk protection is conceptualised and the policies adopted to implement this objective have important repercussions for poor and disadvantaged groups. The SDGs do not provide guidance on this matter. Two priorities of pro-poor financial risk protection are to significantly reduce or preferably eliminate out-of-pocket fees for health services, at least for primary health care services, and to provide protection from catastrophic expenditures. Out-of-pocket user fees, which are a dominant source of financing for health care in low-income countries, have a disproportionate impact on the poor who must pay considerably larger proportions of their incomes for health care than more affluent households. Every year some 100 million people, most of whom live in low-income countries, are pushed into poverty as a result of excessive or catastrophic spending on health care.[37] Therefore providing protection from catastrophic health expenditures, calculated as the proportion of people who spend more than 40% of their income on health-related costs, is a high priority. The SDGs do not address this issue and the indicators adopted related to financial risk protection, as discussed below, do not permit appropriate assessment.

A third dimension of target 3.8, access to quality essential health services and access to safe, effective, quality and affordable essential medicines and vaccines, also has a human rights counterpart. The creation of conditions which would assure to all medical service and medical attention in the event of sickness is one of the four steps the International Covenant on Economic, Social and Cultural Rights enumerates for state parties to undertake to realise the right to health.[38] Similarly, the Convention on the Rights of the Child has a provision to ensure necessary health care to all children with an emphasis on the development of primary care and another provision to ensure appropriate prenatal and postnatal health care for expectant mothers.[39] These requirements are framed as legal obligations for all state parties, and not as optional goals, albeit with a recognition that they will often need to be implemented gradually with steps taken to the maximum of available resources.[40]

General Comment 14 notes that investments should not disproportionately favour expensive curative health services which are often accessible only to a small, privileged fraction of the population rather than primary and preventive health care which can benefit a far larger proportion of the population.[41] The three part strategy set forth by the WHO Consultative Group on Equity and Universal Health Coverage offers a pro-poor approach consistent with these human rights requirements. First, categorise services into priority classes on the basis of such criteria as cost-effectiveness, priority to the worse off, and financial risk protection. Second, expand coverage for high-priority services to everyone. High-priority services are defined in the document as those that tend to be the most effective and to benefit the worse off. And third, as coverage is expanded, take special measures to ensure that disadvantaged groups, such as low-income groups and rural populations, are not left behind.[42] There are no such requirements or even recommendations to proceed in this manner in the SDGs.

To achieve universal health coverage many, perhaps most, countries will need major initiatives and investments devoted to health systems strengthening. After decades of inadequate funding and insufficient investment in health institutions and services the health systems of many countries are seriously weakened and sometimes dysfunctional. Often these problems disproportionately affected poor and disadvantaged communities. According to WHO, the health systems in many countries remain underfunded and struggle to provide even basic health services. In addition, many countries continue to face major shortages of trained health workers, particularly in rural areas.[43] Target 3.8 does not directly address the need for health system strengthening so as to provide geographically accessible, affordable and good quality health services.

Several subsidiary health targets, if implemented, could contribute to the process of health system strengthening: the development of vaccines and medicines for the communicable and non-communicable diseases that primarily affect developing countries and providing access to affordable essential medicines, which is discussed below, and substantially increasing health financing and the recruitment, development, training and retention of the health workforce in developing countries. Increasing health financing does not have an indicator even though it would be relatively easy to measure government budgetary allocations for health. The recruitment, development, training and retention of the health workforce is to be measured by an indicator on health worker density and distribution.[44]

There has been considerable controversy about indicators for measuring progress toward universal health coverage. One indicator, coverage of a list of essential health services does not incorporate any disaggregation. A second indicator purporting to measure the impoverishing effect of health spending on the poorest and most marginalised groups has been criticised as inadequate. At the February 2016 meeting of the Inter-Agency and Expert Group on Sustainable Development Indicators the proposed indicator was changed from the fraction of the population protected against catastrophic/impoverishing out-of-pocket health expenditure[45] to the number of people covered by health insurance or a public health system per 1,000 population.[46] Aware that health insurance does not necessarily eliminate high out-of-pocket payments, human rights and civil society groups reacted with alarm to this substitution and called for urgent action to change the indicator for universal health coverage to one which provides a more meaningful measure of financial risk protection for the poorest groups.[47] WHO and the World Bank then proposed substituting the 'proportion of the population with large household expenditures (e.g. greater than 25%) on health as a share of total household expenditure or income'.[48] However, the 21 December 2016 compilation of indicators still lists the number of people covered by health insurance or a public health system per 1,000 population with the addendum that it is 'under possible refinement'.[49]

Development of vaccines and medicines and providing access to affordable essential medicines[50]

One of the subsidiary targets for Goal 3 is to support the research and development of vaccines and medicines for the communicable and non-communicable diseases that primarily affect developing countries and to provide access to affordable essential medicines and vaccines, in accordance with the Doha Declaration on the TRIPS Agreement and Public Health. The 2001 Doha Declaration affirms the right of developing countries to use the provisions in the Agreement on Trade-Related Aspects of Intellectual Property Rights (TRIPS) regarding flexibilities to protect public health, and, in particular to be able to provide access to medicines for all.[51] Such flexibilities provide ways to obtain lower-cost medicines by overcoming some patent restrictions. Patents, the most common form of intellectual property applied to pharmaceuticals, accord patent holders the right to exclude others from making, using, selling, offering to sell and importing the patented invention into a country where it is protected. Patented drugs tend to be considerably more expensive than their unpatented generic counterparts because the monopoly accorded to patent holders confers the freedom to price their products at high levels that often puts drugs beyond the means of the poor and lower-income countries.

Achieving access to medicines, particularly essential medicines, is fundamental to the right to health. The availability and access to pharmaceuticals are intrinsic to reducing morbidity and mortality rates and enhancing the quality of life. General Comment 14 identifies the provision of essential drugs as defined under the WHO Action Programme on Essential Drugs as a core obligation of state parties to the International Covenant on Economic, Social and Cultural Rights.[52] Essential drugs refer to the medicines that address the priority needs of the population. The general comment also designates the provision of immunizations against the major diseases affecting the population to be an obligation of comparable priority.[53] Anand Grover, the second Special Rapporteur on the right to health, specified in his 2009 report that states have an obligation under the right to health to ensure that medicines are available, financially affordable and physically accessible to everyone in their jurisdiction.[54]

The provision of the SDGs dealing with developing vaccines and medicines and providing access to affordable essential medicines addresses an important global need. Currently approximately two billion people, some one-third of the world's population, do not have access to the medicines necessary for their health care. Moreover, there has been little improvement in the availability or affordability of medicines in developing countries in recent years.[55] The burden of paying for pharmaceuticals is particularly onerous in low- and middle-income countries where 50% of the cost of medicines is usually paid for by the patient or the patient's family. Many people in industrialised countries also cannot afford lifesaving but costly drugs when their health systems of health insurance do not underwrite the costs or require high co-pays for medicines.[56]

It is estimated that improving access to essential medicines could save some 10 million lives each year. Providing meaningful incentives for the development of new medications for the world's poor could reduce the disease burden even further.[57] The often cited figure 10/90 refers to the pattern in which only 10% of global funds for research and development are invested in the diseases affecting less developed countries in which 90% of the global disease burden occurs. Data indicate that of the 1,556 new medicines developed between 1975 and 1999 only 46 were for hitherto neglected diseases in poor countries, and between 2000 and mid-2009 only 26 new medicines and vaccines addressing neglected diseases were marketed.[58]

There are many obstacles to the realisation of improved access to appropriate and needed medicines in health systems in which for-profit corporations dominate the pharmaceutical sector and market mechanisms govern decisions about what kinds of medicines are developed and how they are priced. The incentive structure in the pharmaceutical sector skews research and development of medicines and vaccines to those products that can bring the greatest profits and not those of greatest need. The companies that dominate the pharmaceutical sector focus on products for markets in developed countries, particularly the United States because these markets are considered to be more profitable. It is assumed that poor people and low-income countries cannot afford high-priced pharmaceuticals. The profit orientation has also generated a business model that encourages the development of 'me-too' drugs, products that largely duplicate the composition and the mechanism of action of existing drugs with little additional therapeutic benefit because such drugs are less expensive to develop and viewed as offering substantial profits. Additionally the profit orientation also encourages massive investments in promotional activities directed at physicians and advertising in countries where it is permissible to do so that then reduces the funds available for research. Moreover, the tremendous economic resources of the major pharmaceutical corporations confer considerable political power and the ability to influence public policy on such matters as the formulation and imposition of international trade agreements that protect pharmaceutical patents.[59]

Public health and human rights experts, including Anand Grover, the second Special Rapporteur on the right to health, have identified the existing intellectual property laws, particularly the strict global minimum standards established under the 1994 Agreement on Trade Related Aspects of Intellectual Property Rights (TRIPS), as a significant impediment to greater access to medicines in low- and middle-income countries and a major contributor to their high cost.[60] The TRIPS Agreement both sets mandatory minimum standards for national protection of intellectual property and requires that patents be available for inventions in all fields of technology including pharmaceuticals. Membership in the World Trade Organisation, which is linked with acceptance of the TRIPS Agreement, also makes countries subject to enforcement measures, including potential trade sanctions, for failure to comply with TRIPS standards. However, such strict intellectual property models appropriate for advanced market economies tend to disadvantage less developed countries because intellectual property protection for products developed by companies in industrialised countries usually increases their cost, constrains product development and restricts access.[61]

When the TRIPS Agreement was formulated some low- and middle-income countries lobbied to have the agreement incorporate a number of flexibilities to mitigate the adverse impact of a strong patent regime on access to medicines, and the TRIPS Agreement does include a number of such provisions, but the policies of the major industrialised countries and large pharmaceutical corporations made it difficult for developing countries to use these provisions. These problems motivated the formulation of the Doha Declaration on TRIPS and Public Health which affirms that the all of the flexibilities of the TRIPS Agreement 'can and should be interpreted and implemented in a manner supportive of WTO Members' right to protect public health and, in particular, to promote access to medicines for all'.[62] However, the US government and some European governments have promoted TRIPS-plus trade agreements which eliminate these flexibilities and applied diplomatic pressure and threatened to impose trade sanctions or file complaints in the World Trade Organisation (WTO) when governments have adopted measures to prioritise public health in ways that limit the intellectual property rights and privileges of businesses headquartered in their countries. Therefore the Doha Declaration has not facilitated a significant increase in the use of TRIPS flexibilities to increase access to medicine.[63] Research conducted in 2012 of trends in the compulsory licensing of pharmaceuticals, one of the primary means that countries use to override patent protection by the government authorising an entity other than the patent holder to produce a patented product, identified only 24 instances initiated by 17 countries up to then. Most of these compulsory licenses were issued between 2003 and 2005, involved drugs for HIV/AIDS and took place in upper middle-income countries. None occurred in low-income countries,[64] possibly because they lacked the capacity to manufacture pharmaceuticals.

For this subsidiary target to be meaningful it would have to address the structural issues blocking access to affordable and appropriate medicines noted above, but it does not. Developed countries resisted the considerable efforts by developing countries to have the SDGs address structural macroeconomic, trade and finance issues and to reaffirm the right of developing countries to use the TRIPS flexibilities to the fullest extent. The intense negotiations over this issue nearly toppled the process of developing the SDG agenda.[65] In the end provisions of the SDGs, particularly the section on the means of implementation and the global partnership, basically affirm the current corporate dominated neoliberal world order.[66] While language reiterating the Doha Agreement on TRIPS flexibilities applying to access to medicines and vaccines was included in the SDGs, a means to enable developing countries to use the TRIPS flexibilities to protect public health and to improve access to medicines was not.

There is no indicator proposed as yet to measure the proportion of the population with access to affordable medicines and vaccines on a sustainable basis. Nor is there a firm commitment to provide one. The December 2016 report on global SDG indicators notes it is under possible refinement.[67]

The social determinants of health

There is increasing evidence that health status, both on an individual level and for communities, is shaped by a wide range of nonmedical factors. Studies, such as the landmark report of the World Health Organisation's Commission on the Social Determinants of Health, have provided greater visibility for the significant role of specific social determinants, such as education, income, environmental conditions, housing and nutrition, in influencing health outcomes and thereby contributing to existing and growing health inequalities both within and between societies.[68] Importantly, the framing of the right to health has always been broader than just a right of access to health care. Article 12 of the International Covenant on Economic, Social and Cultural Rights directs state parties to the improvement of all aspects of environmental and industrial hygiene.[69] The Convention on the Rights of the Child stipulates that the right to health includes access to nutritious food, clean drinking water and environmental sanitation.[70] In addition, the Committee on Economic, Social and Cultural Rights' General Comment 14 interprets the right to health as an inclusive right extending not only to timely and appropriate health care but also to the underlying determinants of health. According to the text, these include safe and potable water and adequate sanitation, an adequate supply of safe food, nutrition and housing, healthy occupational and environment conditions and access to health-related education and information. Providing these underlying determinants is considered to be a core obligation that is immediately realisable and not dependent on the availability of resources.[71]

As noted above, the SDGs incorporate a full list of social determinants of health, but they do so as independent goals and targets, and not as factors shaping health outcomes. This means that policies adopted to further these objectives will be unlikely to assess their implications for health. Moreover, like the health targets, none of them promotes a human rights approach. Goals related to the social determinants of health in the SDGs are listed below:

- Goal 1: End poverty in all its forms everywhere;
- Goal 2: End hunger, achieve food security and improve nutrition and promote sustainable agriculture;
- Goal 4: Ensure inclusive and equitable quality education and promote lifelong learning opportunities for all;
- Goal 5: Achieve gender equality and empower all women and girls;
- Goal 6: Ensure availability and sustainable management of water and sanitation for all;
- Goal 10: Reduce inequality within and among countries;
- Goal 13: Take urgent action to combat climate change and its impacts.

In contrast with the indicators for the health-related targets, some of the targets listed under these goals do call for disaggregation.

Conclusion

Writing before the adoption of the SDGs a group of human rights advocates who had unsuccessfully lobbied for the adoption of a right to health approach in Goal 3 anticipated,

> rather than creating a transformative post-2015 agenda, by continuing the MDG route of divorcing rights from development goals there is real risk the post-MDG agenda will be anything but transformative – but regressively reduced to meeting basic needs, to meeting (even more) targets and sub-targets, as opposed to overcoming in-country development inequities.[72]

This is exactly what has occurred. Moreover, the refusal to adopt a human rights approach also reduces prospects for people's participation in decision-making around implementation of the goals and their ability to hold their government accountable. It also creates the likelihood that despite the rhetoric adopted the most vulnerable and disadvantaged groups will once again be left behind.

Notes

1. 'Transforming Our World: The 2030 Agenda for Sustainable Development', Resolution adopted by the General Assembly on 25 September 2015, UN Doc. A/RES/70/1.
2. 'Transforming Our World', para. 8.
3. Ibid., para. 3.
4. Katherina Stepping and Nicole Rippin, 'Goal 3: Ensure healthy lives and promote well-being for all at all ages', in *The Sustainable Development Goals of the Post 2015 Agenda: Comments on the OWG and SDSN Proposals*, eds. Markus Loewe and Nicole Rippin (Bonn: German Development Institute, 2015), 21–25, https://www.oecd.org/pcd/DIE__Comments__on__SDG__proposals__150226.pdf.
5. Convention on the Rights of the Child, adopted by the United Nations General Assembly on 20 November 1989 and entered into force on 2 September 1990, UN Doc.A/RES/44/25, article 24.
6. Committee on the Rights of the Child, *General comment No. 15 (2013) on the right of the child to the enjoyment of the highest attainable standard of health (art. 24)*, UN Doc. CRC/C/GC/15, Introduction.
7. UNICEF, 'A Post-2015 World Fit for Children', 2015, https://www.unicef.org/agenda2030/files/Post_2015_OWG_review_CR_FINAL.pdf (accessed March 19, 2017).
8. *The Millennium Development Goals Report 2015*, 32–3.
9. UNICEF, 'A Post-2015 World Fit for Children'.
10. UN Statistical Office, 'Tier Classification for Global SDG Indicators', 10 November 2016, https://unstats.un.org/sdgs/iaeg-sdgs/tier-classification/ (accessed March 15, 2007).
11. Rebecca Cook, Bernard Dickens and Mahmoud Fathalla, *Reproductive Health and Human Rights: Integrating Medicine, Ethics, and Law* (Oxford: Oxford University Press, 2003), 8–10.
12. UN, Convention on the Elimination of All Forms of Discrimination against Women, New York, 1979, 34 UN GAOR Suppl. No. 21, A/34/46 at 193, UN Doc A/Res/34/180.
13. Committee on the Elimination of All Forms of Discrimination against Women (CEDAW), General Recommendation 24, UN GAOR 1999, UN Doc. A/54/38/rev. 1.
14. Committee on Economic, Social and Cultural Rights (CESCR), General comment No. 22 (2016) on the right to sexual and reproductive health (article 12 of the International Covenant on Economic, Social and Cultural Rights, UN Doc. E/C.12/CG22.
15. Ibid.
16. Ibid, article 5.
17. World Health Organisation (WHO), 'Health in 2015: From MDGs to SDGs', 2015, www:who.int/gho/publications/mdgs-sdgs/en/ (accessed April 6, 2016).
18. Ibid., 232.
19. WHO, 'World Health Statistics 2016: Monitoring Health for the SDGs', 74, www.who.int/gho/publications/world_world_health_statistics2016/en/.
20. WHO, 'Health in 2015'.
21. Independent Accountability Panel, *Old Challenges, New Hopes: Accountability for the Global Strategy for Women's, Children's and Adolescents' Health*, 2016, 22, iapewec.org/downloads/IAP_Report_September2016.pdf (accessed November 23, 2016).
22. Ibid., 74–5.
23. *The Millennium Development Goals Report 2015*, 41–42.
24. Ibid., 237.
25. Alicia Ely Yamin, 'Sexual and Reproductive Health, Rights, and MDG 5: Taking Stock, Looking Forward', in *The Millennium Goals and Human Rights: Past, Present and Future*, ed. Malcolm Langford, Andy Sumner and Alicia Ely Yamin (New York: Cambridge University Press, 2013), 232.

26. Alicia Ely Yamin and Vanessa M. Boulanger, 'Why Global Goals and Indicators Matter: The Experience of Sexual and Reproductive Health and Rights in the Millennium Development Goals', *Journal of Human Development and Capabilities* 15 (2014): 218–31.
27. UN Statistical Office, Tier Classification for Global SDG Indicators, 10 November 2016, unstats.un.org/sdgs/files/meetings/iaeg-sdgs-m (accessed March 10, 2016).
28. The section on Universal Health Coverage references two other of my publications: Audrey R. Chapman, 'Assessing the Universal Health Coverage Target in the Sustainable Development Goals from a Human Rights Perspective', forthcoming in *BMC International Health and Human Rights*; 'Editorial: Contributions of Human Rights to Universal Health Coverage', *Health and Human Rights Journal* 18 (2016): 1–5.
29. Chapman, Assessing the Universal Health Coverage Target and Contributions of Human Rights.
30. WHO, 'Health in 2015'.
31. Ibid., para 26.
32. WHO, 'Health in the Post-2015 Development Agenda', World Health Assembly, A66/47, 1 May 2013.
33. Committee on the Rights of the Child, General Comment 15 on the right to health, CRC/C/GC/15, para. 72.
34. CESCR (2000) General Comment No. 14, *The right to the highest attainable standard of health (article 12 of the International Covenant on Economic, Social and Cultural Rights)*, 2000, para 12 (b) (iii), UN Doc. E/C.12/2000/4.
35. Ibid., para 12 (b) (iii).
36. Ibid.
37. WHO, *World Health Report: Health Systems Financing, the Path to Universal Coverage* (Geneva: WHO, 2010), 12.
38. International Covenant on Economic, Social and Cultural Rights, Article 12, para 2 (d).
39. Convention on the Rights of the Child, Article 24, paras 2 (b) and 2 (d)
40. International Covenant on Economic, Social and Cultural Rights (1966) Adopted and opened for signature, ratification and accession by United Nations General Assembly Resolution 2200 A (XXI) of 16 December and entered into force 3 January 1976, UN Doc. A/6316, para. 2.1; Convention on the Rights of the Child, para. 4.
41. International Covenant on Economic, Social and Cultural Rights, para 19.
42. WHO Consultative Group on Equity and Universal Health Coverage, 'Making Fair Choices on the Path to Universal Coverage', 2014, 37, www.who.int/choice/documents/ (accessed November 10, 2015).
43. World Health Organization, 'Health in 2015', 193–4, 45–6.
44. UN Statistical Office, 'Tier Classification for Global SDG Indicators', 8.
45. UN Statistical Commission (2016), Report of the Inter-Agency and Expert Group on Sustainable Development Goal Indicators, UN Doc. E/CN.3/2016/2, 18.
46. UN Statistical Commission (2016) Report of the Inter-Agency and Expert Group on Sustainable Goal Indicators.
47. A. Marriott and M. M. Kamal-Yanni, 'Last Minute Change to the UHC Indicator for the SDGs is Raising Alarm Bells!', *Global Health Check*, 7 March 2016, http://www.globalhealthcheck.org/?p=1854.
48. Consultation on Possible Refinements of Indicators Identified by the Inter-agency and Expert Group on Sustainable Development Goal Indicators, https://unstats.un.org/...consultation.../Consultation%20on%20Possible%20Refinement (accessed November 10, 2016).
49. UN Statistical Office, 'Tier Classification for Global SDG Indicators', 7.
50. Parts of this section are based on chapter 6 of my book, *Global Health, Human Rights and the Challenges of Neoliberal Policies* (Cambridge: Cambridge University Press, 2016).
51. World Trade Organization, Ministerial Conference Fourth Session, Doha, November 9–14, 2001, Declaration on TRIPS Agreement and Public Health, T/MIN(01)/DEC/2.
52. CESCR, General Comment No. 14, para. 43d.
53. Ibid., para. 44.

54. Anand Grover, *Report of the Special Rapporteur on the right of everyone to the enjoyment of the highest attainable standard of physical and mental health*, Human Rights Council, 2009, A/HRC/11/12, para. 11.
55. MDG Gap Task Force Report, *The Global Partnership for Development: Making Rhetoric a Reality* (New York: United Nations Publications, 2012), xvi.
56. Audrey R. Chapman, *Global Health, Human Rights, and the Challenge of Neoliberal Policies* (Cambridge: Cambridge University Press, 2016), 202–03.
57. Grover, *Report of the Special Rapporteur on the right of everyone*, para 14.
58. MDG Gap Task Force Report, *The Global Partnership for Development*, 71.
59. Chapman, *Global Health, Human Rights*, 204–206.
60. Grover, *Report of the Special Rapporteur on the right of everyone*, para 7.
61. Ibid., para 23.
62. World Trade Organization, Ministerial Conference Fourth Session, Doha, 9–14 November, Declaration on the TRIPS Agreement and Public Health, T/MIN(01)/DEC/2 (2001), para 4.
63. Carlos M. Correa and Duncan Matthews, 'The Doha Declaration Ten Years on and Its Impact on Access to Medicines and the Right to Health' (discussion paper, United Nations Development Programme, 2011), 20, http://www.undp.org/content/dam/undp/library/hivaids/Discussion_Paper_Doha_Declaration_Public_Health.pdf
64. Reed Beall and Randall Kuhn, 'Trends in Compulsory Licensing of Pharmaceuticals since the Doha Declaration: A Database Analysis', *PLoS Medicine* 9 (2012): e1001154.
65. Global Policy Forum, 'Means of Implementation nearly toppled process of SDG agenda', July 23, 2014, https://www.globalpolicy.org/component/content/article/252-the-millenium-development-goals/52671-means-of-implementation-nearly-toppled-process-of-sdgs-agenda.html (accessed March 29, 2016).
66. 'Transforming Our World', paras 67–9.
67. UN Statistical Office, 'Tier Classification for Global SDG Indicators', 8.
68. Commission on the Social Determinants of Health, *Closing the Gap in a Generation: Health Equity through Action on the Social Determinants of Health* (Geneva: WHO, 2008).
69. International Covenant on Economic, Social and Cultural Rights (1966) adopted and opened for signature, ratification and accession by United Nations General Assembly Resolution 2200A (XXI) of 16 December, entered into force on 3 January 1976, UN Doc. A/6316, Article 12.
70. Convention on the Rights of the Child, Article 24.
71. CESCR, General Comment No. 14, paras 11 and 43.
72. Claire E. Brolan, Peter S. Hill and Gorik Ooms, '"Everywhere But Not Specifically Somewhere": A Qualitative Study On Why the Right to Health Is Not Explicit in the Post-2015 Negotiations', *BMC International Health & Human Rights* 15 (2015): 22. doi:10.1186/212914-015-0061-z.

Disclosure statement

No potential conflict of interest was reported by the author.

Neglecting human rights: accountability, data and Sustainable Development Goal 3

Carmel Williams and Paul Hunt

ABSTRACT

In this paper we examine the Sustainable Development Goal 3 through the lens of state obligations to respect, protect and fulfil people's human rights entitlements. We critique some of the *Transforming Our World: The 2030 Agenda for Sustainable Development* 'follow-up and review' arrangements for the health goal, SDG3. To assist in this analysis, we draw from a tripartite conceptualisation of accountability and focus particularly on monitoring and review. We use a human rights framework to explore whether the agreed SDG3 indicators for 'follow-up and review' promote the collection of data that could demonstrate health rights entitlements are being respected, protected and fulfilled. We find there are gaps through which breaches of human rights could fall undetected, especially around participation and quality health care. We find statistics are frequently absent in countries and communities most 'left behind', and suggestions that Big Data could fill these statistical gaps ignore the realities of poor information systems and the digital divide. We conclude that well resourced countries have human rights obligations to provide assistance where needed to national statistics offices to improve their capacity to contribute to human rights accountability mechanisms.

Introduction

The Sustainable Development Goals (SDGs), adopted in September 2015 by all UN Member States, have an explicit grounding in human rights, as outlined in the preamble of *Transforming Our World: The 2030 Agenda for Sustainable Development*.[1] In the third paragraph of the preamble, it is stated: 'The 17 Sustainable Development Goals and 169 targets ... seek to realize the human rights of all and to achieve gender equality and the empowerment of all women and girls.'[2]

The SDGs have an overarching objective to lift everyone out of poverty, reduce inequality between and within countries and importantly, to use their catchphrase, ensure 'no one [is] left behind'. Such a goal has a close fit with the human rights equality imperative that 'All human beings are born free and equal in dignity and rights'.[3]

In adopting the SDGs, States explicitly reaffirmed their commitment to international law and emphasised that the *2030 Agenda* 'is to be implemented in a manner that is consistent with the rights and obligations of States under international law'.[4] These commitments and obligations have both domestic and international implications, and include duties relating to international assistance and cooperation (IAC) which is a feature of both international human rights law,[5] as well as a specific goal in the SDGs (SDG17 Partnership for the Goals). To achieve the equality sought by the SDGs, and to ensure that human rights are realised for all, there is an acknowledged obligation on wealthier economies to support poorer ones.[6] This important obligation should be a feature of global accountability, as the SDGs are not achievable without such support.

The responsibility to mainstream human rights

However, it would be a mistake to focus entirely or exclusively on the underpinning of the SDGs themselves as a basis on which to argue the SDGs carry human rights responsibilities. The UN has mandated human rights mainstreaming across the global organisation, led by the UN Office of the High Commissioner for Human Rights and the UN Human Rights Council, and this necessarily applies to the implementation of activities and policies relating to the achievement of the SDGs.[7]

A crucially important framework, vital to the mainstreaming of all human rights, is that human rights must be respected, protected and fulfilled. As explained in the context of health, a state's duty to respect means it must refrain from interfering with the enjoyment of the right to health; the duty to protect places an obligation on states to prevent third parties from interfering with the enjoyment of the right to health; and fulfilling this right requires states to adopt the necessary measures – from legislation to budgets to community health practice – to progressively realise the right.[8]

The UN Committee on Economic, Social and Cultural Rights not only adopts the respect, protect and fulfil framework, but also adds considerable operational detail about the obligations on states (and other duty bearers), for example in paragraphs 34 to 37 of General Comment 14.[9] This Comment details the meaning of the right to health, and it gives rise to the framework employed in many UN guidelines and other papers, which incorporates the legal obligation on states to make health-related facilities and services available, accessible, acceptable and of good quality. All of these insights are highly relevant to the SDGs.

To summarise: for each of these reasons, from international human rights law, to the mandated human rights mainstreaming in all UN activities, to the duties on States to respect, protect and fulfil rights, and finally to the specifics arising from General Comment 14 as well as other UN guidelines, the activities and policies of SDGs carry human rights implications. The SDGs could not, in isolation, fulfil every human rights entitlement. However, what is crucial, and what this paper sets forth, is that SDG accountability must encompass human rights, including the duties to respect, protect and fulfil. Accordingly, in this paper, we examine the SDG follow up and review mechanisms in the light of human rights, especially the right to health.

SDGs: follow-up and review

The means through which progress towards achieving the SDGs will be monitored and reviewed is outlined in the *2030 Agenda*, in a section entitled 'Follow-up and Review':

A robust, voluntary, effective, participatory, transparent and integrated follow-up and review framework will make a vital contribution to implementation and will help countries to maximize and track progress in implementing this Agenda in order to ensure that no one is left behind.

Operating at the national, regional and global levels, it will promote accountability to our citizens, support effective international cooperation in achieving this Agenda and foster exchanges of best practices and mutual learning.[10]

Subsequent to the adoption of the SDGs a series of indicators has been selected by the Inter-agency and Expert Group on Sustainable Development Goal Indicators (IAEG-SDGs) to monitor each specific target.[11] Much consultation and debate has gone into the development of the indicators and especially so since the Millennium Development Goals (MDGs) indicators had been robustly critiqued.[12] In their Power of Number series, Sakiko Fukuda-Parr, Alicia Ely Yamin and Joshua Greenstein illustrate the unintended consequences resulting from choice of indicators in the MDGs.[13]

However, monitoring alone, and the voluntary and weak monitoring called for in the *2030 Agenda*, is insufficient to hold states accountable for their human rights obligations relating to the SDGs; rather, as explained more fully in the next section, monitoring is just one step towards accountability.[14] If SDGs are simply monitored, using the agreed indicators, human rights failings can be overlooked, intentionally or otherwise. For example, if a state were to introduce punitive measures against women who fail to give birth in approved facilities, they would likely show improvement on SDG 3.1.2, with an increased number of births taking place under supervised care. However, if this indicator is achieved without women's consent or in the absence of culturally acceptable care being provided, then it breaches women's human rights entitlements.

It is therefore critically important that human rights principles and law are incorporated into, and considered by, the mechanisms through which states are held accountable for achievement of the SDGs. For this to happen accountability cannot be limited to a technocratic exercise; it should be as transparent, accessible and participatory as possible.[15] As we find in this article, the present voluntary monitoring requirements for the SDGs fail to achieve these standards and, in several ways, fall short of effective accountability.

In our first section following this introduction, we signal the recognised importance of the 'accountability challenge' within global governance for health and outline why we adopt the conceptualisation of accountability identified by the Commission on Information and Accountability for Women's and Children's Health (COIA). In our second section we explain the tripartite conceptualisation of accountability – monitoring, review and remedial action – which is informed by human rights and was adopted by COIA in 2011. Focusing on the review component, we ask whether or not the *2030 Agenda*'s global 'follow-up and review' arrangements for SDG3 are consistent with the Commission's conceptualisation of accountability. We conclude they are not, except in relation to women's, children's and adolescents' health, and we suggest a way of addressing this shortcoming of review. Having critiqued the process of review, the third section of our paper turns to the practicalities of monitoring, more specifically we examine the monitoring requirements for SDG3 to see if they adequately address respect, protect and fulfil right to health obligations. We assess SDG3's monitoring effectiveness by applying the key elements of the right to health, and suggest that the monitoring is deficient from this perspective. Our fourth section considers the data that is required to fulfil the monitoring of SDG3, and finds it is inadequate, falling short of capturing right to health obligations, especially regarding respecting and protecting human rights. Our fifth section responds to suggestions that Big Data can plug gaps in the data needed for SDG3 monitoring, and finds otherwise – that using Big Data to monitor SDG3 could have serious negative human rights implications, failing to count the people already left behind. We conclude that a human rights approach to monitoring SDG3 must firstly strengthen national statistics offices' capacity to gather data with the support of international assistance and cooperation, and then develop additional indicators to monitor right-to-health elements, such as quality of care, participation and empowerment, and financing of health systems. We also observe that statistics and Big Data are unlikely to paint a complete picture of whether SDG activities have respected, protected and fulfilled human rights; rather, multidisciplinary approaches to monitoring, including qualitative methods, will remain of fundamental importance.

Accountability challenges in global governance for health

Julio Frenk and Suerie Moon identify three major governance challenges for global health, one of which is the 'accountability challenge', in particular 'the lack of clear mechanisms for the accountability of nonstate actors'.[16] Ilona Kickbusch and Martina Szabo identify six key challenges, one of which is 'how can the private sector become more accountable?'[17] We agree that a critical challenge in global governance for health, such as in relation to SDG3, is accountability and we suggest this challenge extends to states and non-state actors.

This raises the question, what is meant by accountability? In this article we adopt the tripartite conceptualisation of accountability – monitoring, review and remedial action – provided by the Commission on Information and Accountability for Women's and Children's Health.[18] We use this conceptualisation for two reasons. First, it was identified and adopted by a high-level political body (i.e. COIA) which set out accountability arrangements for Millennium Development Goals 4 and 5, close predecessors of SDG3; thus, it is highly relevant to, and has considerable political legitimacy within, the fields of development and health. Second, the conceptualisation dispels the confusion between monitoring and accountability that has sometimes constrained effective accountability in development and health. We elaborate on both these points in the next section. Accordingly, we use COIA's conceptualisation of accountability to examine aspects of monitoring, review and SDG3. More particularly, we look at the adequacy of data for monitoring SDG3 and whether or not there is global independent review of all stakeholders in relation to their SDG3 'pledges, promises and commitments'.[19]

We discuss and recognise that the roots of the COIA's conceptualisation of accountability lie, at least in part, in the Westphalian arrangement of nation states and thus, it might be argued, this notion of accountability is not well-suited for global governance. While national law is weighted towards coercion, and international law towards cooperation, nonetheless we suggest the COIA's conceptualisation of accountability has enormous relevance and importance to global governance for health. This view is informed by the COIA's work, as well as the increasing prevalence of accountability as monitoring, review and remedial action in global governance, including global health.[20]

Accountability, independent review and SDG3

In this article we analyse, through a right to health 'lens', the role of data, including Big Data, in monitoring SDG3. Although effective monitoring is crucial, it is not an end in itself, it is a means to evaluate progress and enhance accountability. In this section we locate data and monitoring within the COIA's conceptualisation of accountability. As we demonstrate, human rights have helped to shape this understanding of accountability. We then ask: are the *2030 Agenda*'s follow-up and review arrangements for SDG3 consistent with COIA's conceptualisation of accountability? Sub-national, national, and regional accountability are crucial, but in this paper we focus on global accountability arrangements for SDG3.

Accountability as monitoring, review and remedial action

Concerned by slow progress towards Millennium Development Goals 4 (child health) and 5 (reproductive and maternal health), the UN Secretary-General, Ban Ki-moon, launched his *Global Strategy for Women's and Children's Health* in September 2010.[21] Because the *Strategy* did not establish accountability arrangements, the Secretary-General asked the Director-General of WHO to 'chair a process to determine the most effective international institutional arrangements for global reporting, oversight and accountability on women's and children's health, including through the UN system'.[22]

In December 2010, WHO established a Commission on Information and Accountability for Women's and Children's Health. Supported by two expert Working Groups, the 30-member Commission was high-level: for example, it included 11 current Presidents, Prime Ministers or Ministers, as well as other prominent leaders in global health, including from civil society. In 2011, the Commission produced its final report, *Keeping Promises, Measuring Results*, which included 10 recommendations.[23] For present purposes, the recommendations are less important than the conceptualisation of accountability adopted by the Commission, which informed its analysis and recommendations.

For decades, many health and development professionals tended to equate monitoring, or tracking progress, with accountability.[24] In this way, they eviscerated the concept of accountability. The COIA report corrected this misconceptualisation. It highlighted that accountability consists of three components: monitoring, review and remedial action.[25] The COIA emphasised that monitoring is not accountability, but one important step towards accountability.

Monitoring: Monitoring is familiar to health and development professionals and, according to the COIA, it means 'providing critical and valid information on what is happening, where and to whom (results) and how much is spent, where, on what and on whom (resources)'.[26] It is well-established that data have a crucial contribution to make towards effective monitoring. If data are inaccurate, incomplete or entirely absent, effective monitoring will usually be impossible. Moreover, effective accountability depends upon effective monitoring. In short, inadequate data usually leads to ineffective monitoring which, in turn, leads to ineffective accountability. In this article, our main focus is the adequacy of data, and therefore the effectiveness (or otherwise) of monitoring and accountability, in relation to SDG3.

Review: After its discussion of monitoring, the COIA explains that review has two limbs. The first is familiar to health and development professionals: 'analyzing data to determine whether ... health has improved.'[27] For example, such data analysis may lead to the conclusion that the health of some populations has not improved, but it will not connect this finding to the commitments and responsibilities of any party. Many tend to be less familiar (and less comfortable) with the second limb of review: 'analyzing ... whether pledges, promises and commitments have been kept by countries, donors and non-state actors.'[28] This takes a crucial step beyond limb one. For example, the review may conclude the data show that the health of some populations has deteriorated (limb one), but also that this state of affairs is inconsistent with the 'pledges, promises and commitments' of 'countries, donors and non-state actors' (limb two). In other words, second limb review invites the conclusion that one or more parties have neither honoured their 'pledges, promises and commitments' nor discharged their responsibilities. This is intrinsically different from both monitoring and the COIA's first limb of review. Notably, 'pledges, promises and commitments' encompasses those in relation to human rights and, crucially, second limb review is not confined to states but also 'donors and non-state actors'.[29] By extending review to 'non-state actors', COIA addresses one of the major accountability challenges identified by Frenk and Moon, and Kickbusch and Szabo.[30]

The COIA adds that review is 'a learning process that involves recognizing success, drawing attention to good practice, identifying shortcomings and, as required, recommending remedial actions'.[31] This is not far from what Lynn Freedman calls 'constructive accountability' and 'the commitment to an on-going public, transparent process of assessment, change and reassessment'.[32]

Two additional points about the 'review' component of the COIA's approach require brief elaboration: First, the COIA firmly recognised the importance of *independent* review. It explicitly recommended an independent global oversight body in relation to MDGs 4 and 5, the independent Expert Review Group (iERG), which was duly established by the Secretary-General until MDGs were replaced by SDGs.[33] Although our focus is global arrangements, it is relevant to note that, in relation to national oversight, the COIA also recommended ways 'to increase the independence of review', such as the appointment of a health ombudsperson.[34] For its part, the iERG emphasised the imperative of independent review.[35] The Secretary-General's *Global Strategy for Women's and Children's Health* (for 2010–2015 and the MDGs) was followed by his *Global Strategy for Women's, Children's and Adolescents' Health* (for 2016–2030 and the SDGs) and this new *Global Strategy* explicitly builds upon the COIA's understanding of accountability and establishes an independent review body, the Independent Accountability Panel (IAP), which is, effectively, the successor to iERG.[36] So it is clear that the COIA conception of accountability includes a formal independent element.

Peter Godwin and Sujaya Misra are critical of such independent review; for example, they argue that '[i]n practice, establishing total independence is virtually impossible'.[37] But they appear to discount the many national and global independent review bodies composed of individuals who take instructions neither from those nominating or appointing them, nor from any other person or organisation, and who exercise their professional, autonomous judgment in good faith and thereby make a distinctive and invaluable contribution towards effective accountability. Nonetheless, Godwin and Misra favour 'open-source' accountability whereby all stakeholders hold each other to account, an arrangement that clearly favours interest groups that are well-resourced over the long-term.[38] Space does not permit a full critique of Godwin and Misra's view but, given the scale and complexity of the SDGs, we prefer diverse accountability arrangements, what Kate Donald calls 'a web of accountability' which, in keeping with the COIA prescription, includes independent review, along the lines of iERG, IAP, UN human rights treaty-bodies and special rapporteurs.[39]

Second, if a global independent review body is established, to whom should it report? The Commission required iERG to report to the Secretary-General, but neither iERG nor Godwin and Misra found this a satisfactory arrangement.[40] As the iERG put it, the 'Secretary General has our report but no mechanism to deal with it'.[41] Taking this shortcoming on board, the reporting arrangements for the IAP were formulated differently. IAP is required to report to the Secretary-General *and the Board of the Partnership for Maternal Neonatal and Child Health* (PMNCH), which consists of 30 members from among the Partnership's membership. Board members represent different constituencies, including donor governments and foundations, 'partner governments' (Indonesia, Tanzania, Nigeria and India in 2017), UN agencies, the private sector and NGOs. On a discretionary and less convincing basis, the IAP's reports may be considered elsewhere, for example, other stakeholders 'will be encouraged to discuss the report' and 'the report could also be considered' by UN human rights treaty-bodies and others.[42] The important point we take from this is that lessons were learnt from the iERG's experience, for example, formal independent review must have one or more suitable political body or process to which it is required to report otherwise there is a risk that its outputs will disappear without attracting significant attention. In the case of the IAP, the political body is the PMNCH Board, whether or not it is a 'suitable' political body is a question that lies beyond this article.

At the end of this section we recommend, in relation to SDG3, a formal independent review reporting into suitable political bodies or processes.

Remedial action: The COIA also discusses the third component of accountability: remedial action. Of the three components, this is the least developed by the COIA. Sometimes it uses the term 'act', sometimes 'remedial action'.[43] The latter is to be preferred because it alludes to the idea of redress or remedy. The COIA notion of remedial action may be summarised as measures to put things right, as far as possible, if they have not gone as promised or planned. As we mention below, the COIA understanding of 'remedial action' has been the subject of criticism.

In conclusion, we suggest it is important to distinguish these three components of accountability. Essentially, accountability is a process to ensure that commitments are kept. Such review cannot take place without monitoring. And review becomes meaningless without remedial action. Each component has a critical and distinctive role to play. If they are not distinguished, there is a risk that one or more will be neglected, for example, there has been a tendency to neglect review within development and global health. Worse, if the three components are not distinguished, there is a risk that one, such as monitoring, will be conflated with accountability. If this happens, those who made the commitments – the duty-bearers – are likely to escape meaningful accountability. We will now explore further the COIA's conceptualisation of accountability from a human rights perspective before using it as a 'lens' to consider the global follow-up and review arrangements for SDG3.

Is it a human rights conception of accountability?

At one level, the roots of the COIA understanding of accountability lie in international human rights. For example, the 'review' and 'remedial action' components of the COIA approach to accountability can be traced to the Universal Declaration of Human Rights which guarantees everyone 'a fair ... hearing by an independent and impartial tribunal, in the determination of ... rights and obligations' (article 10), as well as 'an effective remedy' if 'fundamental rights' are violated (article 8).[44] Moreover, a paper prepared in anticipation of the COIA called for a 'three-step accountability process' and its analysis drew explicitly and extensively from international human rights law and practice, including UN human rights treaty-bodies.[45]

In early 2011, PMNCH made a submission to the COIA called 'A review of global accountability mechanisms for women's and children's health' which presents accountability as monitoring, review and remedy or action.[46] It, too, draws heavily from international human rights law and practice, including the Universal Periodic Review. As already noted, the COIA had two working groups, one of which advised the COIA to understand accountability as monitoring, review and remedy and, when making its case, the working group explicitly drew from international human rights law and practice.[47] In summary, at one level, there is a clear link between international human rights and the COIA conceptualisation of accountability.

However, at another level, the roots of the COIA's understanding of accountability stretch back beyond the emergence of contemporary international human rights to the Enlightenment, such as Montesquieu's doctrine of the separation of powers which includes an independent judiciary to hold accountable the other branches of government.[48] The IAP recognises this in its discussion of what it calls 'act and remedy' and 'remedial action': 'In a democratic society, the executive branch and parliament are expected to act based on monitoring and independent review findings.'[49] Indeed, these ideas about democratic governance, such as independent review of those in authority, can be traced beyond the Enlightenment to Ancient Greece and Rome.[50] So it may be an overstatement to credit international human rights with the *idea* of accountability as monitoring, review and remedial action, but there is evidence, as we have seen, that international human rights law and practice helped to shape the COIA's approach and was also one of the vehicles by which this notion of accountability was introduced to, and then adopted by, the COIA. International human rights may not have conceived the COIA's understanding of accountability, but they were the midwife that delivered this idea into the world of global women's and children's health.

Criticisms and impact

There have been some voices critical of the accountability arrangements established for the *Global Strategy* of 2010. Godwin and Misra, for example, have a number of criticisms, such as the 'very weak' governance structures of iERG.[51] They also argue that '[m]uch of the iERG's focus ... has been on independent assessment of the *tracking* element, rather than on holding to account as defined by the CoIA'[52] (emphasis in original). However, their critique does not extend to the COIA's conceptualisation of accountability (but rather its implementation), on the contrary their definition of accountability 'reflects the [Commission's] "framework" of "monitor, review and action"'.[53] In their discussion of remedies within a human rights-based approach to health, Alicia Yamin and Rebecca Cantor regret that the CoIA framework ... does not call for judicial remedies.[54] Their criticism appears to be of the COIA's definition of remedial action, rather than its understanding of accountability as monitoring, review and remedial action. In short, Godwin and Misra, and Yamin and Cantor, do not reject the COIA's tripartite conceptualisation of accountability, but signal how it can be improved.

The COIA's report has had a significant impact on the global accountability architecture for women's and children's health. In 2015, Julian Schweitzer wrote that the COIA 'definition of accountability – a cyclical process of monitoring, review, and action that emphasizes human rights principles of equality, non-discrimination, transparency and participation – is now widely accepted in global health'.[55] As we have seen, in accordance with one of the report's recommendations, the Secretary-General established iERG with responsibility to hold accountable 'all stakeholders' (not only states) for their commitments arising from his *Global Strategy*.[56] Also, the Secretary-General's *Global Strategy for Women's, Children's and Adolescents' Health (2015–2030)* explicitly builds upon the COIA's conception of accountability and sets out the IAP which has various responsibilities, such as 'review [ing] ... all commitments to the Global Strategy (including policy, financial and non-financial commitments) and their implementation by multi-stakeholder commitment makers'.[57] Notably, like its predecessor, IAP is required to hold accountable both state and non-state stakeholders. In its first report, the IAP affirms, uses and deepens the COIA's tripartite conception of accountability, in particular, it develops the component on remedial action.[58]

In summary, the COIA report, as well as experience gained from its implementation, confirms that accountability consists of monitoring, review and remedial action; data make a crucial contribution to monitoring; review includes 'analyzing ... whether pledges, promises and commitments have been kept by countries, donors and non-state actors'; review should include (but not be confined to) some form of formal independent review; the reports emerging from such review must feed into one or more suitable political bodies or processes; and international human rights helped to shape the COIA approach to accountability. Some of these points will enable us to determine whether or not the global follow-up and review arrangements for SDG3 are consistent with the COIA's human rights-shaped conceptualisation of accountability.

Follow-up and review of the SDGs

Our Introduction has already provided an overview of the follow-up and review arrangements for the SDGs. However, before we can effectively assess them in relation to the COIA's human rights-shaped conceptualisation of accountability, we need to provide some more detail. The foundations of the follow-up and review arrangements are laid in *Transforming our World* and developed in a recent General Assembly resolution (70/ 299).[59] There are arrangements at three levels: national, regional and global. In this section, we continue to focus on the global.

A High-Level Political Forum, under the auspices of the General Assembly and Economic and Social Council, has the central role of overseeing a network of follow-up and review arrangements. Meeting for eight days each year, the Forum receives 'State-led' voluntary national reviews; an annual progress report on the SDGs prepared by the

Secretary-General 'on the basis of the global indicator framework, data produced by national statistical systems and information collected at the regional level'; a quadrennial Global Sustainable Development Report; and many other reports and submissions, including from civil society.[60] The concept for the Global Sustainable Development Report is instructive: prepared every four years by 'an independent group of scientists', the report will be 'scientific and analytical, focused on the science-policy interface'.[61] Additionally, a 'myriad' other UN bodies and forums review progress in specific areas addressed by the SDGs, including the World Health Assembly and UN Human Rights Council.[62]

Is the follow-up and review for SDG3 consistent with COIA's conceptualisation of accountability?

As already observed, Schweitzer finds that the COIA's understanding of accountability is 'widely accepted in global health'[63] and so it is pertinent to ask whether or not the follow-up and review arrangements for SDG3 are consistent with the COIA's understanding of accountability. One would think that what was good for MDGs 4 and 5 (between 2011 and 2015) is also good for SDG3 (post-2015).

Given space constraints, we put aside the component of remedial action. In the following paragraphs of this section, we will focus our remarks on the review component of the COIA's understanding of accountability, while the remainder of this article critiques the adequacy of data in the monitoring component.

The follow-up and review arrangements established under *Transforming Our World* and subsequent documents, such as General Assembly resolution 70/299, do not establish a formal independent review reporting to a political body or process. The voluntary country reviews are important, but they are not independent, they are 'State-led'. The Global Sustainable Development Report is independent but it is not responsible for 'analyzing … whether pledges, promises and commitments have been kept by countries, donors and non-state actors' as called for in the COIA accountability framework (i.e. second limb review). Neither is this the function of the Secretary-General's annual progress reports. Civil society commentaries are invaluable, but they are not formal independent reviews with an established mandate. UN human rights treaty-bodies, special rapporteurs and similar mechanisms (for example, within the ILO) have an important role to play, however they are not part of the follow-up and review architecture established under *Transforming Our World*.

The IAP has the features of formal independent review anticipated by the COIA. However, its mandate is confined to women's and children's health which, although crucial, is only part of SDG3. It is too early to assess whether or not the IAP is discharging, in practice, its responsibilities for second limb review.

Confining ourselves to the review component of accountability, we are now in a position to answer the question posed at the beginning of this section: are the global follow-up and review arrangements for SDG3 consistent with the Commission's conceptualisation of accountability? Our answer is 'no', except in relation to women's, children's and adolescents' health, as set out in the *Global Strategy for Women's, Children's and Adolescents' Health (2015–2030)* and in light of the IAP's responsibility to provide independent review.

How could global accountability for SDG3 be improved? In 2016, the Secretary-General and President of the World Bank convened a High Level Panel on Water, consisting of 11 sitting Heads of State and Government, which focuses on SDG6.[64] We suggest that a High

Level Panel on Health is convened which focuses on SDG3, in the context of other health-related SDGs. The Health Panel's reports would be considered by the HLPF, World Health Assembly and similar bodies. We also suggest that a formal independent review body is established to report to, and deepen the deliberations of, the Health Panel. This review body should also report to other forums, such as the World Health Assembly and Human Rights Council. As already discussed, it is important that formal independent review bodies report to one or more political bodies or processes, such as the High Level Panel on Health. The review body would probably be along the lines of IAP and, to avoid overlap, a suitable accommodation between the two bodies would be needed. Perhaps a revised IAP could be given review responsibilities, not only of women's, children's and adolescents' health, but SDG3 in its entirety. In any event, a High Level Panel on Health, supported by a formal independent review body, would help to bring the follow-up and review arrangements for SDG3, and other health-related SDGs, into conformity with the COIA's conceptualisation of accountability.

Now we turn to the monitoring component of the COIA's understanding of accountability. We examine the indicators identified by the UN for monitoring SDG3 and ask if they comply with the requirements of the right to health.

A right to health lens on SDG3 monitoring

There are health implications arising from each of the SDGs but SDG3 is the main health goal. It has 13 targets, and a total of 26 indicators (see Table 1, and Audrey Chapman's article in this issue).

The Special Rapporteur on the right to the highest attainable standard of mental and physical health, Dainius Puras, identifies key alignments between the right to health and various SDG targets. Importantly however, Puras notes that the *2030 Agenda* does not explicitly state that health is a human right.[65] While conceding that SDG3.8 (*Achieve universal health coverage, including financial risk protection, access to quality essential health-care services and access to safe, effective, quality and affordable essential medicines and vaccines for all*) has been regarded as a practical expression of the right to health, Puras cautions that not all paths to universal health coverage are consistent with human rights requirements.[66] He refers to targets 3.7 (*By 2030, ensure universal access to sexual and reproductive health-care services*) and 3.8, which do not confer priority to the poor and marginalised in the process of expanding health coverage. This, he suggests, can give rise to health strategies that prioritise improving access to health care for already privileged groups especially those employed in the formal sector who are more likely to benefit from work related insurance schemes. He writes: 'Likewise, countries with centralized and expansive health coverage might soon proclaim achievement of universal health coverage, even while some of their most vulnerable subgroups are left with health care that is abusive, coercive and/or of poor quality.'[67]

Drawing on a right-to-health lens which is based on General Comment 14[68] and developed by Hunt et al.,[69] we assess whether the SDG indicators for health capture the key elements of the right to health, such as AAAQ (availability, accessibility, acceptability, quality of health services); participation; progressive realisation and maximum available resources; non-discrimination, equality and vulnerability; international assistance and cooperation; laws; and accountability (see Box 1). We focus on indicators, not the

Table 1. Applying a right to health lens to SDG3 indicators.

Target	Indicator	Disaggregators	What right to health elements are measured by the SDG indicators
Goal 3. Ensure healthy lives and promote well-being for all at all ages[a]			
3.1 By 2030, reduce the global maternal mortality ratio to less than 70 per 100,000 live births	3.1.1 Maternal mortality ratio	Age, place of residence	Progressive realisation, Non-discrimination (on basis of age and location only)
	3.1.2 Proportion of births attended by skilled health personnel	Age, parity, place of residence, socioeconomic status, and type of provider	Progressive realisation, Availability, Accessibility, Non-discrimination[b]
3.2 By 2030, end preventable deaths of newborns and children under 5 years of age, with all countries aiming to reduce neonatal mortality to at least as low as 12 per 1,000 live births and under-5 mortality to at least as low as 25 per 1,000 live births	3.2.1 Under-five mortality rate	Place of residence, sex, socioeconomic status *Also: by cause, including pneumonia, diarrhoea, and malaria*	Progressive realisation, Availability, Accessibility, Non-discrimination
	3.2.2 Neonatal mortality rate	Age in days/weeks, birth weight, place of residence, sex, socioeconomic status	Progressive realisation, Availability, Accessibility, Non-discrimination
3.3 By 2030, end the epidemics of AIDS, tuberculosis, malaria and neglected tropical diseases and combat hepatitis, water-borne diseases and other communicable diseases	3.3.1 Number of new HIV infections per 1,000 uninfected population, by sex, age and key populations	General population, Key populations (men who have sex with men, sex workers, people who inject drugs, transgender people, prisoners), Age groups (0–14, 15–24, 15–49, 50+ years), for key populations < 25, 25+ years), mode of transmission (including mother-to-child transmission), place of residence, sex	Progressive realisation, Availability, Accessibility, Non-discrimination
	3.3.2 Tuberculosis incidence per 1,000 population	Age, HIV status, sex	Progressive realisation, Availability, Accessibility, Non-discrimination
	3.3.3 Malaria incidence per 1,000 population	Age, sex, place of residence, season (year and month)	Progressive realisation, Availability, Accessibility, Non-discrimination
	3.3.4 Hepatitis B incidence per 100,000 population	Place of residence, exposure to the birth dose hepatitis B vaccine (official records), exposure to three doses of hepatitis B vaccine	Progressive realisation, Availability, Accessibility, Non-discrimination
	3.3.5 Number of people requiring interventions against neglected tropical diseases	Disaggregation by disease; age; sex and urban/rural is optional	Progressive realisation, Availability, Accessibility
3.4 By 2030, reduce by one third premature mortality from non-communicable diseases	3.4.1 Mortality rate attributed to cardiovascular disease, cancer, diabetes or chronic respiratory disease	Place of residence, sex	Progressive realisation, Availability, Accessibility

(*Continued*)

Table 1. Continued.

Goal 3. Ensure healthy lives and promote well-being for all at all ages[a]			
Target	Indicator	Disaggregators	What right to health elements are measured by the SDG indicators
through prevention and treatment and promote mental health and well-being	3.4.2 Suicide mortality rate	Place of residence, sex, age	Progressive realisation, Availability, Accessibility
3.5 Strengthen the prevention and treatment of substance abuse, including narcotic drug abuse and harmful use of alcohol	3.5.1 Coverage of treatment interventions (pharmacological, psychosocial and rehabilitation and aftercare services) for substance use disorders	The current reporting of ARQ allows for disaggregation by the settings, type of intervention and for the population groups. The indicators can be further modified to include disaggregation by gender and specific age groups.	Progressive realisation, Availability, Accessibility, Non-discrimination[b]
	3.5.2 Harmful use of alcohol, defined according to the national context as alcohol per capita consumption (aged 15 years and older) within a calendar year in litres of pure alcohol	Sex, age	Progressive realisation
3.6 By 2020, halve the number of global deaths and injuries from road traffic accidents	3.6.1 Death rate due to road traffic injuries	Age, per motor vehicle (fatalities per 10 000 motor vehicles), sex, socioeconomic status	Progressive realisation
3.7 By 2030, ensure universal access to sexual and reproductive health care services, including for family planning, information and education, and the integration of reproductive health into national strategies and programmes	3.7.1 Proportion of women of reproductive age (aged 15–49 years) who have their need for family planning satisfied with modern methods	Age, marital status, place of residence, socioeconomic status – This indicator may be disaggregated by geographical area, age, education, rural or urban residence, poverty status and other characteristics that are relevant in the national context. Such analysis can identify population sub-groups where levels of unmet need are highest to help guide programmes aimed at improving access to family planning and other reproductive health services.	Progressive realisation, Availability, Accessibility, Non-discrimination
	3.7.2 Adolescent birth rate (aged 10–14 years; aged 15–19 years) per 1,000 women in that age group	Marital status (when possible, also capture girls <15 years), place of residence, socioeconomic status	Progressive realisation, Availability, Accessibility, Non-discrimination
3.8 Achieve universal health coverage, including financial risk protection, access to quality essential health care services and access to safe, effective, quality and affordable essential medicines and vaccines for all	3.8.1 Coverage of essential health services (defined as the average coverage of essential services based on tracer interventions that include reproductive, maternal, newborn and child health, infectious diseases, non-communicable diseases and service capacity and access, among the general and the most disadvantaged population)	By equity stratifier: sex, age, socioeconomic position, geographic; by type of indicator (child full immunisation, ARV therapy, TB treatment, hypertension treatment, skilled birth attendance, etc.);	Progressive realisation, Availability, Accessibility, Non-discrimination
	3.8.2 Proportion of population with large household expenditures on heath as a share of total household expenditure or income		Progressive realisation, Availability, Accessibility, Non-discrimination

(Continued)

Table 1. Continued.

Goal 3. Ensure healthy lives and promote well-being for all at all ages[a]

Target	Indicator	Disaggregators	What right to health elements are measured by the SDG indicators
3.9 By 2030, substantially reduce the number of deaths and illnesses from hazardous chemicals and air, water and soil pollution and contamination	3.9.1 Mortality rate attributed to household and ambient air pollution		Progressive realisation
	3.9.2 Mortality rate attributed to unsafe water, unsafe sanitation and lack of hygiene (exposure to unsafe Water, Sanitation and Hygiene for All (WASH) services)		Progressive realisation, Availability, Accessibility, Quality, Non-discrimination
	3.9.3 Mortality rate attributed to unintentional poisoning		Progressive realisation
3.a Strengthen the implementation of the World Health Organisation Framework Convention on Tobacco Control in all countries, as appropriate	3.a.1 Age-standardised prevalence of current tobacco use among persons aged 15 years and older	Age, sex, other relevant sociodemographic stratifiers where available	Progressive realisation
3.b Support the research and development of vaccines and medicines for the communicable and non-communicable diseases that primarily affect developing countries, provide access to affordable essential medicines and vaccines, in accordance with the Doha Declaration on the TRIPS Agreement and Public Health, which affirms the right of developing countries to use to the full the provisions in the Agreement on Trade-Related Aspects of Intellectual Property Rights regarding flexibilities to protect public health, and, in particular, provide access to medicines for all	3.b.1 Proportion of the population with access to affordable medicines and vaccines on a sustainable basis	Facility type, facility managing authority (public/private), specific type of medicine/commodity (e.g. priority medicines for women and children, vaccines, ART, family planning, essential NCD medicines)	Progressive realisation, Availability, Accessibility, Non-discrimination
	3.b.2 Total net official development assistance to medical research and basic health sectors	For provider and recipient country; by type of finance, and by type of resources provided. Some data are also available on the policy objectives targeted by individual projects	IAC[c]
3.c Substantially increase health financing and the recruitment, development, training and retention of the health workforce in developing countries, especially in least developed countries and small island developing States	3.c.1 Health worker density and distribution	Cadre, place of employment – rural/urban	Availability
3.d Strengthen the capacity of all countries, in particular developing countries, for early warning, risk reduction and management of national and global health risks	3.d.1 International Health Regulations (IHR) capacity and health emergency preparedness		

Key
[a]Source: UN Statistics, http://unstats.un.org/sdgs/files/metadata-compilation/Metadata-Goal-3.pdf (accessed November 29, 2016).
[b]Non-discrimination, equality, vulnerability.
[c]International assistance and cooperation.

105

targets, because the indicators are the fundamental measure for which data are collected as part of the process of SDG follow-up and review.

Box 1.   Right to health analytical lens as applied to SDG3 indicators. (See note 69)

1. Relevant national and international human rights laws, norms and standards
2. States are obliged to progressively realise the right over time and subject to their maximum available resources
3. All health services, goods and facilities shall be available, accessible, acceptable and of good quality ('AAAQ')
4. Health services and underlying determinants must be non-discriminatory, promote equality and protect the marginalised and vulnerable
5. The right to health requires that there is an opportunity for the active and informed participation of individuals and communities in decision-making that affects their health
6. Low- and middle-income States have a responsibility to seek international assistance and cooperation, while high-income States have responsibilities towards the realisation of the right to health in developing countries
7. Transparent, accessible and effective accountability mechanisms, consisting of monitoring, review (including independent review) and remedial action.

Our analysis seeks to explore whether SDG3 indicators capture that people's health rights entitlements are being respected, protected and fulfilled. We do not expect any single indicator to capture every element of the right to health; rather, once all the indicators are examined, it is important that all elements have been assessed at least once. If there is an aspect of the right to health that remains unaddressed by the SDG indicators, it will require careful alternative monitoring and review to ensure that breaches of this human right are not occurring. Although it is arguably unrealistic that SDG3 should *fulfil* every right to health entitlement, it is important that monitoring and review show that rights are being respected, protected and not violated. For monitoring and review to satisfy human rights accountability, they must detect breaches – for example, if more women experience childbirth with a skilled attendant, in accordance with SDG indicator 3.1.2, but the attendant does not treat women with respect, or does not provide quality care, then this is not human rights progress despite the indicator improving.

Right-to-health view of SDG3 indicators

In this section we present the key findings of our right-to-health assessment of the SDG3 indicators. We examined each SDG3 indicator with a view to assessing which elements of the right to health are captured (Table 1). The disaggregates are those included in the UN Stats metadata tables, as recommended by WHO to UN Statistics.[70]

Target 3.1 commits States to *By 2030, reduce the global maternal mortality ratio to less than 70 per 100,000 live births*. Its associated indicators include 3.1.1 *maternal mortality ratio*, and 3.1.2 *proportion of births attended by a skilled health professional*. Maternal mortality ratio is disaggregated by age and place of residence, and births attended by a skilled health professional by age, parity, place of residence, socioeconomic status and type of provider.

Applying our right-to-health lens, we suggest providing data to satisfy any of these indicators enables assessment of progressive realisation of the right to health because they are reported either annually, biennially or every five years, enabling progress to be tracked. So these indicators, and most others, are scored as having the potential to measure progressive realisation.

The maternal mortality indicator 3.1.1 does not seek disaggregated data about where women gave birth, that is, in a health facility or elsewhere. In the absence of this disaggregated information, the indicator is unable to provide information about whether health services were available, accessible, acceptable and of good quality to all women, or whether services were provided on a non-discriminatory basis, and therefore available to the poorest women and those most likely to die in childbirth. As the indicator seeks disaggregated data based on age and place of residence, it is possible to hold states to account over obligations not to discriminate against those two criteria only.

Indicator 3.1.2 – the percentage of births attended by skilled health professionals – includes WHO's advice on disaggregators by age, parity, place of residence, socioeconomic status and type of provider. This enables human rights assessments to be made about the availability of skilled health professionals, access to them, and whether there is discrimination against women on the basis of age, location, poverty and number of children they have. As the type of provider is also sought, this provides additional information about distribution of the health workforce, but it falls short of being a measure of quality of care.

Other key elements of the right to health assessment addressed by various indicators include:

3.3.1 *Number of new HIV infections per 1,000 uninfected population, by sex, age and key populations.* The disaggregated data required includes key populations, age, residence, and mother-to-child transmission, which enables monitoring of discrimination against vulnerable and marginalised populations. It is marked as a non-discrimination indicator in Table 1.

3.3.3. *Malaria incidence per 1,000 population.* A decrease in malaria incidence could show increased access to health information (how to prevent malaria), and in Table 1 it is therefore marked as an accessibility indicator.

Only one indicator was judged as providing any information about quality: 3.9.2 *Mortality rate attributed to unsafe water, unsafe sanitation and lack of hygiene* – thus this measure of quality is for an underlying determinant of health, not a health care service or facility.

3.b.2 *Total net official development assistance to medical research and basic health sectors* provides some of the information needed to monitor international assistance and cooperation.

3.d.1 *International Health Regulations (IHR) capacity and health emergency preparedness* is the only attempt in the SDG indicators to capture a state's legal commitment towards honouring its international health obligations.

Overall, we conclude that *if data are provided to populate all these indicators*, and disaggregated as suggested by WHO to UN Statistics,[71] inferences could be made about the progressive realisation of the right to health, the availability and accessibility of health services, including in an equal and non-discriminatory way to vulnerable people, and the quality of some underlying determinants of health (not health care). There may also be some indication of international assistance and cooperation obligations being met, although that indicator requires greater clarity. There is no indicator that monitors compliance with legal obligations arising from the right to health.

The SDG3 indicators are therefore capturing only a partial measure of the impact that SDG3 may have on people's right to health entitlements and duty-bearers' corresponding obligations. The indicators are not therefore providing all the information necessary to show that people's health rights entitlements are being respected and protected. This is discussed further in the next section.

Identification of missing indicators

There are some elements of the right to health analysis that are not addressed at all by the SDG indicators. These include whether the right to health is legally acknowledged and whether people find the health services they receive to be culturally acceptable, and of good quality. There is no indicator which captures the human rights meaning of participation and empowerment of people to engage with the health system, and nor do the indicators reflect understandings of human rights obligations as legal obligations.

Well functioning and inclusive health systems are the core institutions through which the right to health can be fulfilled.[72] As the Special Rapporteur states in his SDG report, without focused investment in health system strengthening, there is little prospect of much progress on the health-related SDGs, including addressing the growing burden of non-communicable diseases, universal health coverage, and other targets.[73] Target 3.c *Substantially increase health financing and the recruitment, development, training and retention of the health workforce in developing countries, especially in least developed countries and small island developing States* has an indicator that measures only the density and distribution of health workers, not health financing. WHO has advised that health financing should be at least 5% of GDP and 15% of the total government budget, so that the health system can be strengthened to expand coverage to all and provide a publicly funded package of priority health services based on people's needs.[74] It would also appear an oversight not to have an indicator to measure this target to increase health financing, and one that is critical to achieve other SDG3 targets. Such an indicator is necessary for human rights monitoring and review and therefore accountability.

We conclude this section by emphasising that even if data were available to populate all the SDG indicators, we would not have a complete picture as to whether people's right to health were being respected, protected and fulfilled. At a minimum, the missing information relates to the acceptability and quality of care, the financing and overall functionality of the health system, the active participation of most vulnerable people and the legal foundations of the right to health. Without this information, effective monitoring and review (and therefore accountability) in relation to the right to health is impossible.

Data for adopted and proposed indicators

In this section we return to the agreed and adopted indicators and ask whether low- and middle-income countries have the data needed to report their SDG progress. We focus mainly on the proposed indicators for target 3.8 (universal health coverage) as the practical expression of the right to health. The relevant indicators are:

- 3.8.1 Coverage of essential health services (defined as the average coverage of essential services that include reproductive, maternal, newborn and child health, infectious diseases, non communicable diseases and service capacity and access, among the general and the most disadvantaged population)
- 3.8.2 Proportion of population with large household expenditures on health as a share of total household expenditure or income.

The suggested data sources for the 16 tracer (i.e. measurable/pre-selected) interventions to monitor Target 3.8.1 include household surveys, health facility surveys, administrative records and a combination of all these sources.[75] Data for Target 3.8.2 come from household surveys conducted by national statistical offices, e.g. budget surveys, income and expenditure surveys and living standards measurement surveys. WHO reports that 109 countries have conducted at least one of these surveys since 2000.[76] Since 2010, only 98 countries have undertaken surveys to monitor family planning coverage, and 121 for antenatal and delivery care.[77] The report states comparable 'estimates' for these indicators are available from other sources in 184 and 194 countries.[78] But caution is required about comparable estimates being made in countries that do not have well functioning health information systems, as estimates may be little more than guesses with little transparency on how they are calculated. WHO acknowledges that many of the indicators are not collected, or routinely and reliably collected, in many of the low- and middle-income countries.[79]

Analyses of indicator data availability suggest that few countries have all the data required, and most low- and middle-income countries are missing vast amounts of it. When the Sustainable Development Solutions Network (SDSN) first proposed SDG indicators in a report for the UN Secretary General they acknowledged the indicators would take time to achieve, but stated 'by 2018 at the latest, we hope the international system, notably the UN organizations and partner institutions (OECD, World Bank, WTO, and others) will have in place an accurate and effective annual monitoring system'.[80]

The optimism appears misplaced when recent reports of data availability are considered. For example, research by the Centre for Global Development found only 25% of the 230 SDG indicators could be found online in a publicly accessible format.[81] Their analysis of the data needed to inform specific SDG3 indictors reveals a deep deficiency in data, across all countries. Although annual monitoring is expected for the SDGs, very few of the health data sets are collected annually in all countries. Neonatal mortality (SDG 3.2.2) is an exception where over 99% of countries have provided data to the World Bank more than 15 times in the past 15 years.[82] The quality of this data – e.g. whether it covers remote areas or undocumented people – is not known. Other indicators fare much worse: 3.7.1, the proportion of women of reproductive age who have their need for family planning satisfied with modern methods, has been surveyed on average only 1.56 times in the past 15 years by only 37.82% of countries.[83]

Not only are data collected infrequently, little is known about the quality of what is gathered, and what precisely is measured. For example, there is variation between countries as to what constitutes a 'skilled health personnel' in the context of childbirth, from fully qualified midwives to traditional birth attendants with perhaps only weeks of informal training. WHO has defined a skilled birth attendant as an

> accredited health professional such as a midwife, doctor or nurse that is trained to proficiency and has the necessary skills to manage a normal pregnancy, childbirth and provide postnatal care as well as the skills to detect, manage and refer any complications in the mother and neonate.[84]

But the household surveys from which this information is collected do not seek that level of information from their informants, and in all likelihood, their informants would not know the qualifications and skill sets of people attending them.

National Statistics Offices in low- and middle-income countries, like many other national institutions in these settings, lack strong systems, a situation frequently referred to in reports on data for the SDGs. The SDSN explored data availability, giving each indicator a preliminary assessment, as has WHO in its World Statistics Report – both identifying significant data gaps.[85] The IAEG-SDGs has categorised 97 indicators as Tier I, meaning these are the only indicators of the 230 adopted that have regularly produced data.[86] Even then, many of the poorest countries are not regularly or reliably collecting this data.

The SDSN report estimated the global cost of improving data information systems to enable annual reporting at $1 billion annually, of which 'at least $100–200 m will be required in incremental ODA [official development assistance]'.[87]

The IAP refers to data gaps in monitoring indicators and urges a concerted effort from the international community and national governments to address them. Reiterating the need for independent accountability, the IAP identifies the need to strengthen the capacities of independent national bodies producing and analysing data, and of civil society to engender the political will so that data is used to promote the right to health through more efficient approaches and equitable policy options. 'We insist on prioritizing building national capacities and strengthening civil society. National capacity is essential for generating the data that is the raw material of accountability at national, regional and global levels.'[88]

There is therefore a need not just for additional indicators to capture the human rights dimensions of SDG3, but also for much support to low- and middle-income countries to gather data for the already agreed indicators. This support is needed to gather the data to hold duty-bearers to account for their domestic and international obligations regarding right to health informed SDGs. Reaching the necessary level of systems development and human resource capacity within national statistics offices will take many years and significant funding support, especially through the human rights requirement of international assistance and cooperation.

Can Big Data plug data gaps and improve right-to-health accountability?

In the absence of reliable, regular, and timely national data from many countries, it has been proposed that Big Data might be explored to fill data gaps. Big Data in this context is not referring to just large administrative data sets from government agencies, but rather, to 'an ecosystem created by the concomitant emergence of "the 3 Cs [Digital Crumbs, Big Data Capacities, Big Data Communities] of Big Data"'[89] (see Box 2).

Box 2. Data Pop Alliance definition of Big Data.*

'Big Data' (capitalised) is this document (and others) refers to the ecosystem created by the concomitant emergence of 'the 3 Cs of Big Data':

The 1st C stands for digital bread **Crumbs** – these pieces of data passively emitted and collected as by-products of people's interactions with and uses of digital devices that provide unique insights about their behaviours and beliefs;

The 2nd C stands of **Big Data Capacities** – what has also been referred to Big Data Analytics, that is the set of tools and methods, hardware and software, know-how and skills, necessary to process and analyse these new kinds of data – including visualisation techniques, statistical machine learning and algorithms etc.;

The 3rd C stands for **Big Data Communities**, which describe the various actors involved in the Big Data ecosystem, from the generators of data to their analysts and end-users – i.e. potentially the whole population.

*Source: 'Opportunities and Requirements for Leveraging Big Data for Official Statistics and the Sustainable Development Goals in Latin America', Data-Pop Alliance (Harvard Humanitarian Initiative, MIT Media Lab and Overseas Development Institute, May 2016).

The Independent Expert Advisory Group on a Data Revolution for Sustainable Development defines Big Data and the data revolution as an explosion in the volume of data, the speed with which data are produced, the number of producers of data, the dissemination of data, coming from new technologies such as mobile phones and the Internet of Things, and from other sources.[90]

It is suggested by some Big Data enthusiasts that Big Data can contribute to SDG monitoring (see Box 3) and that the fusion of new data with traditional data can create more timely and detailed information, useful for improved accountability and transparency.[91] These new data sources, proponents claim, have the potential to produce more relevant and more timely statistics than traditional sources, as 'analyses of comments, search queries, or online posts can produce nearly the same results for statistical inference – more quickly and at lower cost – as household surveys and polls'.[92]

Box 3. Proposed use of Big Data for SDG3 monitoring.*

DataPop Alliance	Big Data examples	What is monitored	How is monitored	Countries	Year	Advantages of using big data
Ensure healthy lives and promote well-being for all at all ages	Internet-based data to identify influenza breakouts	Influenza	Google search queries	US	2009	Real time data, captures disease cases not officially recorded; data available earlier than official data
	Data from online searches to monitor influenza epidemics	Influenza	Online searches data	China	2013	
	Detecting influenza epidemics using Twitter	Influenza	Twitter	Japan	2011	
	Cell-phone data to model malaria spread	Malaria	Cell phone data	Kenya	2012	
	Using social and news media to monitor cholera outbreaks	Cholera	Social and news media	Argentina, Bolivia, Brazil, India, Indonesia Mexico, Philippines, Singapore, Thailand Venezuela	Ongoing	
	Monitoring vaccine concerns to help tailor immunisation programmes	Vaccine concerns	Media reports (e.g. online articles, blogs, govt reports)	144 countries	2013	Data not available otherwise; expensive to collect data through survey
	Monitoring vaccine concerns	Vaccine concerns	Twitter	US	2011	
	Analysis of Twitter used to track HIV incidence and drug-related behaviours	HIV, drugs use	Twitter	US	2014	

*Source: 'Opportunities and Requirements for Leveraging Big Data for Official Statistics and the Sustainable Development Goals in Latin America', Data-Pop Alliance (Harvard Humanitarian Initiative, MIT Media Lab and Overseas Development Institute, May 2016).

Big Data, including administrative data systems, and information technology have enormous potential to promote human rights accountability as it relates to the SDGs and to SDG3. In nearly every aspect of the right-to-health lens used in the analysis of SDG3 indicators in this paper, these forms of technology could make a contribution. Use of GPS and mobile technology can, for example, assist with improving the availability and access of health services through accurate mapping of health services and improved supply chains of medicines.[93] Through the integration of large administration data sets it is possible to understand who is, and is not, accessing the health system, and to disaggregate the characteristics of people who use health care well, as opposed to those who are unable to use it at all; these characteristics might be different education levels, income levels, car ownership, distance between home and health centres and so on.[94] Such information can be used to guide policy, and inform accountability, about making health services more accessible.[95] Similarly, the Internet of Medical Things (collection of medical devices and applications that connect to healthcare IT systems through online computer networks), and simpler technology using mobile phones, can seek direct or indirect feedback from people who have used or are using health services as to whether the service was culturally acceptable, of good quality, and can encourage people to participate more in their health system.[96]

These uses of Big Data and technology require the second and third 'Cs' (see Box 2): the data analytics *capacity* to interrogate and interpret the data, and the *community* – the people from whom data is gathered, as well as the end users. This comprehensive Big Data environment is presently only in existence in high-income countries where there is extensive and comprehensive use of digital facilities by the public, sophisticated electronic information systems used by government agencies, and a highly skilled and educated population available to manipulate and analyse data generated electronically. Low-income countries, and many middle-income countries, as we explore below, lack most, if not all, of these components. High-income countries already have national statistics offices that can generate the large data sets of disaggregated information from which monitoring of the SDGs and reporting against agreed indicators is a fairly routine technocratic exercise. So Big Data is not needed in such settings for SDG monitoring purposes. However, Big Data's uses as outlined above may well start to provide richer information which can better inform accountability for the right to health, in so far as it can provide additional information about, for example, quality of care, acceptability of care, participation in the health system.

In later paragraphs we explore the claim that Big Data can help fill data gaps in thematic areas and monitor goals where data are scarce.[97]

Low- and middle-income country digital realities

The President of the World Bank, Jim Yong Kim, has spoken of the gross inequalities in the digital world: 'While people around the world make more than 4 billion Google searches every day, 4 billion people still lack access to the internet.'[98] In this section we are using access to the internet as a proxy for Big Data coverage, as the internet is so fundamental to the first 'C' [digital crumbs] in the definition of Big Data (Box 2). While components of Big Data can be sourced through non-internet-based facilities, including mobile phones that are not connected to the internet, the proposed Big Data uses for

SDG monitoring as outlined in Box 3, depend on internet access (e.g. online searches, social media, online news sources).

Returning to the examples of Big Data's contribution to SDG monitoring in Box 3, it includes lower-middle income countries Kenya, Bolivia and the Philippines, where social media and online searches have been used to monitor cholera and malaria outbreaks, and influenza epidemics in China.[99] But the percentage of the population in each of these four countries with internet access is: Kenya 45%, Bolivia 41.1%, Philippines 43.5% and China 52.2%.[100] This raises questions as to whose ill health is being captured in the reports, and whether disease outbreaks and epidemics in areas where people do not have internet access are reported and responded to.

There are 49 countries in the world where less than 20% of the population has internet access, and 24 countries where only 10% has access (Box 4). These countries with so little digital connectedness are almost all low-income countries, and, as an indication of the weakness of their health systems, they all have high maternal mortality ratios (Box 4).

Box 4. Internet access and health indicators in 24 countries.

	Country	Percentage of population with internet access[a]	Maternal Mortality – deaths /100,000 live births[b]
1	Eritrea	1.1	501
2	Timor Leste	1.2	215
3	Burundi	1.5	712
4	Somalia	1.7	850
5	Guinea	1.8	679
6	Niger	2.1	553
7	Sierra Leone	2.4	1360
8	Myanmar	2.5	178
9	Chad	2.7	856
10	Guinea-Bissau	3.5	549
11	DR Congo	3.9	442
12	Ethiopia	4.2	353
13	Madagascar	4.3	353
14	Central African Republic	4.5	882
15	Tanzania	5.3	398
16	Benin	5.6	405
17	Mozambique	6.4	489
18	Malawi	6.5	634
19	Afghanistan	6.8	396
20	Togo	7.3	368
21	Comoros	7.3	335
22	Congo	7.5	442
23	Liberia	8.6	725
24	Solomon Islands	9.8	114

[a]Internet Live Stats, http://www.internetlivestats.com/internet-users-by-country/ (accessed December 14, 2016)
[b]World Health Organisation, 'World Health Statistics 2016: Monitoring Health for the Sdgs', WHO, http://www.who.int/gho/publications/world_health_statistics/2016/en/ (accessed November 29, 2016).

If the SDG health goals use Big Data as data sources this would give rise to concerns about who the data is reporting on. Such unequal distribution of access to the internet in low- and middle-income countries means that Big Data findings cannot meet critical human rights components, such as equality, non-discrimination and attention to vulnerability. The poorest people in these countries are not using the internet and are not captured by Big Data. They are unlikely to benefit from any direct health service response made to Big Data suggestions of disease outbreaks and epidemics, especially if the diseases reported are not the diseases prevalent in areas where poorer people live. Thus using Big Data in these situations, to identify, direct and prioritise health responses, is discriminating against the people 'off the grid', leaving them even more vulnerable if health resources are directed elsewhere. Rather than achieving the SDG objective of leaving no one behind, use of Big Data in these circumstances could increase inequalities, and fail to respect, protect or fulfil right-to-health entitlements.

There are other human rights risks associated with Big Data, which include privacy, informed consent, data ownership and its use.[101] These are undeniably matters of importance to human rights, requiring suitable safeguards, but they lie outside the scope of this paper and its consideration of Big Data within SDG monitoring.

When Big Data arises from only segments of the population, it is not possible that the information gathered through these technologies will be 'complementing traditional data sources and filling the gaps where they exist'.[102] The countries without high internet coverage are the same countries that are missing the traditional data generated by national statistics offices.

This gives rise to human rights issues relating to inequities between countries. The IAP calls on better resourced countries to support statistics offices in lower resourced countries to enable them to become more effective accountability and oversight institutions.[103] If there is greater momentum and associated funding to support the development, use and extension of Big Data to capture SDG goal attainment, those many countries who do not have Big Data capacity, and whose national statistics offices are underfunded and weak, will get left further behind. There is some evidence that such support for Big Data is occurring. The UN Statistics Inventory of Projects to support research into the use of Big Data and the SDGs includes low income countries.[104] In a project in Cameroon, the description states that it expects use of Big Data to be less costly than classic surveys, but the country needs to build capacities and skills in this new domain in statistics, and it notes the 'challenges seem to be huge in terms of coverage'.[105] Only 18% of the population in Cameroon has internet access.[106]

Any diversion of attention and resourcing away from strengthening national statistics offices so they can at least collect solid data from *all* the people in their countries will result in the most distant and disadvantaged people not being counted, and their health status and rights not being protected. This could have serious consequences on people's health and for their lives, leading to even greater inequalities within and between countries, and is counter to the primary objective of the SDGs, and fails to protect health rights.

Conclusion

Among the key challenges confronting both global governance for health and SDG3 is accountability. Our aim was to critique some of the *2030 Agenda*'s follow-up and review arrangements for SDG3. To assist in this analysis, we drew from the tripartite conceptualisation of accountability which is informed by human rights and was adopted by COIA in 2011.

Charged with enhancing accountability in relation to MDGs 4 and 5, the high-level COIA settled upon a human rights-shaped conceptualisation of accountability consisting of monitoring, review and remedial action. Review has two limbs and the second is especially noteworthy: it analyses 'whether pledges, promises and commitments have been kept by countries, donors and non-state actors'.[107] COIA – and others since – emphasised the importance of *independent* review and the Secretary-General duly established the iERG to provide formal independent review of commitments made by states and non-state actors in relation to MDGs 4 and 5. As the MDGs were replaced by SDGs, the iERG was replaced by the IAP which was established to hold accountable state and non-state stakeholders for their commitments in relation to women's, children's and adolescents' health in the context of the SDGs. Notably, the IAP's remit does not extend to SDG3 in its entirety. Since COIA's conceptualisation of accountability was applied to MDGs 4 and 5, and is now being applied to women's, children's and adolescents' health in the context of the SDGs, it seems most appropriate to use it to assess the existing follow-up and review arrangements for SDG3. Given space constraints, we confined our assessment to monitoring and review (not remedial action), and to global (not national or regional) follow-up and review arrangements for SDG3.

On applying the COIA's review component of accountability to the existing follow-up and review arrangements for SDG3, we demonstrated the inadequacy of the current global review of SDG3 and we recommended its improvement by establishing a formal independent review body, reporting to a High Level Panel on Health, as well as other political bodies and processes. This would be along the lines of the current IAP for women's, children's and adolescents' health which reports to the PMNCH Board, except that our recommended bodies would review all of SDG3, save for that already covered by IAP and PMNCH. Perhaps a revised IAP could be given the review responsibilities, not only of women's, children's and adolescents' health, but SDG3 in its entirety.

We then turned to the monitoring component of the Commission's understanding of accountability. According to the *2030 Agenda*, the SDGs are grounded in human rights. Agreed indicators and their associated data are the primary tools for monitoring the SDGs. We found that if data are available to report accurately on the indicators, then inferences could be made about progressive realisation, and the availability and accessibility of health services including delivery in an equal and non-discriminatory way to vulnerable people. However, the indicators are not designed to collect information to determine if people are, for example, actively participating in the health system, are receiving quality and culturally acceptable care, and if IAC obligations are being met fully. The indicators, therefore, offer only a limited assessment of whether states meet their right to health duties as they pertain to SDG3. This led us to suggest additional indicators are needed to capture right to health elements including ones for acceptable and quality health services, adequate funding, and legal underpinning of the right to health.

There is a dearth of statistical data, especially in low- and middle-income countries, to monitor SDGs. The national statistics offices in these settings require much financial assistance from wealthier nations to strengthen their capacity to monitor the SDGs.

Given the time and cost involved in strengthening national capacity to develop the traditional data collection methods, it has been suggested that Big Data could be used to provide missing data more effectively and at a lower cost. However, in our analysis of countries where there are poor health indicators, such as high maternal mortality, we found most people do not have internet access, and are not engaging in a world where their activities and health needs could be detected by Big Data. We do not see a significant role for Big Data in SDG human rights monitoring in such places because it cannot capture information about the people who need health services the most and whose human rights are not being realised. Furthermore, any investment into Big Data-based projects would not strengthen their poorly functioning national statistics offices which is what is most urgently required for SDG monitoring. Investing in Big Data initiatives in countries that do not yet have basic statistical functionality could increase inequalities between the people who are connected to the internet and the majority who are not. Those connected are likely to have their needs identified and responded to, while the poorer, disconnected people will remain invisible. Even if Big Data support included extending internet coverage and access, the poorest people in those countries will be unlikely to come 'on the grid' before 2030 – the end of the SDG era.

Statistics, and in some countries Big Data, have important roles to play in monitoring SDG3, and helping to hold governments to account for their right to health obligations. But in most low- and middle-income countries the greater need is to strengthen traditional, statistical methods of counting people and monitoring their health. There are in fact two SDG targets (17.18, 17.19), that are consistent with the human rights obligation of IAC, for wealthy countries to provide assistance to national statistics offices. This, we conclude, is a much greater imperative for high-income countries, than investing in Big Data initiatives in countries without strong statistical capacities and institutions.

Meanwhile, in the absence of internet access and any possible engagement with the promises of enhanced accountability through Big Data, and where survey and registration systems are still incomplete, the only way to reach the people who are not 'on the grid' is to walk to their homes and speak to them. Using these old-fashioned, qualitative, ethnographic and mixed methods of social science is necessary if we want to know if these men, women and children are receiving acceptable and quality health care, if they are participating in the health system and if they are able to take action and receive remedy when their rights are breached. We will not find these people amongst the 'data crumbs' that form the basis of Big Data.

This paper's analysis bears upon what Frenk and Moon, and Kickbusch and Szabo, identify as the global health accountability challenge. Formal independent review, effective statistical methods of counting people and monitoring their health, and mixed methods of social science all have a major role to play in improving the accountability of states and non-state actors in global health, as well as enhancing the realisation of human rights.

Notes

1. UN General Assembly, *Transforming Our World: The 2030 Agenda for Sustainable Development* (New York: UN, 2015).
2. Ibid.
3. United Nations, *Universal Declaration of Human Rights*, Article 1 (UN, 1948).
4. UNGA, *Transforming Our World*.
5. Olivier de Schutter et al., 'Commentary to the Maastricht Principles on Extraterritorial Obligations of States in the Area of Economic, Social and Cultural Rights', *Human Rights Quarterly* 34 (2012): 1084–169; Mark Gibney, *International Human Rights Law: Returning to Universal Values*, 2nd ed. (Lanham, MD: Rowman & Littlefield, 2016); Paul Hunt, Judith Mesquita and Rajat Khosla, 'The Human Rights Responsibility of International Assistance

and Cooperation in Health', in *Universal Human Rights and Extraterritorial Obligations*, ed. M. Gibney and S. Skogly. Pennsylvania Studies in Human Rights (Philadelphia: University of Pennsylvania Press, 2010).

6. UNGA, *Transforming Our World*.
7. For a discussion on human rights mainstreaming, see Paul Hunt, 'Configuring the UN Human Rights System in the "Era of Implementation": Mainland and Archipelago', *Human Rights Quarterly* (forthcoming).
8. Committee on Economic Social and Cultural Rights (CESCR), 'General Comment 14: The Right to the Highest Attainable Standard of Health:', 2000, para 33. UN Doc. E/C.12/2000/4.
9. Ibid.
10. UNGA, *Transforming Our World*, para 73.
11. UN Economic and Social Council, *Report of the Inter-Agency and Expert Group on Sustainable Development Goal Indicators* (New York, 2016). UN Doc E/CN.3/2016/2, https://unstats.un.org/unsd/statcom/47th-session/documents/2016-2-IAEG-SDGs-E.pdf (accessed July 14, 2017).
12. Sakiko Fukuda-Parr, Alicia Ely Yamin and Joshua Greenstein, 'The Power of Numbers: A Critical Review of Millennium Development Goal Targets for Human Development and Human Rights', *Journal of Human Development and Capabilities* 15, nos 2–3 (2014): 105–17.
13. Ibid.
14. Paul Hunt, 'SDG Series: SDGs and the Importance of Formal Independent Review: An Opportunity for Health to Lead the Way', *Health and Human Rights Journal*, September 3, 2015, https://www.hhrjournal.org/2015/09/sdg-series-sdgs-and-the-importance-of-formal-independent-review-an-opportunity-for-health-to-lead-the-way/ (accessed July 14, 2017).
15. Ibid.
16. Julio Frenk and Suerie Moon, 'Governance Challenges in Global Health', *New England Journal of Medicine* 368, no. 10 (2013): 936–42, 939, http://www.nejm.org/doi/full/10.1056/NEJMra1109339.
17. Ilona Kickbusch and Martina Szabo, 'A New Governance Space for Health', *Global Health Action* 7 (2014), doi:10.3402/gha.v7.23507, http://www.ncbi.nlm.nih.gov/pmc/articles/PMC3925805/.
18. World Health Organisation (WHO), *Keeping Promises, Measuring Results* (Geneva: Commission on Information and Accountability for Women's and Children's Health, 2011).
19. Ibid.
20. Julian Schweitzer, 'Accountability in the 2015 Global Strategy for Women's, Children's and Adolescents' Health', *British Medical Journal* 351 (2015), http://www.bmj.com/content/bmj/351/bmj.h4248.full.pdf.
21. UN Secretary-General Ban Ki-moon, *Global Strategy for Women's and Children's Health* (New York: United Nations, 2010).
22. Ibid., 15.
23. WHO, *Keeping Promises, Measuring Results*.
24. For example, when the MDGs were established, accountability for them was primarily understood as monitoring progress: see Annex, *Road Map Towards the Implementation of the United Nations Millennium Declaration*, http://www.undp.org/content/dam/undp/library/MDG/english/MDG%20Country%20Reports/MDG%20Reporting%20Guidelines/MDG%20Roadmap%20from%202001.pdf (accessed July 14, 2017).
25. WHO, *Keeping Promises, Measuring Results*, 7.
26. Ibid., 7.
27. Ibid.
28. Ibid.
29. Ibid.
30. Julio Frenk and Suerie Moon 'Governance Challenges in Global Health', *New England Journal of Medicine* 368, no. 10 (2013): 936–42, http://www.nejm.org/doi/full/10.1056/

NEJMra1109339; Ilona Kickbusch and Martina Szabo, 'A New Governance Space for Health', *Global Health Action* 7 (2014), doi:10.3402/gha.v7.23507, http://www.ncbi.nlm.nih.gov/pmc/articles/PMC3925805/.

31. WHO, *Keeping Promises, Measuring Results*, 7.
32. Lynn P. Freedman, 'Human Rights, Constructive Accountability and Maternal Mortality in the Dominican Republic: A Commentary', *International Journal of Gynecology and Obstetrics* 82 (2003): 111–4, 111.
33. WHO, *Keeping Promises, Measuring Results*.
34. Ibid., 16.
35. Independent Expert Review Group on Women's and Children's Health, *Every Woman, Every Child, Every Adolescent: Achievements and Prospects, Final Report* (Geneva: World Health Organisation, 2015).
36. Every Woman Every Child, 'The Global Strategy for Women's Children's and Adolescents' Health (2016–2030) Survive Thrive Transform', in *Every Woman Every Child* (UN, 2015).
37. Peter Godwin and Sujaya Misra, *Report of the External Review of the Accountability Work for Women's and Children's Health* (WHO, 2014), 50.
38. Ibid.
39. Kate Donald, 'Breaking the Accountability Taboo in SDG Negotiations', *Center for Economic and Social Rights*, http://cesr.org/breaking-accountability-taboo-sdg-negotiations (accessed March 17, 2017).
40. Godwin and Misra, *Report of the External Review*.
41. Independent Expert Review Group, *Every Woman, Every Child, Every Adolescent*.
42. Global Strategy for Women's Children's and Adolescent's Health Strategy and Coordination Group, *Independent Accountability Panel: Scope of Work and Terms of Reference for Panelists* (WHO, 2015).
43. WHO, *Keeping Promises, Measuring Results*.
44. UN, Universal Declaration of Human Rights.
45. Paul Hunt, 'A Three-Step Accountability Process for the UN Secretary General's Global Strategy for Women's and Children's Health' (paper presented at the "From Pledges to Action", A Partners' Forum on Women's and Children's Health, Ministry of Health and Family Welfare, Government of India, New Delhi, India, November 12–14, 2010), 15.
46. The Partnership for Maternal, Newborn & Child Health, *A Review of Global Accountability Mechanisms for Women's and Children's Health* (Geneva: WHO, 2011), 9, http://www.who.int/pmnch/knowledge/publications/20110222_global_accountability_final.pdf?ua=1.
47. Working Group on Accountability for Results, 'Final Report' (Commission on Information and Accountability for Women's and Children's Health, 2011).
48. Baron de Montesquieu, 'The Spirit of the Law' (1748).
49. Independent Accountability Panel, *Old Challenges, New Hopes: Accountability for the Global Strategy for Women's, Children's and Adolescents' Health* (UN, 2016), 11, https://www.everywomaneverychild.org/wp-content/uploads/2017/03/IAP_Report_September2016.pdf (accessed August 2, 2017).
50. Aristotle, *Politics*.
51. Godwin and Misra, *Report of the External Review*, 37.
52. Ibid., 30.
53. Ibid., 15.
54. Alicia Ely Yamin and Rebecca Cantor, 'Between Insurrectional Discourse and Operational Guidance: Challenges and Dilemmas in Implementing Human Rights-Based Approaches to Health', *Journal of Human Rights Practice* 6, no. 3 (2014): 451–85, 458.
55. Schweitzer, 'Accountability'.
56. WHO, *Keeping Promises, Measuring Results*.
57. Every Woman Every Child, 'Global Strategy for Women's Children's and Adolescent's Health Strategy and Coordination Group' (Independent Accountability Panel - Scope of Work and Terms of Reference for Panelists, November 12, 2015), http://www.who.int/pmnch/media/news/2015/iap_tors.pdf (accessed August 2, 2017).

58. Independent Accountability Panel, *Old Challenges, New Hopes*, chs 2, 5.

59. UNGA, *Transforming Our World*, paras 72–91.

60. UN Economic and Social Council, *Ministerial Declaration of the High-Level Segment of the 2016 Session of the Economic and Social Council on the Annual Theme 'Implementing the Post-2015 Development Agenda: Moving from Commitments to Results'* (UN ESC, 2016), Annex paras 7–8, https://www.un.org/ecosoc/en/events/2016/ecosoc-high-level-segment-implementing-post-2015-development-agenda-moving-commitments (accessed August 2, 2017).

61. Ibid.

62. Danish Institute for Human Rights, 'Human Rights in Follow-up and Review of the 2030 Agenda for Sustainable Development' (Copenhagen, 2016).

63. Schweitzer, 'Accountability'.

64. UN Economic and Social Council, doc no E/HLS/2016/1, Annex, High Level Panel on Water 'Action Plan' September 21, 2016, https://sustainabledevelopment.un.org/HLPWater (accessed August 2, 2017).

65. UN Special Rapporteur on the Right to Health Dainius Puras, *Right of Everyone to the Enjoyment of the Highest Attainable Standard of Physical and Mental Health* (Geneva: UN General Assembly, 2016).

66. Ibid.

67. Ibid., para 76.

68. CESCR, 'General Comment 14'.

69. Paul Hunt et al., 'The Right to the Highest Attainable Standard of Health', in *Oxford Textbook of Global Public Health*, ed. Roger Detels et al. (Oxford: Oxford University Press, 2015), vol. 6, ch. 4.1.

70. UN Statistics, 'Metadata on SDGs', http://unstats.un.org/sdgs/files/metadata-compilation/Metadata-Goal-3.pdf (accessed November 29, 2016).

71. Ibid.

72. Gunilla Backman et al., 'Health Systems and the Right to Health: An Assessment of 194 Countries', *The Lancet* 372, no. 9655 (2008): 2047–85; UN Special Rapporteur Puras, *Right of Everyone to the Enjoyment of the Highest Attainable Standard*.

73. UN Special Rapporteur Puras, *Right of Everyone to the Enjoyment of the Highest Attainable Standard*.

74. Audrey R. Chapman, 'Editorial: The Contributions of Human Rights to Universal Health Coverage', *Health and Human Rights Journal* 18, no. 2 (2016): 1–5.

75. WHO, *Tier 3 Discussion for 3.8/UHC* (IAEG meeting, Mexico City, 2016).

76. Ibid.

77. WHO, *World Health Statistics 2016: Monitoring Health for the SDGs* WHO, http://www.who.int/gho/publications/world_health_statistics/2016/en/ (accessed November 29, 2016).

78. Ibid.

79. WHO, Tier 3 Discussion for 3.8/UHC (IAEG meeting, Mexico City, 2016).

80. A report to the Secretary-General of the United Nations by the Leadership Council of the Sustainable Development Solutions Network, 7, http://unsdsn.org/wp-content/uploads/2015/05/150612-FINAL-SDSN-Indicator-Report1.pdf (accessed July 14, 2017).

81. Casey Dunning and Jared Kalow, 'What Sdgs Can We Track Now?', in *Views from the Center* 2016 (Centre for Global Development, UK, 2016).

82. Ibid.

83. Ibid.

84. Susan Munabi-Babigumira et al., 'Factors That Influence the Provision of Intrapartum and Postnatal Care by Skilled Birth Attendants in Low- and Middle-Income Countries: A Qualitative Evidence Synthesis', *Cochrane Database of Systematic Reviews*, no. 2 (2015): 2, doi:10.1002/14651858.CD011558.

85. Sustainable Development Solutions Network, *Indicators and a Monitoring Framework for the Sustainable Development Goals*.

86. Ibid.

87. Ibid., 4.
88. Independent Accountability Panel, *Old Challenges, New Hopes.*
89. Data-Pop Alliance, 'Opportunities and Requirements for Leveraging Big Data for Official Statistics and the Sustainable Development Goals in Latin America' (White Paper, Harvard Humanitarian Initiative, MIT Media Lab, and Overseas Development Institute, 2016), 15.
90. Independent Expert Advisory Group on a Data Revolution for Sustainable Development, 'A World That Counts: Mobilising the Data Revolution for Sustainable Development: Report for the UN Secretary General', ed. Data Revolution Group (November 2014).
91. Abdullahi Abdulkadri, Alecia Evans and Tanisha Ash, 'An Assessment of Big Data for Official Statistics in the Caribbean: Challenges and Opportunities', in *A Studies and Perspective Series* (UN ECLAC Subregional Headquarters for the Caribbean, 2016).
92. Data-Pop Alliance, 'Opportunities and Requirements', 11.
93. See for example, Australia Ministry of Foreign Affairs, 'Medical Supply Reform Impact Evaluation Papua New Guinea', Ministry of Foreign Affairs, http://dfat.gov.au/about-us/publications/Pages/medical-supply-reform-impact-evaluation-papua-new-guinea.aspx (accessed November 29, 2016); Dhirendra Pratap Singh, 'Inclusive Growth Is New Mantra', *eHealth*, May 2, 2012, http://ehealth.eletsonline.com/2012/05/inclusive-growth-is-new-mantra/ (accessed July 14, 2017).
94. David Bollier, *The Promise and Peril of Big Data* (Washington, DC: The Aspen Institute, 2010).
95. Simon Ross, 'Virtual Health Information Network – Big Health Data for Epidemiology: Opportunities and Challenges' (paper presented at Big Health Data for Epidemiology Opportunities and Challenges using the SNZ IDI and other sources of 'big data' for epidemiological research in New Zealand, Wellington, January 26, 2016).
96. Dimiter V. Dimitrov, 'Medical Internet of Things and Big Data in Healthcare', *Healthcare Informatics Research* 22, no. 3 (2016): 156–63; Maged N. Kamel Boulos et al., 'How Smartphones are Changing the Face of Mobile and Participatory Healthcare: An Overview, with Example from Ecaalyx', *BioMedical Engineering OnLine* 10, no. 24 (2011); Timothy W. Kenealy et al., 'Telecare for Diabetes, Chf or Copd: Effect on Quality of Life, Hospital Use and Costs. A Randomised Controlled Trial and Qualitative Evaluation', *PLOS One* (2015).
97. Data-Pop Alliance, 'Opportunities and Requirements'.
98. World Bank, *World Development Report 2016 'Digital Dividends Overview'* (Washington, DC: World Bank, 2016).
99. Data-Pop Alliance, 'Opportunities and Requirements'.
100. Zendesk, 'Internet Live Stats', http://www.internetlivestats.com/internet-users-by-country/ (accessed December 12, 2016).
101. See for example, Cathy O'Neil, *Weapons of Math Destruction* (New York: Crown, 2016).
102. Abdulkadri, Evans and Ash, 'An Assessment of Big Data for Official Statistics in the Caribbean'.
103. Independent Accountability Panel, *Old Challenges, New Hopes.*
104. Big Data UN Global Working Group, 'Big Data Project Inventory' (UN Dept of Economic and Social Affairs, Statistics Division), http://unstats.un.org/bigdata/inventory/?selectID=201435 (accessed November 29, 2016).
105. Ibid.
106. Zendesk, 'Internet Live Stats'.
107. WHO, *Keeping Promises, Measuring Results.*

Disclosure statement

No potential conflict of interest was reported by the authors.

Funding

This work was supported by the UK's Economic and Social Research Council [grant number ES/M010236/1].

Economic growth, full employment and decent work: the means and ends in SDG 8

Diane F. Frey

ABSTRACT

This article examines SDG 8 'Promote sustained, inclusive and sustainable economic growth, full and productive employment and decent work for all'. It critically examines the goal from two perspectives, the business approach advocated by the International Organisation of Employers (IOE) and the human right to full employment and decent work advocated by the International Trade Union Confederation (ITUC) and human rights NGOs. While full employment and decent work are indeed prominent in SDG 8, the 2030 Agenda embraces market-centred institutional arrangements that may present obstacles to achieving the goal. Specifically, grafting the human rights to full employment and decent work onto a business-oriented economic growth agenda in SDG 8 calls into question whether the 2030 Agenda enshrines full employment and decent work as human rights obligations of states or merely as benefits of economic growth. The article concludes that the ambiguity in SDG 8 presents both opportunities for human rights monitoring and accountability but also enhanced legitimacy for the business approach.

Introduction

A central question following the adoption of the new Sustainable Development Goals (SDGs) in September 2015 is whether they can finish the task of eliminating poverty initiated under the Millennium Development Goals (MDGs). Access to greater income through work remains central to the elimination of poverty as the International Labour Organisation (ILO) concluded in its 2016 World Employment Social Outlook (WESO) report.[1] In 2015, at the end of the 15-year period under the MDGs, approximately 10% of the world's workers lived on less than $1.90 per day.[2] In addition, the ILO estimated that, in 2012, nearly two billion people lived on less than the $3.10 per day measure of 'moderate poverty' in the developing world, and over 300 million people lived in relative poverty, defined as less than 60% of the median income in their respective countries in the developed world.[3]

According to the United Nations Development Programme (UNDP), only about half of workers globally were in formal waged or salaried employment in 2014. The UNDP estimates that more than 1.5 billion workers worldwide are trapped in informal and vulnerable employment.[4] Most underemployed and underpaid workers work informally.[5] Additionally, the UNDP estimates that there were 204 million people worldwide, including 74 million young people out of work in 2015.[6] The prevalence of informal vulnerable work, however, calls into question the usefulness of official unemployment statistics. Low levels of official unemployment, combined with the absence of unemployment insurance in many developing countries, are more indicative of vulnerable and informal work than high rates of formal employment and decent work.[7]

In this context, this article critically evaluates SDG 8, which states: 'Promote sustained, inclusive and sustainable economic growth, full and productive employment and decent work for all.' SDG 8 is accompanied by 10 targets, which address both economic growth and full employment and decent work. Target 8.5, for example, states: 'By 2030, achieve full and productive employment and decent work for all women and men, including for young people and persons with disabilities, and equal pay for work of equal value.'[8] On the other hand, Target 8.1 addresses economic growth, and states: 'Sustain per capita economic growth in accordance with national circumstances and, in particular, at least 7 per cent gross domestic product growth per annum in the least developed countries.'[9] The merger of a goal on the human rights to full employment and decent work with a goal on economic growth presents a perplexing combination.[10]

There are strong reasons for optimism based on the inclusion of full employment and decent work in the SDGs, as well as some of the targets and indicators, which measure progress towards achieving full employment and decent work. In particular, the targets and indicators build upon well established norms in international law, which provide detailed guidance for monitoring and accountability. Nevertheless, the context and formulation of SDG 8 give cause for concern because it is embedded in potentially conflicting visions of development. Corporate interests represented by the International Organisation of Employers (IOE) advanced a market-centred business approach.[11] From this perspective, governments are not human rights duty bearers. Instead they are enterprise enablers. Governments create a good business environment in which successful enterprises and economies will sustainably grow, prosper and create jobs. In contrast, human rights and labour groups envision a rights-based partnership in which all actors at the global and national level are accountable for their contributions to development and the creation of decent work for all.[12]

By joining economic growth with full employment and decent work, SDG 8 therefore raises many issues. How are these two aspects of SDG 8 connected? Are they interdependent or independent? Why are the goals of full employment and decent work linked to economic growth in SDG 8, rather than poverty in SDG 1 as they were in MDG 1? The article argues for recognising that the SDGs, like human rights, are 'growth neutral' rather than 'growth dependent'. The global community must commit to achieve the SDGs – including full employment and decent work – whether or not there is economic growth. Importantly, economic growth is merely one of the *means* that might, but does not always, lead to the *end* of more jobs and better work conditions.[13] As the World Bank recognises, slower growth may be offset with and even overcome by greater redistribution and narrowing of inequality.[14]

The conflict between corporate and human rights visions of and prescriptions for development is not new. Five years before the adoption of the SDGs, Wolfgang Sachs, in *The Development Dictionary: A Guide to Knowledge as Power*, argued that the concept of development 'can mean just about everything' and invites such fundamental incongruence.[15] He states:

> [Development] is a concept of monumental emptiness, carrying vaguely positive connotation. For this reason, it can be easily filled with conflicting perspectives. On the one hand, there are those who implicitly identify development with economic growth, calling for more relative equity in GDP. Their use of the word 'development' reinforces the hegemony of the economic world-view. On the other hand, there are those who identify development with more rights and resources for the poor and powerless. Their use of the word calls for de-emphasizing growth in favour of greater autonomy of communities. For them, development speech is self-defeating; it distorts their concern and makes them vulnerable to hijack by false friends. Putting both perspectives into one conceptual shell is a sure recipe for confusion, if not a political cover-up.

After this introduction, part 2 of the article explains international standards on full employment and decent work established by the ILO and international human rights instruments. Part 3 examines SDG 8 and its targets. Part 4 discusses divergent approaches to development illustrated by arguments of international corporate actors such as the IOE, and labour and human rights actors, especially the International Trade Union Confederation (ITUC). The article examines their perspectives through messages they developed consultation process. Part 5 discusses the pitfalls of joining in SDG 8 the goal of full employment and decent work with economic growth. It argues that raising economic growth to the level of a goal is imprudent because it (1) confuses the *ends* and *means* of development, (2) is vaguely articulated and contested and (3) is not likely to succeed. The article concludes with a discussion of the challenges presented by the merged goal.

International standards on full employment and decent work

Prior to the adoption of the SDGs in 2015, the ILO and international human rights treaties established standards for full employment and decent work. Thus the SDGs incorporate at least to some extent these standards. A basic outline of these standard is useful to the analysis of SDG 8 and its targets.

The ILO soft law on full employment and decent work

Access to decent work that respects human dignity, secures an adequate livelihood and supports individuals and their families to fully develop their capacities and talents is a unifying interest shared by people globally. It is also an objective shared by the United Nations (UN) human rights system and the ILO.[16] Nevertheless, the idea and implementation of full employment and decent work would be nothing more than vague aspirations without consensus around their specific normative meanings. The ILO first developed a specific normative concept of decent work in the 1999 Decent Work Agenda and defined it along four dimensions or pillars. Since the introduction of the ILO Decent Work Agenda, the ILO, the United Nations General Assembly, many national governments and union constituents, including the ITUC, have championed it. The four pillars were conceptually drawn from existing ILO Conventions and were subsequently formally adopted in 2008 in the ILO Declaration on Social Justice for a Fair Globalisation and a resolution of the United Nations General Assembly

(UNGA).[17] Although considered soft law, the Decent Work Agenda encompasses rights that are recognised in international treaties, including ILO Conventions and the International Covenant on Economic, Social and Cultural Rights.[18] The decent work pillars are outlined in Table 1.

The human right to full employment and decent work

The duties of states and the rights of people with regard to full employment and decent work are also embedded in three cornerstones of the human rights system: (1) the UN Charter, (2) the Universal Declaration of Human Rights (UDHR) and (3) the International Covenant on Economic Social and Cultural Rights (ICESCR). The UN Charter obligates every member of the UN to promote higher standards of living, full employment, conditions of economic and social progress and universal respect for human rights.[19] The UDHR, adopted in 1948, incorporated Charter rights and added many additional work-related rights, including the right to decent work, to just and favourable conditions of work, to protection against unemployment, to social security, to equal pay for equal work, to just and favourable remuneration ensuring an existence worthy of dignity and supplemented if necessary by social protection, the right to rest and leisure, to reasonable limits on work hours, to periodic holidays with pay and to form trade unions. Further, the enjoyment of these rights is to be free of all forms of discrimination.[20]

The rights to full employment and decent work were subsequently implemented through human rights treaties, most comprehensively in the ICESCR in 1966. The ICESCR is also the most widely applicable work rights treaty with 164 state parties. Its coverage encompasses approximately 93% of the world's population.[21] The most significant non-ratifying parties include the United States, Myanmar, Saudi Arabia, Malaysia and Mozambique, which collectively account for only 6.3% of the world's population. The main provisions relevant to full employment and decent work in the ICESCR are outlined in Table 2.

Table 1. ILO decent work pillars.[a]

Rights at Work	This pillar incorporated the ILO 1998 Declaration of Fundamental Principles and Rights at Work, which set four 'core' labour standards. (a) freedom of association and the right to collective bargaining, (b) the elimination of forced or compulsory labour, (c) the abolition of child labour, and (d) the elimination of discrimination in employment.
Fostering Employment	This pillar requires policies, goals and strategies to achieve full employment with appropriate pay as a means of poverty reduction. Notably, the idea of *decent work* transcends narrowly defined waged employment to encompass a 'concern for all workers' and all of the forms of work that contribute to society, including nonpaid family work, all forms of informal paid work, self-employment and agricultural work.[b]
Social Protection	This pillar requires policies to prevent oppressive working conditions and workplace injuries and to establish meaningful forms of social protection such as paid holidays, and social security in case of old age, sickness, disability, unemployment, pregnancy or other conditions that prevent a person from working.
Social Dialogue	This pillar requires tripartite consultation, negotiation and whenever possible agreement between workers and their employers at every level of society, from workplace level up to national level consultation, on social policies, including employment policy to provide meaningful worker voice and resolve conflicts peacefully.

[a]ILO, *Decent Work: Report of the Director-General* (Geneva: International Labour Conference, 87th Session, 1999), http://www.ilo.org/public/english/standards/relm/ilc/ilc87/rep-i.htm (accessed July 23, 2017)
[b]Ibid. Section 1 A Concern for All Workers.

The Committee on Economic, Social and Cultural Rights (CESCR) supervises the implementation of the ICESCR by countries that have ratified it.[22] The CESCR has further elaborated state obligations for the right to full employment and decent work in four General Comments.[23] It does not, however, require any particular economic system or specific policies to achieve full employment and decent work. Indeed, the CESCR does not establish 'an absolute and unconditional right to obtain employment'.[24] Instead, it requires that the system is democratic, that all human rights are respected and that countries take 'deliberate, concrete and targeted steps by all appropriate means to progressively realize the rights' in the ICESCR.[25] In addition, countries must 'act' using the maximum of available resources and 'as expeditiously and effectively as possible'.[26] Under the ICESCR, there is also a presumption that States should not take retrogressive measures without full justification.[27] Finally, with respect to informal employment, the CESCR requires that State parties take the

> requisite measures, legislative or otherwise, to reduce to the fullest extent possible the number of workers outside the formal economy, workers who as a result of that situation have no protection. These measures should compel employers to respect labour legislation and declare their employees as formally employed thus enabling the latter to enjoy all the rights of workers.[28]

Integrating the ILO and human rights standards

In elaborating the normative content of work rights under the ICESCR, the CESCR noted that the human right to work coincides with the ILO's notion of decent work, meaning that the work respects fundamental human rights in terms of working conditions and provides workers with sufficient income to support themselves and their families.[29] The CESCR also embeds the human right to decent work in relevant ILO labour standards.[30] Among these ILO standards is Convention No. 122 on Full Employment Policy (1964),[31] which has been ratified by 111 countries. Under the Convention, countries are obligated to take steps as outlined in Table 3.[32]

As with the ICESCR, Convention No. 122 does not specify the policy measures and steps to be taken to achieve full employment. Instead, non-binding recommendations provide detailed suggestions to help countries implement their full employment policy.[33] Recommendation No. 122 states employment policy aims should be 'clearly

Table 2. ICESCR Full Employment and Decent Work.[a]

Article 6: The right of everyone to the opportunity to gain a living by work that is freely chosen. States have the obligation to take appropriate steps to safeguard this right, including through adopting policies and techniques to achieve steady economic, social and cultural development, and full and productive employment under conditions safeguarding fundamental political and economic freedoms.

Article 7: The right to just and favourable conditions of work, fair wages, equal remuneration for work of equal value, particularly for women, a decent living for workers and their families, safe and healthy working conditions, equal opportunity for promotion, the right to rest and leisure, periodic holidays with pay and reasonable limitations on work time.

Article 8: The right of everyone to form and join trade unions and the right of trade unions to function freely, including the right to strike with limitations on these rights allowed only if necessary in a democratic society in the interest of national security or public order or for the protection of the rights and freedoms of others.

Article 9: The right of everyone to social security, including social insurance.

[a]International Covenant on Economic, Social and Cultural Rights, (ICESCR) adopted 16 December 1966, GA Res. 2200 A (XXI), UN GAOR, 21st Sess., Supp. No. 16, UN Doc.A/6316 (1966), 993 UNTS 3 (entered into force January 3, 1976).

Table 3. ILO Convention 122 Employment Policy (1964).[a]

(1) Declare an 'active' policy goal of 'full, productive and freely chosen employment' with the aim of ensuring work for all who are available for and seeking it.
(2) Ensure that work, to the greatest extent possible, provides every person the opportunity to qualify for a job to which they are well suited and which best uses their skills.
(3) Ensure that employment policy provides employment opportunities irrespective of race, colour, sex, religion, political opinion, national extraction or social origin.
(4) Consider the 'mutual relationships between employment objectives and other economic and social objectives.'
(5) Engage in regular consultation with employers and workers as well as those affected by the policies and employment objectives.

[a]ILO Convention No. 122.

and publicly defined' and include 'quantitative targets for economic growth and employment'.[34] Further, it encourages governments to help the unemployed and underemployed during all periods of unemployment to meet their basic needs and those of their dependents.[35] It also anticipates state parties adopt public works and other public investment as levers to manage employment in the economy.[36] The recommendations present a flexible and expansive list of policies and tools that countries may, but are not required to, consider much less implement.[37]

SDG 8 on economic growth, full employment and decent work

The human rights to full employment and decent work address poverty-producing problems of underemployment, vulnerable employment and unemployment. They have, however, been formulated to provide flexibility for countries to determine how best to progressively achieve them. As such, these rights are consistent with the Agenda 2030 notion that countries have 'different approaches, visions, models and tools' at their disposal.[38] In sum, respecting, protecting and fulfilling the rights to full employment and decent work entail the critical challenge of selecting from among many policy options to manage the vortex in which economic policy and human rights obligations interact.

For example, it is widely recognised that the absence of economic growth contributes (in varying degrees) to worsening unemployment.[39] Yet, there have also been periods of increasing unemployment during 'better-than-expected' growth.[40] The relationship between economic growth and employment is not a linear relationship. Instead, policy choices matter. Pursuit of policies that flexibilise labour markets, weaken labour unions and increase inequality, for example, make levels of employment more, rather than less, reliant on growth.[41] Similarly, the relationships between poverty reduction, economic growth and inequality are complex.[42] In terms of human development, the UNDP has found that 'employment can no longer be considered a derivative of economic growth'[43] and further that the link between 'work' and 'human development' is also not automatic.[44] In sum, the UNDP concludes that it is implementing the decent work agenda that will enhance human development.[45]

Full employment and decent work were prominent in the consultation process to select the SDGs. The ILO, ITUC, human rights NGOs and several countries championed establishing a stand-alone goal on full employment and decent work that would incorporate all four of pillars of the Decent Work Agenda.[46] Ultimately, this objective was only partially successful. Full employment and decent work were raised from an MDG target to the level

Table 4. Goal 8 – Promote sustained, inclusive and sustainable economic growth, full and productive employment and decent work for all.[a]

Targets and Means of Implementation	Decent Work Pillar
Target 8.1 Sustain per capita economic growth in accordance with national circumstances and in particular at least 7% gross domestic product growth per annum in the least developed countries	
Target 8.2 Achieve higher levels of economic productivity through diversification, technological upgrading and innovation, including through a focus on high-value added and labour-intensive sectors	
Target 8.3 Promote development-oriented policies that support productive activities, decent job creation, entrepreneurship, creativity, and innovation, and encourage the formalisation and growth of micro-, small- and medium-sized enterprises, including through access to financial services	• Fostering Employment • Social Protection
Target 8.4 Improve progressively, through 2030, global resource efficiency in consumption and production and endeavour to decouple economic growth from environmental degradation, in accordance with the 10-Year Framework of Programmes on Sustainable Consumption and Production, with developed countries taking the lead	
Target 8.5 By 2030, achieve full and productive employment and decent work for all women and men, including for young people and persons with disabilities, and equal pay for work of equal value	• All Four Pillars
Target 8.6 By 2020, substantially reduce the proportion of youth not in employment, education or training	• Fostering Employment
Target 8.7 Take immediate and effective measures to eradicate forced labour, end modern slavery and human trafficking and secure the prohibition and elimination of the worst forms of child labour, including recruitment and use of child solders, and by 2025 end child labour in all its forms	• Rights at Work
Target 8.8 Protect labour rights and promote safe and secure working environments for all workers including migrant workers, in particular women migrants, and those in precarious employment	• Rights at Work • Social Protection
Target 8.9 By 2030, devise and implement policies to promote sustainable tourism that creates jobs and promotes local culture and products	• Fostering Employment
Target 8.10 Strengthen the capacity of domestic financial institutions to encourage and expand access to banking, insurance and financial services for all	
Means of Implementation	
8.a Increase Aid for Trade support for developing countries, in particular least developed countries, including through the Enhanced Integrated Framework for Trade-related Technical Assistance to Least Developed Countries	
8.b by 2020, develop and operationalise a global strategy for youth employment and implement the Global Jobs Pact of the ILO	• Potentially All Four Pillars

[a]UNGA.[47]

of a goal in the SDGs; however, they were combined with a goal on economic growth. SDG 8 and its targets are show in Table 4.

The ILO notion of full employment and decent work in SDG 8 is apparent, as all four decent work pillars are included. Indeed, the ILO welcomed the adoption of the SDGs, noting decent work is 'now an integral part of the new universal agenda for sustainable development'.[48] Similarly the ITUC observed that its broad objectives were 'for the most part reflected across the declaration and in the SDGs and Targets'.[49] Instead of a stand-alone goal on full employment and decent work for all, linked to poverty reduction as it had been in the MDGs, however, SDG 8 delinked full employment and decent work from poverty and instead merged it with 'sustained, inclusive and sustainable economic growth'. One obvious drawback of joining the two goals is that there are fewer targets devoted to full employment and decent work than if this had been a stand-alone goal. Another anomaly is that SDG 8 raises economic growth from a *means* to achieve development to a *goal* of development. It is not clear why economic growth is a goal in itself for sustainable development.[50]

Two approaches to full employment and decent work

The merged goal presents a puzzle and a challenge. On its face, it incorporates commitments to full employment and decent work along with the different pillars of decent work championed by human rights groups and the ITUC. At the same time, the goal incorporates many of the desires of corporate interests to prioritise an economic-growth and market-centred approach. Evidence of the sharply divergent views and priorities can be seen in exploring the contrasting messages of the advocates involved in the consultations on the SDGs.

The market-centred approach

Market fundamentalism has been described as 'a heterogeneous set of institutions consisting of various ideas, social and economic policies, and ways of organizing political and economic activity'.[51] Typically, these approaches include minimalist levels of taxation, business regulation and welfare, maximal freedom of mobility for international capital and reliance on markets rather than non-market policy or collectively bargained solutions to solve problems. An essential element of this is a flexible labour market with low levels of regulation, decentralised and individualised relations between employers and workers, and therefore, weak unions and the absence of collective bargaining.[52] Underpinning the logic of this market-centred approach is the presumption that states must play an active role in creating and maintaining the best possible environment for businesses because they, not the government, are the engines of economic growth and prosperity. The logic holds that under these conditions, a market-driven system creates a level of employment quantity and quality that is the most efficient.[53]

The market-centred approach is profoundly at odds with many aspects of SDG 8's treatment of full employment and decent work. Under the market-centred approach, governments intentionally avoid full employment to control inflation.[54] The ascendency of this inflation-centric perspective overthrew the prior Keynesian regime that prevailed from the 1930s through the 1960s, during which the rights to full employment and decent work were incorporated into human rights treaties and ILO Conventions. The decline of full employment as economic policy orthodoxy corresponded with rising inflation in the 1970s in the US and UK as well as the rise to power of Reagan and Thatcher.[55]

Transnational corporate actors have put forward policy prescriptions at the UN for many years.[56] The consultation process leading to the SDGs created an unprecedented opportunity to consolidate and expand corporate influence far beyond the SDGs. Arguably corporate influence has achieved a fundamental realignment of international governance in the SDGs in which transnational corporations are full and perhaps more powerful partners than UN institutions and their government constituents in the new development agenda.[57] The SDG process opened many paths to corporate participation and influence, including two seats on the UN Secretary General's High Level Panel (HLP),[58] a UN Global Compact initiative and report to the Secretary General, a thematic group in the Sustainable Development Solutions Network (SDSN) devoted to 'Redefining the Role of Business for Sustainable Development', as well as significant participation in the other thematic groups and 21 seats on the SDSN's leadership council.[59] In addition, a Business and Industry Major Group represented organised corporate interests before the UNGA Open

Working Group on the SDGs responsible for facilitating consultations on the post-2015 agenda.[60]

Transnational corporate actors advanced thematic messages and recommendations in the SDG process that can be summarised as emphasising (1) economic growth, (2) development of new technologies so that economic growth can be decoupled from environmental and resource limits, (3) a central role for business relative to the public sector and (4) the relegation of government's role to providing an 'enabling environment' for businesses by implementing supportive policies, such as ensuring open trading and procurement systems, peace and infrastructure, as well as preventing market disturbances, civil unrest and social deprivations.[61] Overall, there is a conflation of the notion of 'business sustainability' with broader social aims of 'sustainable development', livelihoods and social and economic equity.[62] In addition, corporate actors sought to strengthen and make permanent their role in partnerships and collaborations as legitimate stakeholders along with governments, civil society and other social actors.[63]

The IOE is the largest network of private employer organisations and was a key actor in the SDG consultations. It represents employer interests on labour and social policy at the ILO as well as at the UN and other multilateral organisations. Founded in 1920, it seeks to 'provide an international forum to bring together, represent and promote the interests of national employers' organisations and their members throughout the world in all labour and socio-economic policy issues'.[64] It is composed of 150 business federations and organisations worldwide.[65] With respect to the SDGs, the IOE worked alone as well as through the Global Compact, the Global Business Alliance and other business interests to influence the SDG proceedings with its own messages outlined below.[66]

The IOE's market-centred approach to employment and decent work puts private enterprises at the centre of sustainable development with the promise of jobs, incomes, livelihoods, poverty eradication, economic and social equity and political stability as dividends of business success.[67] The market is the central means to achieve full employment and decent work, which result from the ability of private enterprises to invest and undertake creative innovative solutions.[68] The quantity and quality of social goods, such as employment, are commensurate with the degree to which businesses succeed and grow.[69] From the IOE perspective, states should therefore recognise and support the central role of business.[70] Based on this diagnosis, the IOE advocates that open, transparent and corruption-free governments adopt policies that aim to ensure business success, by creating and maintaining a business-friendly and enabling environment that supports business investment, innovation and growth.[71] If government policy delivers the enabling environment, then business will deliver on poverty reduction, social equity and livelihoods.

The idea of decent work as a right, including the obligation of governments to commit to full employment, rights at work, social protection and worker voice at company or society level, is absent from the IOE's messages. Instead, regulations that impact working conditions are suspect and should be evaluated for their potential negative impact on employment levels and formalisation,[72] putting full employment at odds with decent work. Moreover, acknowledgment of the need for specific mechanisms to hold businesses and governments accountable for full employment and decent work is also absent.

Human-rights-centred approach

Like businesses, the UN human rights system, human rights NGOs and labour groups were active in influencing the SDG process. The Human Rights Council (HRC) adopted multiple resolutions throughout the consultation process including a 2012 resolution, which called upon the SDGs to be built around 'fundamental respect for human rights'.[73] HRC High-level panel discussions resulted in recommendations including to the UN Secretary General's High Level Panel of Eminent Persons on mainstreaming human rights into the post-2015 agenda.[74] The heads of the 10 UN treaty bodies also actively advocated for integrating human rights obligations into the SDGs as well as the use of specific human rights indicators that would enable an assessment of progress on realising human rights and could also make use of national and international human rights mechanisms.[75] The UN Office of the High Commissioner for Human Rights also advocated, coordinated and supported efforts to embed the SDGs in human rights.[76] UN Special Rapporteurs, which are part of the United Nations Special Procedures, offered collective and individual thematic messages on the need to frame the SDGs goals and measures of success generally in terms of national and international participation and accountability mechanisms.[77] For example, the Special Rapporteur on extreme poverty and human rights advocated for inclusion of social protection floors and unpaid care work.[78]

In addition, the ITUC, along with the Center for Economic and Social Rights and 47 other NGOs, created their own messaging, partially overlapping with the official human rights bodies.[79] The approach advocated by the ITUC and human rights NGOs puts human rights and government obligations for upholding them at the centre of sustainable development.[80] Effectively addressing poverty, inequality and ecological devastation, is possible, from their perspective, if human rights become the substantive aim of sustainable development along with commitments to reform the structural drivers of inequality, poverty and ecological devastation.[81] From the human rights perspective, governments need to emphasise human rights-based processes, such as transparency and participation, in developing social and economic policies, including those addressing the role of government and business in fulfilling the rights to full employment and decent work.[82] In addition, all stakeholders should be held accountable for their impacts on economic and social rights including full employment and decent work. The ITUC and human rights NGOs also advocated for policies and an enabling environment supportive of human rights.[83] Policy priorities included regulation of businesses, protection of marginalised populations and responsibility for implementing social and economic rights at least at minimum essential levels.[84] The enabling environment to support the human rights approach also includes protection of human rights defenders and access to justice for people living in poverty and other excluded groups.[85]

Market-centred versus the human rights-centred approaches

The underlying values and messages of the business and human rights advocates are sharply contradictory. This is evident in their respective diagnoses and analyses of the global problems to be solved by the SDGs. The human rights groups advocate for realising a broad array of civil and political, as well as economic, social and cultural rights.[86] In contrast, the IOE diagnoses the problems to be low incomes, poverty, inadequate human development, lack of jobs, economic and social equity as well as economic and political instability.[87] Yet it ultimately focuses more narrowly with the message that what is good for business will be good for people, the planet and the achievement of the SDGs.[88] The IOE omits most human rights and focuses on the rule of law, property rights and equal opportunity.[89] Under both approaches, one of the greatest obstacles to achieving full employment and decent work is the informal economy. The two approaches, however, hold sharply divergent views about the nature of the problem. From the business perspective, the problem lies with legal and administrative regulatory barriers that must be removed to create a business-friendly environment, thus facilitating formalisation.[90] In contrast, the human rights perspective posits that it is the lack of access to secure decent work itself that coerces workers to accept informal work.[91]

Based on these divergent ideas about the problems, the two approaches advocate for dramatically different policy solutions. For the market-centred approach, the central solution is economic growth, and growth requires that companies be allowed to thrive.[92] This in turn, requires business friendly regulations that omit or treat formal accountability mechanisms and regulations as suspect.[93] For the human rights approach, deregulating businesses is contrary to the state's role and duty to protect human rights by holding private actors accountable.[94] Human rights activists urged governments to enhance regulations of corporations and reminded governments of their duty to ensure that companies respect human rights and the environment.[95] While the business perspective articulates the need for deeper investment in a corporate market-led approach, the human rights messages argued that such an approach is contributing to many of the detrimental structural drivers they seek to eliminate such as tax avoidance, burdensome debt and unfair intellectual property systems.[96] A comparison of the business approach and the Human Rights NGO and ITUC approach is shown in Table 5.

Perspectives on economic growth

The ITUC and human rights NGOs advocated for inclusion a stand-alone goal on full employment and decent work in the 2030 agenda.[98] For their part, business stakeholders championed economic growth to be a stand-alone goal. As a result, there were separate discussions on the two proposed goals and therefore the ITUC and human rights NGOs did not directly challenge the market-centred approach embodied in the economic growth proposal.[99] It was only very late in the consultations on the SDGs that the two proposed goals were merged into SDG 8. By combining the two goals near the end of the consultations, there was little time to consider the implications of the incongruent combination.

With respect to the SDGs, the inclusion of a goal on growth and its merger with the human rights to full employment and decent work is problematic. Three concerns must be considered in elevating economic growth in the SDGs to the status of a goal, whether alone, or in combination with full employment and decent work. Raising economic growth, even 'sustained, sustainable economic growth', as described in SDG 8, to the level of a goal is imprudent because it (1) potentially confuses the *ends* and *means*

Table 5. Comparison of key messages of businesses and human rights NGOs on the SDGs.[a]

	Business Approach (IOE)	Human Rights NGOs Approach
Problems Addressed	Poverty, inadequate human development, lack of jobs, low incomes, lack of economic and social equity as well as economic and political instability	Poverty, inequality and ecological devastation
Solutions Offered	Businesses invest and initiate innovative solutions	Human rights realisation as the aim of the SDGs Structural reform to address drivers of inequality, poverty and ecological devastation
State Role	Businesses as primary drivers of development	States as primary duty-holders in development
Processes	Sound, open and transparent government, free from corruption Investment and partnership opportunities accessible to all	Transparent and participatory policymaking, including budget, financial, and tax policies. Disaggregated data at country-level as defined by rights-holders. Accountability for human rights

Policies	Policies to support business
	
	• Development aid to small and medium size enterprises
	• Fiscal, economic and regulatory policies to create a better business environment
	• Removal of regulatory barriers preventing formalisation
		Policies to support human rights
		
		• Regulation of private actors, especially business and private financial actors
		• Protection of rights of poor, marginalised and excluded
		• Policies to fulfil the minimum essential levels of economic, social, and cultural rights through:
		  ○ Social protection floors
		  ○ Universal health coverage
		  ○ Food security
		  ○ Decent Work

Enabling Environment	Business enabling • Support economic growth • Support pro-business regulations • Protect property rights • Protect rule of law • Efficient law enforcement systems	Human rights enabling • Empower civil society • Protect human rights defenders • Eradicate barriers to justice for poor and marginalised groups • Prosecute tax evasion, environmental crimes and human rights violations

[a]Table is based on comparison of IOE Guidance Paper[97] and HR Joint Statement.

of development, (2) is vaguely articulated and contested and (3) is not likely to succeed while obscuring real challenges and potentially transformative solutions.

The ends and means of development

As Jean Drèze and Amartya Sen stated 15 years ago, economic growth may be a *means* to achieve human rights and human development but it is not an *end* in itself.[100] Elevating 'economic growth' to the status of an SDG unnecessarily confuses the well-accepted and long-standing commitment of UN member states to human development and human rights as the *ends* of development.[101] Rather than calling for promotion of economic growth, the UN Charter obligates states 'to promote conditions of economic and social progress'.[102] Economic growth is one possible *means* to fulfil this obligation. Nevertheless, 'economic growth' does not equate to 'progress' in terms of human development or human rights. In the absence of economic growth, UN member states' obligations for full employment and other economic and social rights remain.

Like the UN Charter, the ICESCR obligates states to 'take appropriate steps to safe-guard' the right of everyone to 'gain a living by work that is freely chosen' by adopting policies and techniques to achieve steady 'economic, social and cultural development'.[103] The ICESCR human rights goal is framed as 'development' and it has social and cultural as well as economic elements. Economic growth is one of the *means* that could enable such development but economic growth is at best the *means* and not the normative goal. As under the UN Charter, in the absence of economic growth, State parties to the ICESCR must still safeguard the right of everyone to gain a living by work that is freely chosen.

Compliance with the ICESCR requires taking deliberate steps and using maximum available resources to realise economic and social rights irrespective of economic growth.[104] This is especially true with respect to the right to full employment and decent work. In times of low growth or recession, the government must provide specialised services to assist people in finding employment, remove discriminatory barriers in labour markets, protect work-related human rights, maintain just and favourable conditions of work, social protection from unemployment and provide government jobs pro-grammes.[105] In fact, the need for governments to 'take steps' to progressively achieve full employment and decent work is most important when there is no economic growth, as for example during the Great Depression of the 1930s in the United States.[106]

Economic growth is a vague and contested concept

A great deal of effort has gone into forging a consensus on what 'economic growth' means in the SDGs. The 2015 UN resolution formally adopting the SDGs, expresses their trans-formative intent across a range of outcomes including the productive capacity of least developed countries,[107] the human race,[108] the lives of all[109] and the world.[110] The SDGs' 'transformative goals and targets' are the source of these larger transformations.[111] The UN resolution makes 'economic growth' central in the transformation process, men-tioning it explicitly 10 times.[112] Another source of transformation is that the separate goals and targets are not considered silos but rather 'interrelated' with a new approach that recognises that poverty eradication, inequality, environmental preservation, sustained, inclusive and sustainable economic growth and fostering social inclusion are 'interdependent'.[113]

There was once broad unanimity on the concept of 'sustainable development' dating from the 1987 Brundtland Commission report *Our Common Future*.[114] In the original consensus, 'sustainable development' acknowledged that there are limits to growth and trade-offs between growth and equity.[115] However, under the weight of corporate influ-ence, acknowledgement of these limits and trade-offs has largely been erased. They are no longer 'fully reflected in the normative codes of conduct used by, and promoted for, the business community'.[116] Even if 'sustained, inclusive and sustainable economic growth' in the SDG 8 represents a transformative new consensus, it may well 'drift' the way of 'sustainable development' if it is untethered to international human rights norms.

The World Bank links poverty, inequality and environmental preservation to 'sus-tained, inclusive and sustainable economic growth'.[117] It argues that there is a consensus that sustained and sustainable economic growth is achievable for all countries through a set of ingredients to be artfully combined by wise leaders and policymakers within their own national realities.[118] The Bank also supports the notion that inequality can be addressed 'without compromising growth' and with benefits for 'poverty reduction and shared prosperity' albeit with the proviso that it must be 'done smartly'.[119] In addition, it supports the proposition that 'green growth' is 'necessary, efficient and affordable'.[120]

Despite the World Bank's efforts, there is legitimate cause to question whether 'sustained, inclusive and sustainable economic growth' in SDG 8 represents a new consensus and whether it is distinguishable from neoliberal growth. Just as they were able to bring about a change in the meaning of sustainable development in the Brundtland Commission Report, corporations have sought to influence the meaning of 'sustained, inclusive and sustainable economic growth' in SDG 8.[121] They have also encouraged other actors to adopt corporate understandings and notions such as 'sustainable development'.[122]

From the point of view of the ITUC and human rights NGOs, governments and businesses will need to overturn the neoliberal model's over-reliance on exports, financialisation and consumer borrowing as a source for economic growth.[123] In addition, from their perspective, a 'new transformative model' would reverse the 'deliberate and systemic' erosion of human rights, such as collective bargaining, employment protections and minimum wages. Based on human rights, 'sustained, inclusive and sustainable economic growth' will be transformative if businesses adapt their approach to make employment creation a reality.[124] In fact, the ITUC has long advocated an alternative to neoliberal growth based on structural transformation. It maintains that corporate influence, with support of many governments and elites, 'have taken us down paths that are unsustainable and continue to create global obstacles to the implementation of the agenda'.[125] Instead, the ITUC envisions a model of growth based on rising wages and a more equal distribution of income to increase domestic demand for goods and services and build resilient economies.[126]

Economic growth is not likely to succeed and obscures other solutions

Finally, it is unwise to rely on economic growth to eradicate poverty because it is not likely to succeed, and it may obscure other solutions. David Woodward, a United Nations Conference on Trade and Development (UNCTAD) advisor, has demonstrated that it would cost $4.57 trillion dollars, equal to approximately 6.8% of the global GDP to move the 62.3% of the world's population above a $5-per day poverty line.[127] Relying on pro-poor economic growth to generate $4.57 trillion dollars would require GDP growth in excess of $11,500 trillion and take between 123 and 209 years to accomplish at current rates of economic growth.[128] In an increasingly carbon-constrained world, this level of GDP growth would require a 2000-fold increase in production and consumption and would be achieved 'at a glacial' pace and in a 'grotesquely inefficient' manner.[129] As Woodward notes, we would have a better and quicker chance of raising $4.57 trillion dollars and achieving the $5-per day poverty line with redistribution of world GDP rather than reliance on pro-poor shares of economic growth.[130] It is unclear whether SDG 10 on reducing inequality within and among countries will meaningfully impact this calculation.[131]

The idea that wise leaders, using artfully mixed ingredients, will create 'sustained, inclusive and sustainable economic growth' leading to full employment and decent work is attractive but nevertheless unrealistic.[132] It obscures the challenges we face and the transformative solutions that are needed. Undoubtedly economic growth and employment are related but managing the relationship is 'very difficult'.[133] Economic growth is assumed to be the solution but growth may be 'un-economic' contributing to human and environmental ills rather than development, progress and prosperity.[134] Efforts to decouple growth from its detrimental environmental and human impacts have been 'insufficient'.[135] Ecological economists argue that growth is not infinitely sustainable even if it is the 'supreme goal of all nations'.[136] Employment without growth is not even currently 'seriously discussed'.[137] Nevertheless, attention is beginning to focus on reducing dependence on and transforming conceptions of neoliberal growth.[138] Full employment and decent work should be included in that transformative vision, and the ILO is well placed to lead this effort through social dialogue within the framework of Convention No. 122.[139]

Conclusion

Corporations and human rights activists will potentially have powerful levers for their positions in the merged SDG 8. For business advocates, there is a transformative aspect to the SDGs. For the first time, the global development agenda explicitly includes targets on economic growth (target 8.1), enterprise creation (target 8.3), productivity (target 8.2), technological innovation (target 8.2) and consumption (target 8.4). The IOE welcomed the fact that enterprise creation and entrepreneurship 'lie at the heart of sustainable development'.[140] From the IOE's viewpoint, the SDGs will support their efforts to encourage the ILO and national governments to focus on policies that create and sustain businesses, and support market solutions and regulatory and tax regimes that are 'sound and fair' from business's point of view. Sound and fair policies include reductions in 'government spending, non-wage labour costs, over-prescriptive standard setting, and over-regulation of employer activity'.[141] If growth lags and fails to deliver sufficient numbers of jobs, then corporate interests will be well placed to argue that the policy environment has not been made sufficiently business friendly.

For their part, human rights and labour activists can point to the SDG 8 commitment to achieve full employment and decent work for all by 2030. SDG 8 targets include taking immediate and effective measures to eradicate forced labour, modern slavery and trafficking (target 8.7), as well as to protect labour rights (target 8.8). Other aspects of decent work are promotional in SDG 8; for example, target 8.8 aims to 'promote,' rather than 'achieve,' safe and secure working environments. Nevertheless, there are also indicators that can be useful as accountability tools and are directly related to all four decent work pillars. These include tracking informal employment (indicator 8.3.1), average hourly earnings (indicator 8.5.1), unemployment (indicator 8.5.2), youth not in education, employment or training, child labour (indicator 8.6.1), frequency rates of fatal and non-fatal workplace injuries (indicator 8.8.1) and total government spending on social protection and employment programmes as a proportion of the national budgets and GDP (indicator 8.b.1).

From a human rights perspective, the SDGs might have also called for delinking full employment and decent work from economic growth – but these two goals have now been married into SDG 8 until 2030. Only time will tell whether this means that corporate interests will continue to outweigh those of human beings in the new global agenda for sustainable development.

Notes

1. ILO, *World Employment Social Outlook: Transforming Jobs to End Poverty* (WESO) (Geneva: International Labour Office, 2016), iii, xiv.
2. Sustainable Development Knowledge Platform, 'Goal 1 End Poverty in All Its Forms Everywhere', https://sustainabledevelopment.un.org/sdg1 (accessed January 9, 2017).
3. ILO WESO, xiii.
4. United Nations Development Programme (UNDP) Report on Work, *Human Development Report 2015: Work for Human Development* (New York: UNDP, 2015), 63 (hereafter UNDP 2015 Report on Work).
5. Ibid.
6. Ibid.,5.
7. ILO, WESO, 51.
8. UNGA, *Transforming Our World: The 2030 Agenda for Sustainable Development*, resolution adopted by the General Assembly on September 25, 2015, UN Doc A/RES/70/1 (2015), Target 8.5 p. 19/35.
9. Ibid., Target 8.1, p. 19/35.
10. Diane F. Frey and Gillian MacNaughton, 'Full Employment and Decent Work in the Post-2015 Development Agenda', in *International Norms, Normative Change, and the UN Sustainable Development Goals*, ed. Noha Shawki (Lanham MD: Lexington Books, 2016), 185–201, 195–6.
11. IOE, 'Guidance Paper: The Post-2015 Development Agenda and its Impact on Business' IOE Guidance Paper, undated, http://www.ioe-emp.org/fileadmin/ioe_documents/publications/Policy%20Areas/sustainability/EN/_2015-08-26__C- (accessed December 25, 2015).
12. Jens Martens, 'The 2030 Agenda: A New Start Towards Global Sustainability', in *Spotlight on Sustainable Development, 2016: Report by the Reflection Group on the 2030 Agenda for Sustainable Development*, ed. Barbara Adams et al. (2016), 12, https://www.2030spotlight.org/en/published.
13. In a similar vein, rethinking economic growth and well-being has been undertaken in David Griggs et al., 'An Integrated Framework for Sustainable Development Goals', *Ecology and Society* 19, no. 4 (2014): 49.
14. World Bank Group, *Poverty and Shared Prosperity 2016: Taking On Inequality* (Washington DC: The World Bank, 2016), 2
15. Wolfgang Sachs, 'Preface to the New Edition', *The Development Dictionary: A Guide to Knowledge as Power*, 2nd edn (London: Zed Books, 2010), x.
16. ILO, Declaration on Social Justice for a Fair Globalization, adopted by the International Labour Conference, 97th Session, Geneva, June 10, 2008; UNGA, Resolution on the International Labour Organization Declaration on Social Justice for a Fair Globalization, adopted by the General Assembly December 19, 2008, UNGA Res. 63/199.
17. Ibid.
18. Gillian MacNaughton and Diane F. Frey, 'Decent Work for All: A Holistic Human Rights Approach', *American University International Law Journal* 26, no. 2 (2011): 441–83.
19. UN Charter, http://www.un.org/en/sections/un-charter/un-charter-full-text/, arts 55–6.
20. UNGA Universal Declaration of Human Rights, 217 A (III), http://www.refworld.org/docid/3ae6b3712c.html, arts 2, 22, 23, 24,
21. Author's calculation based on cross referencing data from Worldometers, Current World Population by Country, http://www.worldometers.info/world-population/population-by-country/, and United Nations Office of The High Commissioner of Human Rights, Status of Ratification International Covenant on Economic, Social and Cultural Rights, http://indicators.ohchr.org

22. See Office of the High Commissioner of Human Rights (OHCHR), http://ohchr.org/en/hrbodies/cescr/pages/cescrindex.aspx

23. UN CESCR, General Comment 3: The Nature of The State Party Obligations, UN Doc. E/1991/23 (1990); UN CESCR, General Comment 18: The Right to Decent Work, UN Doc. E/C.12/GC/18 (2005), UN CESCR, General Comment 19: The Right to Social Security, UN Doc. E/C.12/GC/19 (2007); UN CESCR, General Comment 23: Just and Favourable Conditions of Work, UN Doc., E/C.12/GC/23 (2016).

24. CESCR General Comment 18, para. 6.

25. CESCR General Comment 3, paras 3, 4, 8.

26. Ibid., para. 9.

27. Ibid. See also UN CESCR, 'An Evaluation of the Obligation to Take Steps to the "Maximum of Available Resources" under the Optional Protocol to the Covenant', 38th Sess., UN Doc. E/C.12/2007/1, 2007.

28. CESCR General Comment 18, para. 10.

29. Ibid., para. 7.

30. Ibid., para. 4 referencing ILO Convention No. 122; para. 11 referencing ILO Convention No. 158.

31. ILO Convention 122, Ratifications, ILO Normlex, http://www.ilo.org/dyn/normlex/en/f?p=NORMLEXPUB:11300:0::NO:11300:P11300_INSTRUMENT_ID:312267:NO.

32. ILO Convention No. 122 (1964), http://www.ilo.org/dyn/normlex/en/f?p=NORMLEXPUB:12100:0::NO::P12100_INSTRUMENT_ID:312267 (accessed March 27, 2017); see also Jean Mayer, 'The Concept of the Right to Work in International Standards and the Legislation of ILO Member States', International Labour Review 124, no. 2 (1985): 227.

33. ILO (2013) 'Guide on Employment Policy and International Labour Standards' (International Labour Standards Department, Employment Policy Department Code: COC-WEI-NOU, 2013), http://www.ilo.org/wcmsp5/groups/public/---ed_norm/---normes/documents/publication/wcms_233783.pdf; International Labour Conference, 99th Session (2010) Report III(Part 1B) 'General Survey Concerning Employment Instruments in Light of the 2008 Declaration on Social Justice for a Fair Globalization', http://www.ilo.org/wcmsp5/groups/public/@ed_norm/@relconf/documents/meetingdocument/wcms_123390.pdf

34. ILO Recommendation No. 122, 1964, Section II (2) and II (4)(1).

35. Ibid., section II (7)(2).

36. Ibid., Annex I (4)(c).

37. Other ILO Recommendations on employment policy: 83, 99, 168, 169, 188, 189, 193 and 198.

38. UNGA, Transforming Our World, para. 59.

39. Arthur Okun, 'Potential GNP: its Measurement and Significance'. American Statistical Association Proceedings of the Business and Economics Statistics Section of the American Statistical Association (1962): 98–104; World Bank Group, World Development Report 2013: Jobs (Washington DC: The World Bank Group, 2012), 88; Miklós Antal, 'Green Goals and Full Employment: Are they Compatible?' Ecological Economics 107 (2014): 276–86.

40. Louis Emmerij, Richard Jolly and Thomas Weiss, Ahead of the Curve? UN Ideas and Global Challenges (Bloomington: Indiana University Press, 2003), 60 speaking about the 1960s.

41. Antal, 'Green Goals', 80–1.

42. David Woodward, 'Incrementum ad Absurdum: Global Growth, Inequality and Poverty Eradication in a Carbon-Constrained World', World Economic Review 4 (2015): 43–62.

43. UNDP 2015 Report on Work, 17.

44. Ibid., 6.

45. Ibid., 23.

46. See further: ILO Governing Body Six Point Strategy for work on the post-2015 agenda (ILO, September 4, 2013), http://ilo.org/wcmsp5/groups/public/---ed_norm/---relconf/documents/meetingdocument/wcms_221635.pdf

47. UNGA, 'Transforming Our World: The 2030 Agenda for Sustainable Development', Resolution Adopted by the General Assembly on September 25, 2015, UN Doc A/RES/70/1 (2015), https://sustainabledevelopment.un.org/post2015/transformingourworld (accessed July 23, 2017)

48. ILO, '2030 Development Agenda: Major Breakthrough for World of Work' (ILO press release, August 4, 2015), http://www.ilo.org/global/about-the-ilo/newsroom/news/WCMS_388407/lang--en/index.htm

49. Matt Simonds, 'The SDGs Summit and the 2030 Agenda for Sustainable Development', ITUC, September 18, 2015, https://www.ituc-csi.org/sdgs-summit-2030-agenda

50. Martens, 'The 2030 Agenda'; Mark Elder, Magnus Bengtsson and Lewis Akenji, 'An Optimistic Analsysis of the Means of Implementation for the Sustainable Development Goals: Thinking about Goals as Means', *Sustainability* 8, no. 9 (2016), 962, http://www.mdpi.com/2071-1050/8/9/962 (accessed July 23, 2017): 'The confusion between goals and means may be the sharpest in the cases of Goals 8 and 9 … '

51. John L. Campbell and Ove K. Pedersen, 'Introduction: The Rise of Neoliberalism and Institutional Analysis', in *The Rise of Neoliberalism and Institutional Analysis*, ed. John L. Campbell and Ove K. Pedersen (Princeton: Princeton University Press, 2001), 5.

52. Ibid.

53. J. W. Nevile, 'Policies to Minimise the Costs of Unemployment', in *Post-Keynesian Essays from Down Under, Volume III: Essays on Ethics, Social Justice and Economics*, ed. Joseph Halevi, G. C. Harcourt, Peter Kriesler and J. W. Nevile (Houndmills: Palgrave MacMillan, 2016), 47.

54. Fernando J. Cardim de Carvalho and G. Julio López, 'Are Full Employment Policies Obsolete?', *International Journal of Political Economy* 36, no. 3 (2007); Philip Harvey, 'Benchmarking the Right to Work', in *Economic Rights: Conceptual, Measurement, and Policy Issues*, ed. Shareen Hertel and Lance Minkler (Cambridge: Cambridge University Press, 2007), 120.

55. Irfan ul Haque, 'Globalization, Neoliberalism and Labour' (discussion paper 173, United National Conference on Trade and Development [UNCTAD], 2004), http://www.rrojasdatabank.info/globneoliblabour.pdf, p. 6.

56. Jens Martens, 'Corporate Influence on the Business and Human Rights Agenda of the United Nations', (working paper, Bischöfliches Hilfswerk MISEREOR e.V., Aachen, 2014), http://www.misereor.org/fileadmin//user_upload/misereor_org/Publications/englisch/working-paper-corporate-influence-on-business-and-human-rights.pdf.

57. Lou Pingeot, *Corporate Influence in the Post-2015 Process.* Aachen/Berlin/Bonn/New York: Bischöfliches Hilfswerk MISEREOR e V, Brot für die Welt – Evangelischer Entwicklungsdienst Evangelisches Werk für Diakonie und Entwicklung e. V. and Global Policy Forum, 2014, https://www.brot-fuer-die-welt.de/fileadmin/mediapool/2_Downloads/Fachinformationen/Sonstiges/Corporate_influence_in_the_post_2015_process.pdf (accessed July 23, 2017); Regina Scheyvens, Glen Banks and Emma Hughes 'The Private Sector and the SDGs: The Need to Move Beyond "Business as Usual"', *Sustainable Development* 24, no. 6 (2016): 371–382.

58. Pingeot, 'Corporate Influence', 8. High Level Panel representatives Paul Polman, CEO of Unilever, Betty Maina, CEO of Kenyan Association of Manufacturers. The HLP report included thematic consultations and extensive outreach to the private sector including consultation with 250 executive corporate officers in 30 countries.

59. Ibid., 9.

60. See e.g. The Major Group Position Paper, The Business and Industry's vision and priorities for the Sustainable Development Goals, March 2014, https://sustainabledevelopment.un.org/content/documents/3432SD2015%20Position%20Paper_Business%20&%20Industry.pdf

61. Pingeot, *Corporate Influence*, 17–8; Scheyvens et al.

62. IOE, Guidance Paper.

63. Ibid., 19.

64. IOE Website, About the IOE: http://www.ioe-emp.org/about-ioe/ and IOE members: http://www.ioe-emp.org/members/

65. Ibid.
66. IOE, Guidance Paper; Pingeot, 'In Whose Interest?'.
67. Ibid; IOE, Guidance Paper, 6.
68. Ibid.
69. Ibid., 3, 6.
70. Ibid., 6–7.
71. Ibid., 6–7.
72. Ibid., 7.
73. UN Human Rights Council, Agenda item 3, Promotion and protection of all human rights, civil, political, economic, social and cultural rights, including the right to development Resolution adopted by the Human Rights Council, October 9, 2012, A/HRC/RES/21/2, para. 14, https://documents-dds-ny.un.org/doc/RESOLUTION/GEN/G12/173/89/PDF/G1217389. pdf?OpenElement (accessed April 4, 2017); Julia Kercher, 'The Sustainable Development Goals (SDGs): Contributions of the UN Human Rights Council to Debate so far, Background Paper' (background paper, Geneva, Friedrich Ebert Stiftung, undated), http://www.fes-globalization.org/geneva/documents/2015/2015_06_Background Paper HRC and SDGs 2015_FES Layout.pdf, See e.g. the website of the Office of the High Commissioner of Human Rights (OHCHR), http://www.ohchr.org/EN/Issues/MDG/Pages/Intro.aspx (accessed July 24, 2017)
74. HRC 22nd Session on human rights mainstreaming, March 1, 2013, 19, http://www.ohchr. org/Documents/HRBodies/HRCouncil/RegularSession/Session22/AHRC221_English.pdf; HRC 26th Session side event; see also Kercher, 'The Sustainable Development Goals (SDGs)', 2; HRC 28th Session, 3 March 2015 High Level panel discussion on human rights mainstreaming.
75. Kercher, 'The Sustainable Development Goals (SDGs)', 5–6.
76. United Nations Office of the High Commissioner of Human Rights (OHCHR) 'Human Rights and Post-2015 Development Agenda', http://www.ohchr.org/EN/Issues/MDG/Pages/Intro.aspx
77. For example: HRC Special Procedures, (2012) Open Letter from Special Procedures mandate holders of the Human Rights Council to States negotiating the Outcome Document of the Rio+20 Summit, http://www.ohchr.org/EN/HRBodies/SP/Pages/OpenLetterRio20.aspx (accessed April 4, 2017); http://www.ohchr.org/EN/NewsEvents/Pages/DisplayNews.aspx? NewsID=14558 (accessed April 4, 2017); HRC Special Procedures World Press Freedom Day: Free media reinforces the post-2015 goals (2014), http://www.ohchr.org/EN/NewsEvents/Pages/DisplayNews.aspx?NewsID=14558& (accessed April 4, 2017); Also See Kercher, 'The Sustainable Development Goals (SDGs), 5, for full list.
78. United Nations Special Rapporteur on Extreme Poverty and Human Rights, Magdalena Sepulveda Carmona 'The need to include a rights-based approach to Social Protection in the Post 2015 Development Agenda' (undated), http://www.ohchr.org/Documents/Issues/Poverty/SRPovertyPost2015.pdf (accessed April 4, 2017); HRC Special Rapporteur on extreme poverty and human rights, The Post-2015 Development Agenda: Realizing the rights of women living in poverty through commitments on gender equality and unpaid care work Submission by the UN (undated), http://www.ohchr.org/Documents/Issues/Poverty/UCWPost2015Agenda.pdf (accessed April 4, 2017); See also Kercher, 'The Sustainable Development Goals (SDGs)', 4–6; including 31 special rapporteurs support inclusion of freedom of association and 15 special rapporteurs call for inclusion of social protection floors based on human rights and right to social security.
79. Joint Statement: Human Rights for All Post-2015, May 10, 2013, http://www.cesr.org/joint-statement-human-rights-all-post-2015 (accessed April 4, 2017).
80. Ibid., 'Introduction'.
81. Ibid.
82. Ibid., number items 2, 5.
83. Ibid., number item 1.
84. Ibid., number items 1, 4, 5, 8.

85. Ibid., number item 1.
86. Ibid., Introduction.
87. IOE, Guidance Paper, 6.
88. Ibid., 3, for example.
89. Ibid.
90. Ibid., 7.
91. CESCR General Comment 18, para.10.
92. IOE, Guidance Paper, 3, 6.
93. Ibid., 7.
94. Joint Statement: Human Rights for All Post-2015, number 4.
95. Ibid.
96. Ibid., number 2, number 4.
97. IOE, 'Guidance Paper: The Post 2015- Development Agenda and its Impact on Business' and 'Joint Statement: Human Rights for All Post-2015', May 10, 2013, http://www.cesr.org/joint-statement-human-rights-all-post-2015 (accessed April 4, 2017).
98. Compilation Document, (2014) Major Groups and other Stakeholders Dialogue with the Co-Chairs on SDGS, UN Open Working Group, April 2, 2014, https://sustainabledevelopment.un.org/content/documents/3674Compilation%20Document%20on%20Goals%20and%20Targets_April%2011-%20final.pdf (accessed July 24, 2017). Simonds, 'The SDGs Summit and the 2030 Agenda'; Matt Simonds, 'Decent Work for All by 2030: Taking on the Private Sector', in Spotlight on Sustainable Development, ed. Adams et al., 68.
99. Compilation Document, 19. They did however argue that 'decent wages' should be tied to share of national income rather than growth- related concepts of productivity.
100. Jean Drèze and Amartya Sen, India Development and Participation, 2nd edn (Oxford: Oxford University Press 2002), 34.
101. Economic growth may even be contrary to upholding human rights norms. See for example the case of the right to water: Meera Karunananthan, Council of Canadians, in collaboration with Devin Tellatin and the NGO Mining Working Group, 'Whose Rights to Water Will the 2030 Agenda Promote?', in Spotlight on Sustainable Development, ed. Adams et al.,.
102. UN Charter, arts 55–56.
103. ICESCR, art. 6,
104. Ibid., art 2; CESCR 2007, 'An Evaluation of the Obligation to Take Steps' CESCR.
105. CESCR General Comment 18.
106. Harvey, 'Benchmarking the Right to Work'; Diane F. Frey and Gillian MacNaughton, 'A Human Rights Lens on Full Employment and Decent Work in the 2030 Sustainable Development Agenda', Journal of Workplace Rights (April–June 2016): 1–13, doi:10.1177/2158244016649580.
107. UNGA, Transforming Our World, 27.
108. Ibid., preamble.
109. Ibid., preamble; 2.
110. Ibid., para. 2.
111. Ibid.,
112. Ibid., para. 3, 9 (twice), 13, 21, 27, 68 and pp. 14, 19 (twice).
113. Ibid., para. 13.
114. R. Barkemeyer et al., 'What Happened to the Development in "Sustainable Development"?', Sustainable Development 22, no. 1 (2014): 15–32.
115. Ibid., 17.
116. Ibid., 16.
117. The World Bank, Commission on Growth and Development, The Growth Report: Strategies for Sustained Growth and Inclusive Development (2008); https://openknowledge.worldbank.org/bitstream/handle/10986/6507/449860PUB0Box3101OFFICIAL0USE0ONLY1.pdf; World Bank Group, World Development Report 2013: Jobs; The World Bank, Inclusive Green Growth: The Pathway to Sustainable Development, 2012, http://siteresources.worldbank.org/EXTSDNET/Resources/Inclusive_Green_Growth_May_2012.pdf

118. The World Bank, Commission on Growth and Development, *The Growth Report.*
119. World Bank Group, *Poverty and Shared Prosperity 2016: Taking On Inequality*, 3.
120. The World Bank, Commission on Growth and Development, *The Growth Report*, 1.
121. IOE, Guidance Paper.
122. Pingeot, 'In Whose Interest', 10.
123. Simonds, 'Decent Work for All by 2030', 68.
124. Ibid.; see also Paul L. Quintos, *The Post-2015 Corporate Development Agenda*, 2015, 4, http://www.cetri.be/IMG/pdf/the20post-203e50.pdf.
125. Martens, 'The 2030 Agenda', 12.
126. Simonds, 'Decent Work for All by 2030', 68–9.
127. Woodward, 'Incrementum ad Absurdum', 59.
128. Ibid.
129. Ibid.
130. Ibid., 58.
131. UNGA, *Transforming Our World*, Goal 10, p. 21/35; see also Kate Donald, 'Will Inequality Get Left Behind in the 2030 Agenda?', in *Spotlight on Sustainable Development*, ed. Adams et al.; Gillian MacNaughton, 'Vertical Inequalities: Are the SDGs and Human Rights Up to the Challenges', this issue.
132. The World Bank, Commission on Growth and Development, *The Growth Report*, 5.
133. Antal, 'Green Goals', 280–1.
134. Herman E. Daly, *From Uneconomic Growth to a Steady-State Economy: Advances in Ecological Economics* (Cheltenham: Edward Elgar, 2014).
135. Antal, 'Green Goals'; Simonds, 'Decent Work for All by 2030'.
136. Herman E. Daly, 'A Further Critique of Growth Economics', *Ecological Economics* 88 (2013): 20–4, 20.
137. Antal, 'Green Goals', 284.
138. Ibid.; see also Philip A. Lawn, 'Full Employment in a Low-Growth or Steady State Economy: A Consideration of the Issues', *Australian Bulletin of Labour* 28, no. 1 (2002); Kate Raworth, 'A Safe and Just Space for Humanity: Can We Live Within The Donut? (Oxfam Discussion Papers, 2012), https://www.oxfam.org/sites/www.oxfam.org/files/dp-a-safe-and-just-space-for-humanity-130212-en.pdf; Eléonore Fauré, Åsa Svenfelt, Göran Finnveden and Alf Hornborg, 'Four Sustainability Goals in a Swedish Low-Growth/Degrowth Context', *Sustainability* 8 (2016): 1–18.
139. ILO Convention No. 122.
140. IOE Policy Working Group on Employment, http://www.ioe-emp.org/policy-areas/employment/
141. Ibid.

Acknowledgments

The author wishes to acknowledge Gillian MacNaughton for her insightful and extremely helpful comments to drafts of this article and to the editors of this volume and the two anonymous referees for their helpful comments.

Disclosure statement

No potential conflict of interest was reported by the author.

Index

For Product Safety Concerns and Information please contact our EU representative GPSR@taylorandfrancis.com Taylor & Francis Verlag GmbH, Kaufingerstraße 24, 80331 München, Germany

T - #0152 - 160425 - C0 - 246/174/9 - PB - 9780367519797 - Gloss Lamination